고난도 TEPS in TEPS 어휘

박기혁

서울대학교 졸업
(전) 중앙데일리 영자신문 객원 논설위원
(현) 와우패스 무역영어 대표강사
(현) 메가스터디 TEPS 강사
(현) 반포 행복한 어학원 대표

정구영

한국외대 영어과 졸업
동양대학교 겸임교수
한영대 영어설교통역 연구원
강남 YBM e4U 시사영어학원 영어강사

고난도 TEPS in TEPS 어휘

저자	박기혁 · 정구영
초판 1쇄 인쇄	2011년 4월 1일
초판 1쇄 발행	2011년 4월 8일
발행인	박효상
마케팅	이종선, 이태호, 이전희
책임 편집	강성실
편집, 진행	모희진, 이종만, 권희정
디자인	손정수, 윤영선
출판등록	제 10-1835호
발행처	사람in
주소	121-839 서울시 마포구 서교동 378-16 4F
전화	02)338-3555(代)
팩스	02)338-3545
E-mail	saramin@netsgo.com
Homepage	www.saramin.com

※ 책값은 뒤표지에 있습니다.
※ 파본은 바꾸어 드립니다.

고득점을 위한 고강도 훈련

TEPS의 새로운 패러다임

고난도 TEPS in TEPS

박기혁 · 정구영 지음

까다로운 TEPS 어휘를 완벽 대비할 수 있는 정확한 분석과 해법

어휘

VOCAbulary

사람in
saram incom

머리말

이 고난도 문제집은 기존의 문제집보다 난이도가 높은 문제들을 연습하기 위한 것으로서 TEPS에서 진정으로 고득점을 하고자 하는 수험생들을 위해 기획된 것입니다. 모든 공부에는 이론과 실전이 공존해야 합니다. 그래서 이 책은 기본적인 이론 공부를 마친 학습자가 **TEPS의 문법/ 어휘/ 독해** 실전에서 고득점할 수 있도록 기출문제를 바탕으로 실제 시험과 유사한 문제 형태를 유지하되 좀 더 까다로운 수준으로 제작되었습니다.

TEPS는 실용성과 학문성이 절묘하게 결합된 시험으로, 1999년 출범 이래 현재 대한민국 영어 시장에서 완전히 자리매김했다고 평가되고 있습니다. 시행 초기에는 주로 서울대 대학원을 준비하는 이들로 대상이 한정되었으나, TOEIC의 변별력이 떨어지고 TOEFL로 인해 지불되는 로열티 금액이 막대해짐에 따라 그에 대한 반발적인 분위기가 형성되면서 응시 인원이 늘어나기 시작했습니다.

최근에는 외고 등 특목고를 대비하는 상위권 중학생 및 외고 재학생, 대학의 특차전형 입학을 원하는 상위권 중고생, 공기업 취업을 준비하는 대학생, 국가고시 준비생, 로스쿨, 의학 대학원 자격시험(MEET) 및 치과 대학원 자격시험(DEET) 준비생, 신학대학원 준비생 등 다양한 연령대에서 응시하는 시험이 되었습니다.

본 문제집의 내용을 소화한 후에는 수험생 스스로 시사적인 내용이나 학문적인 내용을 다룬 책을 적극적으로 찾아 읽음으로써 단순히 시험 점수를 위한 요령 습득이 아닌 진정한 영어실력 향상을 위해 노력하기 바랍니다.

자신의 꿈을 이루기 위한 발판이 될 TEPS 990점을 달성하는 데 이 책이 좋은 지렛대가 되기 바랍니다. 끝으로 이 책을 출간하는 데 도움을 주신 모든 분들께 감사의 말씀을 전합니다.

저자 일동

TEPS의 구성

TEPS는 청해, 문법, 어휘, 독해 4개 영역에 걸쳐 총 200문항으로 구성되어 있으며 시험시간은 140분이다. 문항반응이론(IRT)에 따라 채점하기 때문에 모든 문제를 맞아도 만점은 990점이고 모든 문제를 틀리더라도 10점은 나온다.

영역	PART별 내용	문항 수	시간/배점
청 해 Listening Comprehension	Part Ⅰ: 문장 하나를 듣고 이어질 대화 고르기	15	55분/400점
	Part Ⅱ: 3 문장의 대화를 듣고 이어질 대화 고르기	15	
	Part Ⅲ: 6–8 문장의 대화를 듣고 이어질 대화 고르기	15	
	Part Ⅳ: 단문의 내용을 듣고 질문에 해당하는 답 고르기	15	
문 법 Grammar	Part Ⅰ: 대화문의 빈칸에 적절한 표현을 고르기	20	25분/100점
	Part Ⅱ: 문장의 빈칸에 적절한 표현을 고르기	20	
	Part Ⅲ: 대화에서 어법상 틀리거나 어색한 부분 고르기	5	
	Part Ⅳ: 대화에서 어법상 틀리거나 어색한 부분 고르기	5	
어 휘 Vocabulary	Part Ⅰ: 대화문의 빈칸에 적절한 단어 고르기	25	15분/100점
	Part Ⅱ: 단문의 빈칸에 적절한 단어 고르기	25	
독 해 Reading Comprehension	Part Ⅰ: 지문을 읽고 질문의 빈칸에 들어갈 내용 고르기	16	45분/400점
	Part Ⅱ: 지문을 읽고 질문에 가장 적절한 내용 고르기	21	
	Part Ⅲ: 지문을 읽고 문맥상 어색한 내용 고르기	3	
총계	13개 PART	200	140분/990점

*IRT(Item Response Theory)에 의하여 최고점이 990점, 최저점이 10점으로 조정됨.

TEPS 등급표

등급	점수	영역	능력검정기준
1+급	901–990	전반	교양있는 원어민에 버금가는 정도로 의사소통이 가능하고 전문분야 업무에 대처할 수 있음.
	361–400	청해	교양있는 원어민에 버금가는 수준의 청해력
		독해	교양있는 원어민에 버금가는 수준의 독해력
	91–100	문법	교양있는 원어민에 버금가는 수준으로 내재화된 문법능력
		어휘	교양있는 원어민에 버금가는 수준으로 내재화된 어휘력
1+급	801–900	전반	단기간 집중 교육을 받으면 대부분의 의사소통이 가능하고 전문분야 업무에 별 무리 없이 대처할 수 있음.
	321–360	청해	다양한 상황의 수준 높은 내용을 별 무리 없이 이해할 수 있는 정도의 청해력
		독해	다양한 소재의 수준 높은 내용을 별 무리 없이 이해할 수 있는 정도의 독해력
	81–90	문법	다양한 구문을 별 무리 없이 신속하게 이해할 수 있을 정도로 내재화된 문법능력
		어휘	다양한 표현을 별 무리 없이 신속하게 이해할 수 있을 정도로 내재화된 어휘력
2+급	701–800	전반	단기간 집중 교육을 받으면 일반 분야업무를 큰 어려움 없이 수행할 수 있음.
	281–320	청해	일반적 상황에 보통수준의 내용을 별 무리 없이 이해하는 정도의 청해력
		독해	일반적 소재에 보통수준의 내용을 별 무리 없이 이해하는 정도의 독해력
	71–80	문법	일반적인 구문을 별 무리 없이 이해하는 정도의 문법능력
		어휘	일반적인 표현을 별 무리 없이 이해하는 정도의 어휘력
2급	601–700	전반	중장기간 집중 교육을 받으면 일반분야 업무를 큰 어려움 없이 수행할 수 있음.
	241–280	청해	일반적 상황에 보통수준의 내용을 대체로 이해하는 정도의 청해력
		독해	일반적 소재에 보통수준의 내용을 대체로 이해하는 정도의 독해력
	61–70	문법	일반적인 구문을 대체로 이해하는 정도의 문법능력
		어휘	일반적인 표현을 대체로 이해하는 정도의 어휘력
3+급	501–600	전반	중장기간 집중 교육을 받으면 한정된 분야의 업무를 큰 어려움 없이 수행할 수 있음.
	201–240	청해	일반적 상황에 보통수준의 내용을 다소 이해하는 정도의 청해력
		독해	일반적 소재에 보통수준의 내용을 다소 이해하는 정도의 독해력
	51–60	문법	일반적인 구문에 대한 의미파악이 어느 정도 가능한 문법능력
		어휘	일반적인 표현에 대한 의미파악이 어느 정도 가능한 어휘력
3급	401–500	전반	중장기간 집중 교육을 받으면 한정된 분야의 업무를 다소 미흡하지만 큰 지장은 없이 수행할 수 있음.
	161–200	청해	일반적 상황에 보통수준의 내용을 이해하기 다소 어려운 정도의 청해력
		독해	일반적 소재에 보통수준의 내용을 이해하기 다소 어려운 정도의 청해력
	41–50	문법	일반적 구문에 대한 신속한 의미 파악이 다소 어려운 정도의 문법능력
		어휘	일반적인 표현에 대한 신속한 의미 파악이 다소 어려운 정도의 어휘력
4+급	301–400 201–300	전반	장기간의 집중 교육을 받으면 한정된 분야의 업무를 대체로 어렵게 수행할 수 있음.
5+급	101–200 10–100	전반	단편적인 지식만을 갖추고 있어 의사소통이 거의 불가능함.

이 책의 구성과 특징

● TEPS 고득점을 위한 고강도 훈련 Actual Training

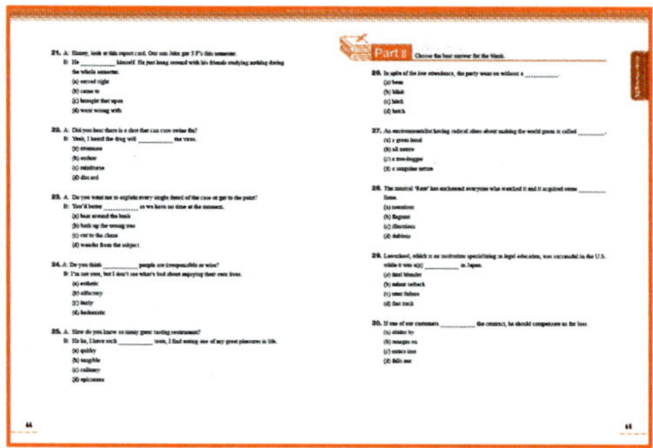

정체된 성적을 끌어올릴 수 있도록, 익숙한 빈출 문제만으로 구성된 기존의 문제집보다 한 차원 높은 문제들로 실제 시험과 동일한 문항수로 구성하였다.

● 문제에 나온 어휘들을 또렷하게 되살려주는 Final Check

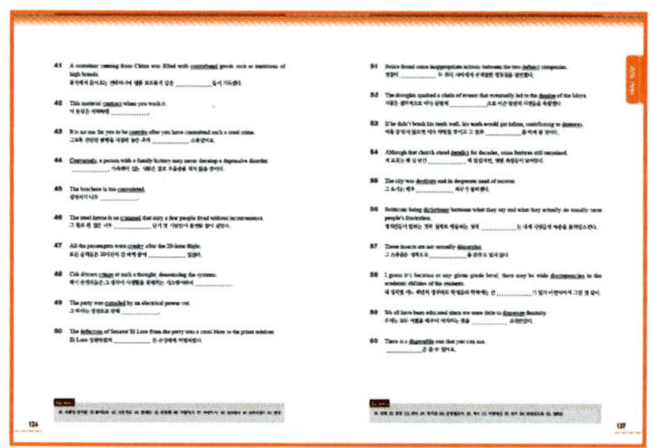

Actual Training에서 나온 주요 어휘들을 마지막까지 확실히 흡수할 수 있도록 연어, 2어 동사, 숙어, 중요 표현 등의 분류에 따라 재배치하였다.

● 필요한 내용이 한눈에 쏙 들어오는 해설지

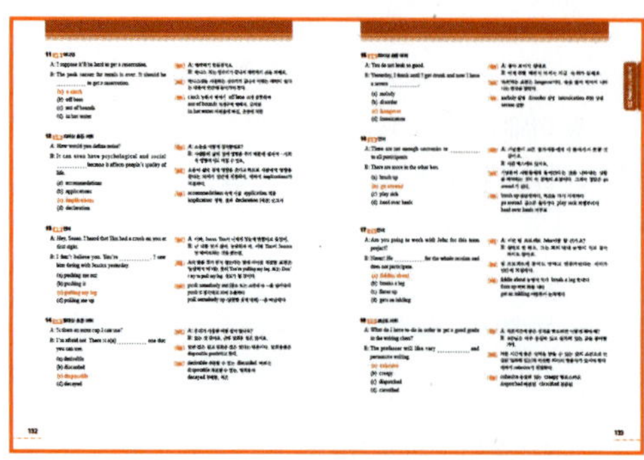

문제와 해설을 함께 보면서 고난도 문제의 핵심을 되짚는 것은 기본이고, 해설 부분을 가리고 다시 한 번 풀어보거나 각 문제의 유형 tag를 참조하여 유형별 학습을 하는 등 다양한 활용을 위해 정답 및 해설에 문제와 해설을 나란히 배치하였다.

Contents

고난도
Actual Training
01

실제 TEPS 시험의 문항수와 동일하게 구성된 고난도 Actual Training을
제한 시간 15분 내에 모두 풀 수 있도록 노력해 보세요!

1. A: Does money buy happiness?

B: Yes, it does. From people who practice what's called the ___________ science. For when economists tackled the question, they started from the observation that when people put something up for sale they try to get as much for it as they can.

(a) cognitive　　　　　　　　(b) histrionic

(c) dismal　　　　　　　　　(d) convalescent

2. A: Does your brother stand on his own two feet?

B: I hope so, but he is still ___________ my parents.

(a) living it up

(b) coalesce into

(c) living off

(d) squaring up to

3. A: You know what? Some climate scientists, trying to muzzle dissenting voices, have fervently spreaded their opinions on conservative blogs. I believe these opinions have fueled widespread suspicion that global warming is an elaborate ___________.

B: It was shocking to hear the news. I wonder what the truth is.

(a) ruse　　　　　　　　　　(b) distraction

(c) candor　　　　　　　　　(d) spate

4. A: What do you think about the future of carbon?

B: The cap-and-dividend would set a price on carbon, thus giving Americans a powerful ________ to burn less filthy fuel.

(a) paucity

(b) plethora

(c) incentive

(d) instinct

5. A: Do you know what Mr. Knox says?

B: Yes I do. He does not ___________ his words. He describes Bush's legacy as dishonest wars, stolen wars, and economic collapse.

(a) expound　　　　　　　　(b) mark

(c) mince　　　　　　　　　(d) abominate

6. A: The criminal justice system is in need of an overhaul.

B: True, it is particularly true of its ___________ policies. Too many people are being put behind bars who do not need to be there.

(a) probation

(b) apprehension

(c) inquisition

(d) incarceration

7. A: As an expert in the economy, what are your prospects for our future?

B: The central bank's policy of zero interest rates, the large stimulus and ensuing deficits would, by some iron law of economics, _______________ the currency and boost the government's long-term borrowing costs.

(a) appreciate

(b) undergird

(c) debase

(d) fiddle

8. A: What do you think about the American television program?

B: I guess it is worthless and ___________.

(a) for kicks

(b) diamond in the rough

(c) for the birds

(d) in there pitching

9. A: In what situation is the Parliament?

B: Two Congressional ___________ arising out of the war on terror have brought the jurisdictional and normative dimensions of the Great Writ of habeas corpus into sharp relief.

(a) statues

(b) status

(c) statures

(d) statutes

10. A: Do you know what *Double X* contributor Amanda Marcotte tries to say?

B: He takes modern guys to ___________ for using Facebook as a "X-rated version of amateur porn."

(a) job

(b) occupation

(c) task

(d) employment

11. A: I was impressed with Nicholas reagarding his patience.

    B: I thought so too. Even when he was beset with something irritating, he used to be calm and ___________.

    (a) restive

    (b) infuriating

    (c) poised

    (d) sinewy

12. A: How can home appliances operate?

    B: They can get electricity from either a battery unit which is sold in convenience stores or from a wall ___________.

    (a) consent

    (b) outlet

    (c) merchandise

    (d) vent

13. A: How come the students alienate the young professor?

    B: He ___________ explanation after he made some blunders in grading process.

    (a) construed

    (b) bereaved

    (c) eschewed

    (d) stipulated

14. A: Why does the Danish boy look so gloomy?

    B: He was alarmed to hear that he could not inherit the family estate on the grounds that he was an ___________ child, born to his father's mistress.

    (a) illegal

    (b) illiterate

    (c) lawless

    (d) illegitimate

15. A : Do you remember when *Harry Potter* came out first?

    B : Of course, I do. It was a(n) ___________ hit.

    (a) irascible

    (b) piqued

    (c) smash

    (d) triggering

16. A: When did the bombing take place?

B: It occurred ____________ the beginning of the graduation ceremony.

   (a) to

   (b) in

   (c) for

   (d) at

17. A: Do you remember the physician that ____________ her injuries following the accident?

B: I'm not certain, but I guess it was Dr. Garner.

   (a) cared

   (b) cured

   (c) redeemed

   (d) treated

18. A: How come you are fond of the restaurant so much?

B: Because they offer such ____________ portions, I treasure it.

   (a) general

   (b) generous

   (c) magnificent

   (d) voracious

19. A: This apple pie is ____________.

B: I just made it myself. Isn't it fantastic?

   (a) white elephant

   (b) black sheep

   (c) out of this world

   (d) skeleton in the closet

20. A: It is imprudent of you to ____________ the get-together.

B: I didn't mean to bother, but it was urgently needed. I couldn't help it.

   (a) interfere

   (b) hurl

   (c) overhaul

   (d) interrupt

21. A: I suppose meeting the deadline is not easy.

    B: You mean you want to ____________, don't you?

      (a) elongate

      (b) expand

      (c) expend

      (d) extend

22. A: What do you do as a coast guard?

    B: In case of emergency on the beach, I use mouth-to-nose ____________.

      (a) rehabilitation

      (b) regurgitation

      (c) resuscitation

      (d) resurrection

23. A: Can you tell me who helped you while you were writing this article?

    B: Of course. I'm most ____________ to Mr. Watson.

      (a) accustomed

      (b) opposed

      (c) qualified

      (d) indebted

24. A: I'm so overweight nowadays.

    B: Why don't you ____________ more often?

      (a) walk out

      (b) work out

      (c) set about

      (d) set back

25. A: The morning walk every day after breakfast is lively and ____________, isn't it?

    B: Yes, I think so, too.

      (a) mediocre

      (b) salubrious

      (c) mortal

      (d) peripheral

Part II **Questions 26-50**
Choose the best answer for the blank.

26. Plenty of investment companies tend to ____________ the probability of legal action for the wrongdoings of their employees.

(a) get over

(b) brace for

(c) give in

(d) let up

27. Historically speaking, a host of tiny island countries have ____________ become a hub for smuggling drugs. In other words, they went bad without any knowledge of it.

(a) methodically

(b) inadvertently

(c) pugnaciously

(d) ferociously

28. David has argued that the economic ____________ were brought about by the surge of oil prices.

(a) recess

(b) doldrums

(c) libel

(d) graft

29. Barring unanticipated events, the ____________ would be ironed out sooner or later.

(a) conservation

(b) arrangement

(c) sanitation

(d) skirmish

30. Purchasing such a costly automobile is a bit ____________ for a woman of her income.

(a) perspicacious

(b) scathing

(c) extravagant

(d) frugal

31. The technology has never been improved or made as ___________ as expected.

(a) scrupulous

(b) state-of-the-art

(c) ludicrous

(d) intangible

32. Few know exactly how to make a lot of money from investment or ___________.

(a) stipend

(b) speculation

(c) conjecture

(d) approbation

33. This site is intriguing and interactive to help children ___________ astronomy.

(a) estrange

(b) unearth

(c) aggravate

(d) appreciate

34. The financial expert has been ___________ a 20% consumer price surge for the entire year.

(a) protracting

(b) projecting

(c) imploding

(d) condoning

35. People in ethnic minorities are generally ___________ economic and educational opportunity, and therefore they often lack self-esteem.

(a) delayed

(b) degenerated

(c) dissembled

(d) denied

36. The President ______________ the cheers of the people on the street, waving his hands.
  (a) booked
  (b) conserved
  (c) acknowledged
  (d) salvaged

37. As a well-known political scientist, he has ___________ the problems of politics throughout his book.
  (a) bewitched
  (b) addressed
  (c) withdrew
  (d) retreated

38. Susan and John met with a travel agent and ___________ airline tickets.
  (a) gathered
  (b) collected
  (c) contained
  (d) comprised

39. Plenty of professors at the university have been warned not to ___________ other peer scholars' thesis.
  (a) capsize
  (b) rebate
  (c) plagiarize
  (d) stack

40. The chairperson has been charged with ___________ of dividends from his corporation.
  (a) supplements
  (b) decrial
  (c) latch
  (d) appropriation

41. Generally speaking, women seem to be more ___________ than men to the adverse effects of alcohol.

(a) specious

(b) sprightly

(c) suspended

(d) susceptible

42. The artist was not a loser. After all, his works were ___________ in a famous gallery.

(a) exhibited

(b) encased

(c) embittered

(d) entranced

43. Owing to ___________ technology, our lives have become more and more convenient.

(a) astute

(b) discrete

(c) rudimentary

(d) cutting-edge

44. Many passengers got completely ___________ after the 20-hour flight.

(a) dilapidated

(b) cranky

(c) destitute

(d) decrepit

45. Regrettably, nobody in her class is supporting her due to her ___________ character.

(a) grudging

(b) grimacing

(c) bellicose

(d) filthy

46. Mr. Baker was cautious to ___________ from the topic of marriage as Susan had just broken up with her boyfriend.
(a) align
(b) quench
(c) dodge
(d) stifle

47. Park has hit five goals this season in the UK but drew ___________ in his country's opening two World Cup qualifiers.
(a) breaks
(b) blanks
(c) brinks
(d) blinks

48. The other day the prosecution in the International Court of Justice announced that it would ___________ charges against the war criminals.
(a) convict
(b) press
(c) accuse
(d) blame

49. In 1994, the Korean Scholastic Aptitude Test was first ___________ to high school students.
(a) arranged
(b) braced
(c) brewed
(d) administered

50. Two days ago, Hurricane Katrina ___________ plenty of trees and telephone poles in New Mexico.
(a) uprooted
(b) foamed
(c) berated
(d) saturated

고난도
Actual Training
02

실제 TEPS 시험의 문항수와 동일하게 구성된 고난도 Actual Training을
제한 시간 **15분** 내에 모두 풀 수 있도록 노력해 보세요!

1. A: Did you get any new items today?

B: No. It seems that I'm going to have to ___________ what I have.

(a) make believe

(b) make up for

(c) make for

(d) make do with

2. A: Did the Bakers quarrel again?

B: Yes, you know, most married couples ___________ with each other over money.

(a) fall back

(b) fall out

(c) get away

(d) hold out

3. A: It was a bad accident, wasn't it?

B: Yes, it's awful that they had to ___________ his leg to get him out. There simply wasn't any other option.

(a) forsake

(b) hoodwink

(c) amputate

(d) palter

4. A: How did the bird manage to run away?

B: Simba the Lion appeared with ___________ timing and he helped her.

(a) hefty

(b) apocryphal

(c) unaffected

(d) impeccable

5. A: The new boy in my class was so ___________ that he didn't even talk to other students.

B: You said it, he has his nose in the air all the time.

(a) hale

(b) snobbish

(c) irresistible

(d) compelling

6. A: If you work in such bad weather, you're going to ____________ your cold.

B: I appreciate your concern.

    (a) ameliorate

    (b) prostrate

    (c) coddle

    (d) exacerbate

7. A: Where and how was Admiral Nelson's funeral held?

B: It was conducted by means of ____________ in England.

    (a) cremation

    (b) incarceration

    (c) bogeyman

    (d) knoll

8. A: Elizabeth said to me that she ____________ your father into attending her birthday party.

B: Yeah, she has a way with words.

    (a) took

    (b) told

    (c) talked

    (d) spoke

9. A: My boy, are you ready to ____________ ?

B: Yes sir, except for the fact that I should buy things for camping.

    (a) put out

    (b) put off

    (c) take off

    (d) set off

10. A: My brother-in-law has ____________ a great deal of money after selling his cosmetics business.

B: It is astounding that he has become a billionaire.

    (a) dislocated

    (b) dislodged

    (c) concocted

    (d) accrued

11. A: He should not have ____________ with the board meeting.

B: I've heard that it was an emergency. He couldn't avoid it.

    (a) interfered

    (b) interrupted

    (c) perpetrated

    (d) bothered

12. A: I discovered that Julia is ____________ in that class.

B: Yes, she will start in a few days.

    (a) registering

    (b) getting

    (c) enrolling

    (d) signing

13. A: Did you watch the final round yesterday?

B: Certainly. It was thrilling. There was a score ____________.

    (a) sitting on a gold mine

    (b) leaving no stone unturned

    (c) at the eleventh hour

    (d) in the hole

14. A: The bookcase that matches these books seems a little too large. Do you have any ____________?

B: I'm sorry, we don't have other items.

    (a) substitutes

    (b) altercations

    (c) garment

    (d) alternatives

15. A: If my memory serves me right, it's not my signature on the check!

B: Do you mean that somebody ____________ it?

    (a) plagiarized

    (b) drew

    (c) forged

    (d) spared

16. A: I believe that the vice president was going on too much about our mistakes at the meeting.

B: The reason is that he is the man who's ___________ responsible when something goes

awry.

(a) held

(b) been

(c) taken

(d) gone

17. A: Have you noticed Professor Kim's hair is ___________?

B: Yes, you can tell he is going bald.

(a) shortening

(b) thinning

(c) slimming

(d) belittling

18. A: Never forget this is a ___________ document.

B: I'll keep that in mind. I mean I'll make sure that no one can see it.

(a) confident

(b) diffident

(c) confidential

(d) draconian

19. A: When you were in law school, did you do your utmost?

B: No. I ___________ to not doing my best.

(a) mean

(b) remember

(c) chide

(d) confess

20. A: How could the city official own such a luxurious house with his modest salary?

B: It is likely that he has received ___________ from contractors, taking advantage of his

position.

(a) doldrums

(b) setbacks

(c) alimony

(d) payoffs

21. A: Why do you go home so early?

    B: If I don't get home on time, my parents will jump down my _____________.

       (a) mind

       (b) heart

       (c) throat

       (d) obloquy

22. A: Do you know his father-in-law is in the hospital?

    B: Yeah, the old man's bones are so ____________ that he broke his legs after falling.

       (a) infirm

       (b) fragile

       (c) flimsy

       (d) feeble

23. A: Have you heard the news?

    B: Yes, I have. They say that the government has decided to ____________ a program of radical reform sooner or later.

       (a) go back on

       (b) kick off

       (c) let on

       (d) wipe out

24. A: Please hand in your ____________ of expenses before you leave.

    B: Okay. I'll have submitted it by the time I call it a day.

       (a) measure

       (b) estimate

       (c) endorsement

       (d) defile

25. A: What was the result of your team last weekend?

    B: To our disappointment, we played to a ____________, but our opponent was last season's champion.

       (a) landslide

       (b) venture

       (c) draw

       (d) neck

Part II   Questions 26-50
Choose the best answer for the blank.

26. According to the weather forecast, there will be a lot of thick morning fog, which will cause poor ___________.
(a) spectrum
(b) spectacle
(c) visibility
(d) vision

27. Because neither company could come to an agreement, compromise over the control of the small island has finally ___________.
(a) found
(b) foundered
(c) founded
(d) flinched

28. Both heavy drinking and smoking could do ___________ damage to your brain.
(a) transient
(b) substantial
(c) meticulous
(d) astute

29. Poor nutrition in the early stages of infancy can ___________ adult growth.
(a) hold up
(b) hold back
(c) get at
(d) get away

30. Your ___________ tactics may compel me to call off the contract because the job must be finished on time.
(a) deferential
(b) nefarious
(c) genteel
(d) dilatory

31. M.M.S.'s bad behavior was unusually ____________, but it's hard to think of a recent catastrophe in the business world that wasn't abetted by inept regulation.

(a) extraneous

(b) innocuous

(c) egregious

(d) decorous

32. The Stock Exchange Commission failed to spot the frauds at Enron and decided to let investment banks take on obscene amounts of ____________.

(a) viceroy

(b) trumping

(c) leverage

(d) indemnity

33. Robert strived to act carefree although he had been laid off, but I don't believe anybody was taken in ____________ how he really felt.

(a) as to

(b) as for

(c) as of

(d) as with

34. The explosion accident at the rubber factory really ____________ home the point that safety rules ought to be abided by.

(a) made

(b) got

(c) ran

(d) brought

35. If you think that the unemployment issue could be swept ____________, it would be self-deception.

(a) under the weather

(b) under the rug

(c) over the cover

(d) below the roof

36. In retrospect, Samuelson said that he left his parents behind in their hometown
at the __________ age of thirteen and made for Chicago so as to pursue his dream.
(a) small
(b) beginner
(c) tender
(d) unassuming

37. The renowned law firm __________ out of the deal after the terrible scandal.
(a) pushed
(b) pulled
(c) kept
(d) carried

38. Mac flunked the course because he __________ off the final exam.
(a) took
(b) headed
(c) blew
(d) made

39. Korean people usually say that Kalbi is so delicious that they are __________ to
everything else.
(a) obsolete
(b) oblivious
(c) ostentatious
(d) obligatory

40. The patient who suffered a stroke did not __________ as rapidly as he anticipated.
(a) reimburse
(b) reclaim
(c) replenish
(d) recuperate

41. The residents were disappointed with the new member of the House of Representatives elected in their ____________.

(a) constituency

(b) electorate

(c) civilization

(d) court

42. The essay was thorough and technically competent but ____________ and colorless; the writer seemed to have no fresh ideas about his subject.

(a) vapid

(b) estranged

(c) adamant

(d) complacent

43. We need perseverance to succeed. All I have to do is ____________ and everything will work out.

(a) get off the hook

(b) bide my time

(c) do justice

(d) fall flat on my face

44. The General Hospital in the decent area has ____________ for as many as two hundred patients.

(a) affiliation

(b) accommodations

(c) embezzlement

(d) domicile

45. To my disappointment, last night's farewell party was ____________ by an electrical power cut.

(a) condensed

(b) compressed

(c) abbreviated

(d) curtailed

46. When the class _____________, it was late compared to the usual time.
(a) get out
(b) lay out
(c) let out
(d) make out

47. The deceitful history of the chief executive officer _____________ just after he stepped down from his position.
(a) measured
(b) enunciated
(c) perused
(d) unfolded

48. The rumor has it that his wife is so wealthy that she not only owns several houses but also has _____________ company holdings.
(a) abject
(b) naught
(c) sizable
(d) murky

49. After closer screening, some doubt was _____________ upon the verity of the suspect.
(a) hauled
(b) hoisted
(c) cast
(d) coiled

50. The unanticipated arrival of his girlfriend from abroad lifted his _____________ spirits.
(a) infuriating
(b) embittered
(c) outright
(d) sagging

고난도
Actual Training
03

실제 TEPS 시험의 문항수와 동일하게 구성된 고난도 Actual Training을
제한 시간 15분 내에 모두 풀 수 있도록 노력해 보세요!

1. A: Did you understand the professor's lecture?

B: No, not a word. I seem to be ____________.

(a) unintelligible

(b) unintelligent

(c) comprehensible

(d) apprehensible

2. A: You know what! Jessey played hookey again.

B: I guess that he is just ____________.

(a) malicious

(b) malfunctioning

(c) malingering

(d) malpracticing

3. A: Why don't you announce your plan?

B: I think it desirable that we await a more ____________ occasion to do it.

(a) procrastinating

(b) preceding

(c) propitious

(d) provocative

4. A: What do you think about him?

B: I could see by his brazen manners that he is ____________.

(a) impeccable

(b) immaculate

(c) innocuous

(d) impertinent

5. A: What's the reason that you chose James for the top sales manager?

B: I guess he seems to have an ____________ ability to talk people into buying things.

(a) giddy

(b) stark

(c) uncanny

(d) emaciate

6. A: I'm disappointed that Harry has been dishonest with me all the time.

B: You said it. I don't give ____________ to anything he says.

    (a) justice

    (b) credence

    (c) visibility

    (d) streak

7. A: Olson is so outgoing that everybody likes him. Is his brother Tom the same?

B: In fact, they couldn't be more different. Tom is so ____________.

    (a) extroverted

    (b) indigent

    (c) taciturn

    (d) extravagant

8. A: How come you didn't get the teaching job in Seattle?

B: I'm sick and tired of moving around. I want to keep my life ____________ from now on.

    (a) up in arms

    (b) in the nick of time

    (c) in the offing

    (d) on an even keel

9. A: I'm concerned that my niece has a speech impediment.

B: I'm sorry, but I believe that you don't have to worry too much. When I was younger, I also had a ____________, and it's OK now.

    (a) shriek

    (b) shackle

    (c) stutter

    (d) streak

10. A: Excuse me, ma'am. Does this flight go directly to LA?

B: No. There's a 30-minute ____________ in Tokyo along the way.

    (a) setback

    (b) redirection

    (c) backtrack

    (d) layover

11. A: Excuse me, sir. Is this the right way to the museum?

     B: Yes, just keep going straight until you come to the ____________ of Abraham Lincoln at the corner there.

       (a) status

       (b) statute

       (c) statue

       (d) stature

12. A: Hey, Joel, congratulations on being appointed the new promotions manager.

     B: Thanks a million! I was so amazed when they ____________ my name.

       (a) promulgated

       (b) announced

       (c) remitted

       (d) proclaimed

13. A: Now that it is hot today, let's have pork for lunch.

     B: Are you serious? Don't you know that I am ____________ to meat.

       (a) disposed

       (b) adverse

       (c) averse

       (d) innocuous

14. A: How do you feel about your new laptop?

     B: I can't make it out. The brochure is too ____________.

       (a) confounded

       (b) preposterous

       (c) prodigious

       (d) convoluted

15. A: How was your birthday party last night?

     B: It was too much. The neighbors complained that we were so ____________ that they couldn't turn in.

       (a) construed

       (b) ovoid

       (c) convalescent

       (d) boisterous

16. A: I shouldn't have broken up with my fiancée.

B: Don't you know "What's done is done."? Why don't you stop ___________ yourself and make a new start?

   (a) torturing

   (b) degrading

   (c) contending

   (d) ingurgitating

17. A: You did a good job on your presentation this morning.

B: I appreciate your help. I always ___________ it to your assistance.

   (a) contribute

   (b) draft

   (c) owe

   (d) trespass

18. A: Do you give your mother a call very often?

B: No. I only call her ___________.

   (a) over the hill

   (b) until the fat lady sings

   (c) once in a blue moon

   (d) top-of-the-line

19. A: Will you be serving refreshments on this flight?

B: Not this moment, but we will be giving some food after we reach ___________ altitude.

   (a) flying

   (b) cruising

   (c) anchoring

   (d) traveling

20. A: Do you hear me? I can't hear you well.

B: I gather that there's some ___________ on the line. I'll call you later.

   (a) mix

   (b) cut

   (c) plight

   (d) static

21. A: I do hope that I'll go skiing on Saturday.

B: Do you want me to lend you ski _____________?

(a) resort

(b) tool

(c) apparatus

(d) gear

22. A: I can't make up my mind whether or not to take the job.

B: Why don't you take it? The annual salary is not so great, but it comes with nice

_____________.

(a) tailgate

(b) allowance

(c) perks

(d) dawdle

23. A: How is the weather outside?

B: It's so cold that you'd better _____________ up if you are to go out.

(a) dress

(b) wear

(c) trudge

(d) bundle

24. A: The President said he's not involved in the sex scandal with the famous actress.

B: He is just trying to _____________ the eyes of the public. Everybody knows it's a big lie.

(a) pull the wool over

(b) come down with

(c) make up

(d) dwell on

25. A: Have you decided to stick with the old insurance policy?

B: No. I believe that I have to _____________ around for others.

(a) juggle

(b) dribble

(c) foam

(d) shop

Part II

26. The religious leaders who are focused on something sacred in the Catholic World banned the practice as ___________.
(a) finicky
(b) sacrilegious
(c) proverbial
(d) prosaic

27. The chair is so ___________ about the method the conference is run that it seems impossible to please him.
(a) nefarious
(b) fastidious
(c) menial
(d) vicarious

28. Employers can require that would-be employees provide ___________ so as to verify their former work performance.
(a) remittance
(b) reimbursement
(c) references
(d) recommendation

29. The grandmother's voice was so ___________ that I could hardly hear her when she died.
(a) fragile
(b) flimsy
(c) feeble
(d) robust

30. The Fifth Amendment in the American Constitution ensures that people can ___________ the right to remain silent.
(a) endow
(b) exercise
(c) estrange
(d) epitomize

31. At length, the defendant ____________ guilty of the crime he had been charged with after a
long denial.

(a) conceived

(b) beseeched

(c) admitted

(d) pleaded

32. If an installment is not paid within 7 days after it is due, a ____________ charge of $20 will
be paid by the purchaser.

(a) tardy

(b) plus

(c) delinquent

(d) down payment

33. Nobody is perfect and we should acknowledge the fact that all the people in the world are
____________ to make errors.

(a) tend

(b) infallible

(c) liable

(d) garrulous

34. I've heard that Mr. Kim was apprehended for sexual harrassment and I want to know all the
____________ of the case.

(a) ebb and flow

(b) ins and outs

(c) odds and ends

(d) part and parcel

35. Ever since I got a job, I have made it a rule to ____________ in at 8:00 a.m. in the morning.

(a) report

(b) punch

(c) roll

(d) position

36. The former President, in an attempt to _____________ his fall in popularity, proclaimed yesterday a plan to create one million new jobs in the battered domestic economy.

(a) staunch

(b) reclaim

(c) spew

(d) relinquish

37. After a little heated discussion, the chair called the meeting to _____________.

(a) halt

(b) end

(c) order

(d) beginning

38. A host of Ireland-born novelists have been writing plenty of literary works _____________ the tale of an impoverished Irish peasant.

(a) talking

(b) relating

(c) making

(d) speaking

39. The conductor once _____________ a famous pianist with a cynical remark that there were for him no stars except those in the universe.

(a) seconded

(b) motioned

(c) cowed

(d) championed

40. E-mail coming from the development of computer technology is virtually a _____________ way of giving and taking information from one side to another at great speed.

(a) airproof

(b) waterproof

(c) shatterproof

(d) foolproof

41. I'm certain that every parent hopes that they won't __________ any of their children.

(a) outgrow

(b) outline

(c) outlive

(d) outnumber

42. __________ are the words displayed at the bottom of a moving picture expounding what it is all about.

(a) Subtexts

(b) Credits

(c) Captives

(d) Captions

43. Ten months after Robert was cast __________ in the English Channel, he returned to his native land.

(a) adroit

(b) adrift

(c) amuck

(d) awesome

44. Nokia started its biggest sale, targeted at raising funds to __________ its bid for next-generation cellular phone licences all around the world.

(a) rebut

(b) surrogate

(c) bolster

(d) solicit

45. In the digital photo world, __________ are possible: if you snap a lousy picture, then delete it and take another shot.

(a) turn-outs

(b) leftovers

(c) do-overs

(d) turn-ons

46. When I was younger, I had a ______________ when a school bus nearly hit me as I was crossing the street.
(a) lion's share
(b) close call
(c) white elephant
(d) black sheep

47. The champion is so nimble that when the bell sounded, he responded with ______________.
(a) albatross
(b) gloat
(c) alacrity
(d) glum

48. The workers ______________ the factory gates during the general strike, lest others should gain access to the demonstration area.
(a) hoisted
(b) retreated
(c) hurled
(d) picketed

49. Mr. Hatoyama asked residents to ______________ a compromise that would keep the base on the island while the government sought to move the Marine Corps air base elsewhere.
(a) backtrack
(b) stake
(c) entertain
(d) dislodge

50. The international organization was created to resolve problems, not to create them; to nurture freedom, not to wait on ______________.
(a) bond
(b) bondage
(c) bandage
(d) boundary

고난도
Actual Training
04

실제 TEPS 시험의 문항수와 동일하게 구성된 고난도 Actual Training을
제한 시간 15분 내에 모두 풀 수 있도록 노력해 보세요!

1. A: Do you know the meaning of ____________?
   B: Yes, I do. It is a short sentence or phrase, usually from a politician's speech, which is broadcast during a news bulletin.
   (a) maxim
   (b) precept
   (c) soundbite
   (d) quote

2. A: Did you attend Alex Gigg's wedding ceremony?
   B: Yeah. I was his bestman, and Professor Goethe ____________ at the wedding.
   (a) officiated
   (b) tumbled
   (c) notarized
   (d) lubricated

3. A: Have you followed the instructor's main point?
   B: No way. I am in the dark about what she was trying to ____________.
   (a) play down
   (b) impart to
   (c) come across
   (d) get across

4. A: Does anybody know whether there is any home remedy to ____________ anemia?
   B: Eat chicken soup and stay in bed all day long. That works.
   (a) catch
   (b) beat
   (c) develop
   (d) contract

5. A: What is the best way to preserve the clean environment?
   B: I ____________ that the Congress should enact the law which keeps people from incinerating any products.
   (a) dilate
   (b) delve
   (c) garble
   (d) gather

6. A: What do usually you do to keep yourself as fit as a ____________?

B: I work out on a regular basis every day.

    (a) shape

    (b) health

    (c) fitness

    (d) fiddle

7. A: If I purchase lots of items, would you make them a little cheaper?

B: Certainly. If you buy more than 20, we can ____________ five percent.

    (a) go off

    (b) come off

    (c) carry off

    (d) knock off

8. A: He has no choice but to ____________ a piece of metal to hold the bones together.

B: I assume it is a very tough operation.

    (a) pull over

    (b) drive up

    (c) take out

    (d) put in

9. A: Did Mary obey her parents?

B: No. She ____________ them when they disapproved of her marriage with Jim.

    (a) went in for

    (b) stood up for

    (c) stood up to

    (d) played up to

10. A: Why don't you hurry up?

B: I see. If we don't ____________, we'll miss the last bus.

    (a) get the nod

    (b) air our grievances

    (c) fill the bill

    (d) get the lead out

11. A: Your daughter looks down in the dumps.

B: She broke my favorite vase, so I blamed her for being carelessness.

I shouldn't have ____________ on her.

(a) gotten it up

(b) asked it out

(c) given it away

(d) taken it out

12. A: Ann told me that she will ____________ the expenses of lunch.

B: Again? No. I suggest that I foot the bill.

(a) claim

(b) cost

(c) bear

(d) keep

13. A: Would it be possible for you to ____________ me to a good attorney?

B: Don't worry about it. I will fix you up with a good lawyer as soon as possible.

(a) show

(b) refer

(c) take

(d) have

14. A: My bosom friend broke the window, but I turned a blind eye to his mistake.

B: ____________ it. Anyway, the window had to be replaced.

(a) Put up

(b) Take away

(c) Get over

(d) Set about

15. A: There still remains robust opposition preventing my progress.

B: I suppose you had better ____________ everything before you make up your mind what to do next.

(a) chew over

(b) catch up

(c) fix up

(d) set about

16. A: Janet has been in hot water since last week.

    B: You can say that again. She is in a ___________ at the moment.

       (a) elusive circumstances

       (b) delectable environment

       (c) digressive one

       (d) no-win situation

17. A: I saw you sleep through the momentous part of the class.

    B: I know. I shouldn't have ___________.

       (a) tossed and turned

       (b) turned in

       (c) snoozed

       (d) been caught napping

18. A: I don't like the job any more, it's just boring.

    B: I hope you will find a job you can ___________ your teeth into.

       (a) extract

       (b) subside

       (c) sink

       (d) bite

19. A: Mr. Bae is running three hotels and two restaurants in total and they pay their own way.

    B: I guess he has cleaned up ___________ from his businesses.

       (a) good paper

       (b) a small fortune

       (c) dud coin

       (d) petty cash

20. A: I'm afraid that I won't be able to get the first prize in the piano competition.

    B: Don't ___________. You never know till you try.

       (a) be brash

       (b) meet trouble halfway

       (c) give yourself airs

       (d) fall into a bias

21. A: How wonderful you are! You've finally done your ___________.

B: I owe you many things. I appreciate your proofreading it.

    (a) letters

    (b) scheme

    (c) hypothesis

    (d) dissertation

22. A: I hope Ms. Roosevelt won't notice the ___________ cup.

B: Don't pull my leg. She's got eyes like a hawk.

    (a) chopped

    (b) churned

    (c) clogged

    (d) chipped

23. A: Have you read James Joyce?

B: Yes, but it's not easy. The implication in his novel took a while to ___________.

    (a) stand in

    (b) sink in

    (c) sleep on

    (d) set on

24. A: Do you like your would-be daughter-in-law?

B: As a matter of fact, she didn't ___________ up to my expectations, but I will accept my son's decision.

    (a) get

    (b) come

    (c) take

    (d) answer

25. A: I guess you really need to take a day off before you ___________ under the strain.

B: Tell me about it.

    (a) strike

    (b) break

    (c) crack

    (d) bust

26. Every time Ann hopes to buy something, she asks me for some money. I guess she thinks that I have money to ___________.
(a) buy
(b) grant
(c) burn
(d) mock

27. Surprisingly, the plants that listen to classical music frequently are likely to be better able to ___________ infection and disease.
(a) faze
(b) withdraw
(c) withstand
(d) fumble

28. I have been concerned that my favorite friends, Tom and Mary, don't have ___________ with each other in the least.
(a) heart
(b) history
(c) mind
(d) chemistry

29. The moment the prodigal son got back home, his mother ___________ her arms around him and gave him a hearty and big hug.
(a) infuriated
(b) wrapped
(c) razed
(d) hugged

30. On the grounds that the rain really ___________ it was no use even though I had an umbrella.
(a) hoisted
(b) sprinkled
(c) pelted
(d) hurled

31. Although David and Susan didn't know that the film would be so ___________ , they wound up laughing for the whole time.

(a) sober

(b) scrupulous

(c) diurnal

(d) hilarious

32. Even though the oral presentation was ___________, it was quite well-organized.

(a) complimentary

(b) convulsant

(c) ambiguous

(d) boisterous

33. To her disappointment, she got abruptly ___________ without any prior notification.

(a) crammed

(b) crushed

(c) sanctioned

(d) sacked

34. Smith had ___________ himself to the issue for the primary purpose of redistribution of wealth.

(a) concealed

(b) addressed

(c) beckoned

(d) demised

35. In autocratic times, the authors ___________ the secret society to dodge crack by the government.

(a) censored

(b) chided

(c) treasured

(d) undermined

36. The presidential election results were ______________ on the grounds of voter fraud.
    (a) negotiated
    (b) nullified
    (c) championed
    (d) ameliorated

37. After an exhaustive and thorough examination of the patient's mental condition, the ______________ prescribed some drugs.
    (a) psychopath
    (b) pharmacist
    (c) psychiatrist
    (d) psychologist

38. When Jane learneds that she was expecting, she wanted to meet with a proficient ___________.
    (a) plastic surgeon
    (b) orthopedist
    (c) dermatologist
    (d) obstetrician

39. On the basis of the incidents with drinking problems which occurred two weeks ago, the school resolved to ______________ the rules that allow serving alcohol on the campus.
    (a) emaciate
    (b) cow
    (c) rescind
    (d) falter

40. A longer war would harm the U.S. at home, ______________ racial tensions on the grounds of the disproportionate number of blacks on the front lines.
    (a) extinguishing
    (b) consummating
    (c) exacerbating
    (d) transacting

41. According to the report, the aircraft set off to_____________ away from the runway due to the inclement visibility.

(a) sway

(b) swing

(c) swerve

(d) swamp

42. It has been so _____________ for us to lose a year's harvest on account of the huge typhoon.

(a) mesmerizing

(b) unnerving

(c) fuzzy

(d) cumbersome

43. Every step forward will meet with more impediments if we are bent on maintaining the

_____________.

(a) pro-choicer

(b) pros and cons

(c) status quo

(d) archetype

44. When a hostage situation takes place, the police have a tight security _____________ around the building.

(a) lane

(b) line

(c) hurdle

(d) cordon

45. According to the research by the sociologist, there are _____________ differences between the East and the West in their support for the death penalty.

(a) ample

(b) stark

(c) profuse

(d) fecund

46. Some researchers announced that when children make some mistakes, for example, breaking a vase or spilling water, if they are chided for them, it contributes to _____________ children's creativity.

(a) circumscribing

(b) digressing

(c) dislodging

(d) infuriating

47. I surmise that without a _____________ of doubt, Mr. Choo will be a member of the all star team.

(a) fracture

(b) room

(c) trace

(d) cream

48. This is a fantastic machine that is designed to fix a _____________ which has taken place in the course of making things.

(a) swatch

(b) paralysis

(c) glitch

(d) laud

49. Edward's father admonished him that if he didn't brush his teeth three times a day after meals, his teeth would get infirm and easily broken, contributing to _____________.

(a) dentures

(b) diarrhea

(c) hepatitis

(d) wisdom teeth

50. Forgetting what he had done in the past, Matt resolved to be _____________ to remember it.

(a) enchanted

(b) hypnotized

(c) bewitched

(d) intrigued

고난도 Actual Training
Training
05

실제 TEPS 시험의 문항수와 동일하게 구성된 고난도 Actual Training을
제한 시간 15분 내에 모두 풀 수 있도록 노력해 보세요!

1. A: The manager says that Tom will ___________.

B: I can understand the manager. Tom is always rude to the customers.

(a) get cold feet

(b) get to the bottom of something

(c) get the boot

(d) get down to brass tacks

2. A: Shanna, what is your religion?

B: My whole family is Catholic but I am still an ___________.

(a) ardent

(b) antipodal

(c) ambience

(d) agnostic

3. A: I've never seen that couple raises their voice at each other before. Have you?

B: Oh, I'm sure they do have an ___________ once in a while.

(a) altercation

(b) alternation

(c) alternant

(d) alignment

4. A: Dad! What are we having for your birthday dinner tonight?

B: I'm sorry Howard, but I'm afraid we will just have to make ___________ with something at home.

(a) do

(b) to

(c) out

(d) believe

5. A: You have a huge issue when you date someone.

B: I know, I try not to ___________ myself too much but it's hard not to.

(a) spurt

(b) dodge

(c) pamper

(d) disentangle

6. A: Part time jobs are a waste of time, don't you think?

B: No. It may seem ____________, but it can be a great experience in life.

  (a) precious

  (b) flaunting

  (c) ephemeral

  (d) external

7. A: How is Shayna these days? Is she still depressed?

B: Yeah, I feel so bad. She used to be so joyful and ____________.

  (a) abstruse

  (b) frigid

  (c) vivacious

  (d) vigilant

8. A: How is your plan for a trip to China going?

B: Ha ha, I finally decided to take the ____________!

  (a) decision

  (b) plunge

  (c) itinerary

  (d) eaves

9. A: How did that theory go?

B: Fortunately the market behaved precisely as assumed, so it finally hit the ____________!

  (a) booze

  (b) brake

  (c) mark

  (d) roof

10. A: I think that Maria has a talent for the piano. She won every musical contest that she attended.

B: Didn't you know that Maria's father is a pianist? She is a ____________.

  (a) chip off the old block

  (b) drop in the ocean

  (c) run-of-the-mill

  (d) all thumbs

11. A: Jenna, how do you want me to pay you back?

    B: Oh! I almost forgot. You can just ___________ the money.

      (a) revere

      (b) retrieve

      (c) remit

      (d) restore

12. A: What is the primary requirement you want from a potential employee?

    B: From many aspects, we first want them to be ___________ in making decisions.

      (a) rebuked

      (b) retentive

      (c) repellent

      (d) resolute

13. A: Is there a problem with the light? It doesn't work.

    B: The electricity was ___________ for hours to change an old cable.

      (a) cut down

      (b) cut off

      (c) cut out

      (d) cut up

14. A: Who have you met recently among our ___________?

    B: Remember Jack who was in our math class? I ran into him the other day!

      (a) altar

      (b) alumni

      (c) alumnus

      (d) alchemy

15. A: Jenny admitted she came close to losing her business.

    B: But, she ___________. She doesn't cry at all.

      (a) gets cracking

      (b) twists her arm

      (c) spills the beans

      (d) keeps a stiff upper lip

16. A: I'm very worried about my son. He doesn't do anything without watching TV.

    B: That's too bad. He is just ___________.

       (a) the pick of the bunch

       (b) turning the table

       (c) pulling his socks up

       (d) marking time

17. A: Did you know you had a sickly ___________ last night?

    B: Really? I really didn't feel good yesterday.

       (a) pallor

       (b) pittance

       (c) magnitude

       (d) iota

18. A: Did you get your results back from the hospital?

    B: Yeah, and I have bad news. Doctors found a ___________ tumor in my breast.

       (a) colossal

       (b) infinite

       (c) malignant

       (d) penurious

19. A: If you put the trash there, a ___________ odor comes into our house.

    B: I'm really sorry, but this is where it's supposed to be.

       (a) cogent

       (b) impregnable

       (c) rancid

       (d) colossal

20. A: How did Kristen get to be in charge of that project?

    B: I don't know, I guess the boss gave her a ___________ for the last time.

       (a) remiss

       (b) crack

       (c) scrutiny

       (d) leave

21. A: Honey, look at this report card. Our son Jake got 5 F's this semester.

B: He ___________ himself. He just hung around with his friends studying nothing during the whole semester.

   (a) served right

   (b) came to

   (c) brought that upon

   (d) went wrong with

22. A: Did you hear there is a shot that can cure swine flu?

B: Yeah, I heard the drug will ___________ the virus.

   (a) attenuate

   (b) endear

   (c) reimburse

   (d) discard

23. A: Do you want me to explain every single detail of the case or get to the point?

B: You'd better ___________ as we have no time at the moment.

   (a) beat around the bush

   (b) bark up the wrong tree

   (c) cut to the chase

   (d) wander from the subject

24. A: Do you think ___________ people are irresponsible or wise?

B: I'm not sure, but I don't see what's bad about enjoying their own lives.

   (a) esthetic

   (b) olfactory

   (c) burly

   (d) hedonistic

25. A: How do you know so many great tasting restaurants?

B: Ha ha, I have such ___________ taste, I find eating one of my great pleasures in life.

   (a) quirky

   (b) tangible

   (c) culinary

   (d) epicurean

Part II   Questions 26-50
Choose the best answer for the blank.

26. In spite of the low attendance, the party went on without a ___________ .

(a) bean

(b) blink

(c) hitch

(d) hatch

27. An environmentalist having radical ideas about making the world green is called _________ .

(a) a green hand

(b) all nature

(c) a tree-hugger

(d) a sanguine nature

28. The musical 'Rent' has enchanted everyone who watched it and it acquired some _________ fame.

(a) notorious

(b) flagrant

(c) illustrious

(d) dubious

29. Lawschool, which is an institution specializing in legal education, was successful in the U.S. while it was a(n) ___________ in Japan.

(a) fatal blunder

(b) minor setback

(c) utter failure

(d) fast track

30. If one of our customers ___________ the contract, he should compensate us for loss.

(a) abides by

(b) reneges on

(c) enters into

(d) falls out

31. Be careful, that pottery was rated as "________" by experts because of its origin and age.

(a) valuable

(b) variable

(c) vaticinal

(d) vagarious

32. The President announced that he would focus on solving the ________ poverty.

(a) abstract

(b) abridged

(c) abject

(d) absurd

33. The U.S. government on Monday ________ sanctions on four people and eight organizations accused of aiding North Korea's government through illicit trade, the Treasury Department said.

(a) slashed

(b) smacked

(c) skimmed

(d) slapped

34. I am warning you for the last time, do not try to hand me a ________.

(a) lemon

(b) bowl

(c) pepper

(d) fiddle

35. Just like any other typical politician, she also gave us a(n) ________ answer.

(a) retorted

(b) nostalgic

(c) equivocal

(d) equivalent

36. I prefer simple designs over flaring and ____________ interior designs.

    (a) mere

    (b) dull

    (c) gaudy

    (d) infantile

37. The ____________ seem to dislike me, for they misapprehend that I overwhelmed them with knowledge.

    (a) pundits

    (b) bandits

    (c) transits

    (d) misfits

38. The greatest concern of Obama was that many of the hard-core supporters would rather lose the election than ____________ the vote.

    (a) court

    (b) entangle

    (c) face

    (d) pry

39. I will give you another copy of our contract for you to ____________ after the meeting.

    (a) procrastinate

    (b) peruse

    (c) perceive

    (d) procreate

40. Are you still waiting for the judge to drop the other ____________?

    (a) boot

    (b) shoe

    (c) sandal

    (d) slipper

41. North Korean spies ______________ into South Korea in order to watch troop movements.

    (a) instigated

    (b) intimated

    (c) intermediated

    (d) infiltrated

42. The man next door was accused of ___________ a convicted felon.

    (a) hankering

    (b) hooting

    (c) harboring

    (d) harrowing

43. The cravings for excitement is deeply ___________ in humankind of all periods.

    (a) rooted

    (b) drooled

    (c) convicted

    (d) awry

44. History is not just a list of events arranged in a careless manner like a ___________ of things.

    (a) dictate

    (b) measure

    (c) heap

    (d) bore

45. One must understand that suffering and failure are not only ___________ but also beneficial.

    (a) inevitable

    (b) inedible

    (c) inert

    (d) inexorable

46. When the company restructured its employment policies, Harper and more than 6,000
fellows found most of their benefits had _____________ through their fingers.
   (a) slipped
   (b) smashed
   (c) spruced
   (d) sizzled

47. Experts announced that bad habits often _____________ up on us while we are not conscious
of them.
   (a) curse
   (b) thrust
   (c) creep
   (d) strike

48. Although I have a handicap, I am _____________ with a fierce resolution to succeed in the
world.
   (a) empowered
   (b) possessed
   (c) convinced
   (d) controlled

49. How can we _____________ those natural resources that can be used to produce nutritious
foods for thousands who are starving?
   (a) squander
   (b) scavenge
   (c) scrounge
   (d) swamp

50. In order to stop the virus from spreading, we must keep suspicious patients in _____________
 from others.
   (a) reconciliation
   (b) usefulness
   (c) quarantine
   (d) nomination

고난도
Actual Training
06

실제 TEPS 시험의 문항수와 동일하게 구성된 고난도 Actual Training을
제한 시간 **15분** 내에 모두 풀 수 있도록 노력해 보세요!

1. A: I really love professor Kim's lectures on physical anthropology. He always helps us understand difficult matters so easily in his lectures.

B: I couldn't agree with you more. Today's lecture was also ____________ and no one needed to ask any questions.

(a) as good as his words   (b) as plain as day

(c) a word out of season   (d) around the corner

2. A: I hate Lisa singing out so loud at midnight. I can't possibly go to sleep and it drives me crazy.

B: You know what? Lisa loves singing alone at midnight but never sings in front of others and always tries to ____________ even when she has to sing.

(a) sink a shoot   (b) have the last word

(c) get out of that   (d) go out of date

3. A: Is there any difference between these apples?

B: Yes, these apples are tree- ____________, so the price is 30% higher.

(a) ripened

(b) fledged

(c) seasoned

(d) harvested

4. A: I guess the monsoon season is finally over.

B: To my sadness, it's not over yet. The National Weather Service said it's just____________ for a moment.

(a) holding off

(b) holding in

(c) holding out

(d) holding up

5. A: It seems you're living quite a busy life!

B: You think so? I am volunteering for a host of ____________ traveling around the country.

(a) pavement

(b) sparks

(c) proceeds

(d) causes

6. A: I'm so sorry, I couldn't make it to the meeting.

B: Never mind, but promise me you will never _____________ your word again.

    (a) go back on

    (b) flare up at

    (c) get hold of

    (d) make up for

7. A: Did you hear that the company is going to downsize our production crew?

B: No, I didn't. That news really _____________.

    (a) brings me down

    (b) trips me up

    (c) runs me down

    (d) holds me down

8. A: My dentist pulled out an intact tooth even though I had paid a high hospital fee.

B: You must feel _____________ advantage of.

    (a) clipped

    (b) given

    (c) taken

    (d) ripped off

9. A: How would you like to be _____________?

B: You can call me Parker.

    (a) anointed

    (b) designated

    (c) named

    (d) addressed

10. A: You will be more economical if you make a list of things to buy before shopping.

B: Don't worry. I make mental _____________ of what I buy whenever I shop.

    (a) willies

    (b) tallies

    (c) rallies

    (d) fillies

11. A: Do I get my money back if I'm not satisfied with this product?

    B: Of course, our refund guarantee is ___________.

       (a) sturdy

       (b) solid

       (c) genial

       (d) potent

12. A: Could I send these glasses to Korea by express mail?

    B: It is possible but you need to write down "___________" on the box because they break easily.

       (a) vulnerable

       (b) fragile

       (c) feeble

       (d) tender

13. A: I'm moving out next week, how can I get my mail ___________?

    B: Please fill out the form and submit it to me.

       (a) received

       (b) remitted

       (c) forwarded

       (d) transmitted

14. A: My check ___________. What's going on?

    B: Let's see. It's because you're overdrawn.

       (a) withdrawn

       (b) bounced

       (c) broke

       (d) bankrupted

15. A: I'm earning a great deal of money. It's the ___________ of my career.

    B: That's great!

       (a) pinnacle

       (b) crest

       (c) vertex

       (d) plateau

16. A: I'd like to have this white T-shirt _____________ because I spilt some black ink on it.

    B: Sure. Is there anything else?

      (a) altered

      (b) bleached

      (c) dry-cleaned

      (d) starched

17. A: The clouds look so _____________.

    B: You're right. I suspect that a heavy rainstorm is coming.

      (a) ambivalent

      (b) ominous

      (c) biped

      (d) affluent

18. A: I feel tired. Can you _____________?

    B: Sure, but I suggest you take a shower before you go to bed. You smell bad.

      (a) hit the spot

      (b) let me up

      (c) play sick

      (d) tuck me in

19. A: Let's _____________ for a present on Sue's birthday.

    B: Good idea. I will contact everyone who adores her.

      (a) keep the chin up

      (b) buy off

      (c) cash in

      (d) chip in

20. A: Why did you spank Marty?

    B: He _____________ despite my warning even when the traffic was very heavy.

      (a) overworked

      (b) retarded

      (c) jaywalked

      (d) underwrote

21. A: Would you stop ___________ me, please?

B: It's too cramped here so I can't help it.

    (a) gushing

    (b) wiping

    (c) hissing

    (d) poking

22. A: How was the food at the new Chinese restaurant?

B: Fantastic! The food was delicious, not to ___________ cheap.

    (a) speak

    (b) state

    (c) mention

    (d) talk

23. A: I've heard that you recently started to play golf. Are you enjoying it?

B: Of course. It's a(n) ___________ from my daily life.

    (a) diversion

    (b) divergence

    (c) evasion

    (d) conversion

24. A: Do you think he is good-looking?

B: Yes, he's tall and has ___________ features.

    (a) engraved

    (b) chiseled

    (c) exempted

    (d) hassled

25. A: Tell me the time and the ___________ of the meeting?

B: It's Lecturer's Common Room, 2 pm next Tuesday.

    (a) vendition

    (b) vendor

    (c) venison

    (d) venue

Part II · Questions 26-50

Choose the best answer for the blank.

26. Desperate to hide the test result, Jack ____________ his parents signature and submitted the sheet back.

(a) forged

(b) forwent

(c) forfeited

(d) foresaw

27. Actress Angelina ____________ a suit against her manager for revealing her private life to the public.

(a) inspected

(b) instituted

(c) inscribed

(d) inverted

28. We must hold our president ____________ for the continuous economic recession.

(a) applicable

(b) accusable

(c) appliable

(d) accountable

29. We have reached a conclusion that any kind of plagiarism will not go __________, and will be punished.

(a) uncensured

(b) uncensored

(c) uncanny

(d) uncaring

30. Some celebrities earn their talents through intense training, but most of them are born with ____________ talents.

(a) excessive

(b) congenital

(c) accused

(d) conceded

31. In order to resolve the ______________ over North Korea's nuclear weapons program, diplomats from six nations gathered at the table.

(a) digression

(b) nomination

(c) impasse

(d) implication

32. Geographers claim that major cities nearby the ocean basin will be ______________ due to natural hazards such as tsunami.

(a) obliterated

(b) obedient

(c) obliged

(d) obeisant

33. A growing number of teenagers these days tend to think that keeping their ______________ is not that important if they use protection.

(a) polygamy

(b) asceticism

(c) celibacy

(d) percept

34. Eight ______________ doctors who used licenses from real doctors were taken into custody.

(a) quota

(b) quorum

(c) quirk

(d) quack

35. It is your responsibility to ______________ if you feel any physical pain. We are not in charge of your accident.

(a) abominate

(b) abort

(c) alleviate

(d) advert

36. According to the statistical view economists have come up with, it alone ____________ the possibility of economic recession.

(a) negates

(b) legitimates

(c) integrates

(d) justifies

37. We not only look at the essay's content, logicality, and grammar, but we also consider the ____________.

(a) bribery

(b) braid

(c) brevity

(d) brevet

38. Politicians who are____________between what they say and what they actually do usually raise people's frustration.

(a) spilt

(b) dichotomous

(c) sporadic

(d) convergent

39. When you are at a workplace, you need to be more serious at your work than giving ____________ opinions during the meeting.

(a) frivolous

(b) ferocious

(c) fervent

(d) felicitous

40. As technology developed, many means of communication became ____________.

(a) oblivious

(b) obsolete

(c) oblique

(d) obliterate

41. Without any survey or research done, it is _____________ to think that the plan could
succeed.

(a) averse

(b) elliptical

(c) ludicrous

(d) immense

42. During the presentation today, could you clearly point out the _____________ feature of your
idea to the investors?

(a) shallow

(b) amiable

(c) introverted

(d) salient

43. Because mistakes are not intentionally made, I do not want to _____________ Bryan for the
accident he caused.

(a) vent

(b) creep

(c) castigate

(d) diffuse

44. An educator's job is not only to provide knowledge but also to _____________ their students
into life.

(a) galvanize

(b) vent

(c) ladle

(d) cram

45. Many immigrant workers were _____________ against the company's owner because of the
excessive workload and delay in paying wages.

(a) moribund

(b) plagued

(c) relieved

(d) incensed

46. The judge should not have been so ______________ with that sex offender at the court last week.

(a) utter

(b) lenient

(c) slothful

(d) overbearing

47. The process in which ____________ cancer cells multiply has not been fully understood by the experts yet.

(a) extinct

(b) vigorous

(c) malignant

(d) vehement

48. If you let them walk, they will sooner or later develop a nasty ____________ for committing a crime again.

(a) coarseness

(b) destituteness

(c) insolvency

(d) penchant

49. Most of the newly released cars these days are ____________ with the latest technology.

(a) replete

(b) replicative

(c) replenished

(d) repopulated

50. The unstable economic and political situation were ____________ to the cause of the conflict between the two countries.

(a) trifled

(b) ancillary

(c) secluded

(d) resilient

고난도
Actual Training 07

실제 TEPS 시험의 문항수와 동일하게 구성된 고난도 Actual Training을
제한 시간 15분 내에 모두 풀 수 있도록 노력해 보세요!

1. A: It is no use for you to be ___________ after you have committed such a cruel crime.

    B: I know, but could you please reconsider?

      (a) rumpled

      (b) dilapidated

      (c) contrite

      (d) deplorable

2. A: An example of ___________ is "You told me that story a thousand times!"

    B: Oh, and another one is "She nodded her head a million times."

      (a) hyperbole

      (b) hibernation

      (c) decrepitude

      (d) induction

3. A: Government's ___________ plan will threaten the country's social security system.

    B: They must plan so that the country develops as time goes by.

      (a) deriding

      (b) myopic

      (c) sporadic

      (d) tenacious

4. A: What is the reason for the troops still remaining there?

    B: I think the ___________ reason for their presence is to keep the peace, but you never know.

      (a) prerogative

      (b) ostensible

      (c) grudging

      (d) grimacing

5. A: How did the ___________ meeting for the concert go?

    B: It went well, all the members were present and they all had great ideas.

      (a) enunciate

      (b) perilous

      (c) prenuptial

      (d) preliminary

6. A: Once you start a conversation with her, you will know that she is very ____________.

B: I realized! She was socializing very well at the party.

(a) acquitted

(b) gregarious

(c) perverse

(d) sedulous

7. A: The brand 'Dior Homme' succeeded in its undertaking thanks to Hedi Slimane.

B: After he left 'Dior Homme', the brand tried to ____________ by recruiting innovative and creative designers.

(a) make dry bones alive

(b) come back alive

(c) keep it alive

(d) keep the matter alive

8. A: I wish you and Jack would stop fighting.

B: We can't help it. I guess we are just ____________ enemies.

(a) unsolicited

(b) implacable

(c) premature

(d) uncharted

9. A: What is your essential point in your job?

B: I always try to be ____________ in keeping the records up-to-date.

(a) dealing

(b) adjunct

(c) abstract

(d) meticulous

10. A: Why do so many politicians lie about what they have done?

B: I guess they are just lying on the ____________ of protecting the country.

(a) pretext

(b) launching

(c) retainment

(d) meddling

11. A: What do you think of my poem?

B: Wow…it's very concise but the words _____________ with such complex and deep

expressions.

(a) resonate

(b) infringed

(c) stifled

(d) pre-empted

12. A: What is the worst thing about your boyfriend?

B: You need to see him at a restaurant… He's a real _____________ eater.

(a) exacerbated

(b) voracious

(c) formidable

(d) incumbent

13. A: I heard that you had a fight with Ms. Kelly the other day. Did you apologize to her?

B: No. Her sharp words _____________ so I don't want to apologize.

(a) took me off

(b) gave a little

(c) rained favors on me

(d) cut me to the quick

14. A: The documentary last night dealt with the _____________ of modern society.

B: That must have been interesting. I've always wanted to make a documentary myself.

(a) introvert

(b) extrovert

(c) decadence

(d) levity

15. A: That infamous construction company got accused again.

B: Again? They are the most _____________ corporation I've ever heard of.

(a) uncanny

(b) nefarious

(c) predominant

(d) preceding

16. A: Were there any complaints with the service?

B: There was one woman who felt one of the workers was too ___________.

   (a) standoffish

   (b) gregarious

   (c) preamble

   (d) staunch

17. A: When Miranda appeared on the catwalk with a fashionable outfit, she ___________.

B: I was also invited to that fashion show and she was really awesome.

   (a) scored in public

   (b) brought down the house

   (c) acted on her own volition

   (d) covered up the stage

18. A: As an educator, what do you think is the most ___________ obstacle to a high quality education?

B: I think the current trend of private education is the biggest factor that deters the development of quality education at public school.

   (a) heartening

   (b) forlorn

   (c) formative

   (d) formidable

19. A: Don't get too close to him. There are rumors ___________ about him.

B: Really? But he seems totally innocuous to me.

   (a) going around

   (b) hanging around

   (c) winding down

   (d) chucking up

20. A: Don't you think the new assignment is too much for us to do by ourselves?

B: I don't know, it's pretty ___________ but I am going to try my best.

   (a) opaque

   (b) lustrous

   (c) onerous

   (d) unhindered

21. A: In order to survive in a highly competitive society, you must try not to be ___________.

B: I know that I need to be more tactful, thanks for your advice.

   (a) hindered

   (b) unheeding

   (c) elucidated

   (d) eluded

22. A: Why do you look at him like that?

B: I don't know, I just don't like his ___________ grin.

   (a) impish

   (b) impious

   (c) imposing

   (d) impoverished

23. A: Most politicians have used spies.

B: Right, they did to ___________ some useful information on the opponent.

   (a) ferret out

   (b) dig up

   (c) gussy up

   (d) map out

24. A: What are you planning on doing after retirement?

B: I want to build a foundation that helps those who are ___________.

   (a) far-fetched

   (b) frivolous

   (c) indigent

   (d) opulent

25. A: Police found some inappropriate actions between the two ___________ companies.

B: Wow, but too bad they don't exist anymore.

   (a) pecuniary

   (b) prissy

   (c) debunked

   (d) defunct

Part II
Questions 26-50
Choose the best answer for the blank.

26. Due to current CEO's bad investment decisions, the company had to go through a
____________ loss.
(a) refined
(b) pecuniary
(c) chagrin
(d) eclectic

27. Although we overcame the critical situation, there is no room to be ____________.
(a) myriad
(b) furtive
(c) complacent
(d) perfunctory

28. The coach has still not made a decision of how he will ____________ me for my inexcusable
behavior.
(a) serene
(b) reprimand
(c) convince
(d) acclimatize

29. Now that you apologize for it, it's ok. But I was so upset when you ____________ and
got angry without any understanding.
(a) accounted for that
(b) jumped the gun
(c) scooped in
(d) distressed yourself

30. The world ____________ South Korea to the skies about organizing the ministerial talks with
North Korea and Russia.
(a) solicit
(b) sojourn
(c) probed
(d) extolled

31. The journalist Cameron Stucky was criticized for being ___________ in his essay written about a politician.

(a) defiled

(b) irrevocable

(c) hard-hitting

(d) tentative

32. We had a special guest to give us a lecture but he kept on talking about topics ___________ to the issue at hand.

(a) pseudonymous

(b) parsimonious

(c) intravenous

(d) extraneous

33. I doubt he can predict the outcome; it's almost impossible with any degree of ___________.

(a) chagrin

(b) certitude

(c) commotion

(d) circumference

34. In his address, the spokesperson made a clever attempt to ___________ the many failures of his company.

(a) gloss over

(b) jump at

(c) dote on

(d) kick off

35. The communist leader lamented, "Why is the road to the West so ___________?"

(a) bumpy

(b) glum

(c) heretical

(d) medicinal

36. Many reporters were striving to find more information about the president's assassination in order to write the ______________ for their newspaper.

(a) olfactory

(b) vicinity

(c) lethargy

(d) obituary

37. Widespread ______________ towards public order and morality among teenagers today is becoming a serious issue.

(a) apathy

(b) minor

(c) conclave

(d) caucus

38. Everyone at the conference was very impressed by the information provided and thought the content really hit the ______________.

(a) air

(b) spot

(c) buffers

(d) bull's-eye

39. Politicians really need to hold their ______________ and discuss the matters thoughtfully rather than make a violent scene.

(a) corner up

(b) course

(c) horses

(d) ground

40. Carter's plan to re-start exports of U.S. beef angers Korean ______________.

(a) rangers

(b) ranchers

(c) rapports

(d) respecters

41. Our company has a strict dress code. It is out of ___________ to wear any inappropriate clothes to work.

    (a) a hat

    (b) upright

    (c) the gate

    (d) bounds

42. They will praise the student even if he is not ___________.

    (a) unassuming

    (b) abusive

    (c) bleak

    (d) agonizing

43. After the company went out of business, everyone started to doubt the former owner's ___________ because of his strange behavior caught by the paparazzi.

    (a) sanity

    (b) sanitary

    (c) sanctuary

    (d) saturation

44. Four people were arrested at the scene while trying to sell illegal drugs under the ___________.

    (a) corporal

    (b) affidavit

    (c) backlash

    (d) counter

45. It was impressive to see how Cindy coped in her new job considering she was up to her ___________ in work.

    (a) lark

    (b) eyes

    (c) tricks

    (d) ears

46. My irresponsible brother-in-law seems to always stay _____________ financially.

   (a) in the works

   (b) in there pitching

   (c) in the soup

   (d) in the bag

47. You should not have _____________ up at the reporter even though you were offended.

   (a) flared

   (b) fired

   (c) skewed

   (d) antiquated

48. There is no good in making a mountain out of a molehill, because this case is something we don't want to make a big _____________ about.

   (a) pose

   (b) fuss

   (c) dirt

   (d) pinch

49. Whenever there is an argument or a disagreement, I always try to sit on the _____________ and try to settle things down.

   (a) rock

   (b) tree

   (c) swing

   (d) fence

50. Thanks to the taxi driver, I was saved by the _____________.

   (a) air

   (b) bell

   (c) hand

   (d) sound

고난도
Actual Training
08

실제 TEPS 시험의 문항수와 동일하게 구성된 고난도 Actual Training을
제한 시간 15분 내에 모두 풀 수 있도록 노력해 보세요!

1. A: Have you ever had a(n) _____________ that someone is hiding something from you?

B: No, never in my life. I'm really slow at catching things.

(a) wink

(b) inkling

(c) eye

(d) itch

2. A: You look so fat. What about doing a little _____________ on your beer belly?

B: I know I've grown fleshy but I don't want to undergo any operations.

(a) nip and tuck

(b) back and belly

(c) Botox injections

(d) breast augmentation

3. A: The government's aim is to make all the companies compete on a _____________.

B: I doubt it since it doesn't have any policies to guarantee the equality of opportunity for reaching new markets.

(a) ground plan

(b) level playing field

(c) high ground

(d) gray area

4. A: Hello Mr.Clark, nice to meet you. I am just going to cut to the _____________ since we don't have much time.

B: Yes sure, let's get down to business right away.

(a) quick

(b) a point

(c) bone

(d) chase

5. A: This new product ready for next month's launch will decide the future of our company.

B: I know, I'll really make a _____________ for its success.

(a) bad break

(b) pitch

(c) tally

(d) big splash

6. A: Why are you mad at me?

B: I'd prefer not to see you ______________ over my share.

   (a) fluttering

   (b) drooling

   (c) squabbling

   (d) snuggling

7. A: Let's set up a modern hospital in a third world country, perhaps one in Africa.

B: Sounds like a good plan but do you think it's realistically and financially ______________ ?

   (a) supercilious

   (b) innate

   (c) autonomous

   (d) feasible

8. A: What ability do you look for the most in hiring a worker?

B: Our company lacks people who are ______________ in computer usage, therefore we need those who are highly proficient in dealing with computers.

   (a) literate

   (b) literary

   (c) literal

   (d) illiterate

9. A: Why did you turn down her offer like that?

B: The idea seemed pretty ingenious, but it was hardly ______________ to what I am looking for.

   (a) blistering

   (b) potent

   (c) dire

   (d) germane

10. A: Although that church stood ______________ for decades, some features still remained.

B: You're right. We can still observe the very detailed decorations on the church wall.

   (a) derelict

   (b) implacable

   (c) snug

   (d) lush

11. A: Everything is closely related to cash these days.

　　B: I think that's why it is believed that poverty is ___________ to the next generation.

　　　(a) consecrated

　　　(b) perspired

　　　(c) perpetuated

　　　(d) procured

12. A: I was really shocked that James beat Chad up.

　　B: Me too, he was so obsequious that no one expected him to be ___________.

　　　(a) riotous

　　　(b) pugnacious

　　　(c) gluttonous

　　　(d) stupendous

13. A: We should respect other people regardless of gender, creed and nation.

　　B: To do that, we must get rid of any ___________ first.

　　　(a) relative concept

　　　(b) compulsive idea

　　　(c) popular opinion

　　　(d) preconceived notion

14. A: Why do you always force me to study but not tell my younger sister to do so?

　　B: I believe that she will follow ___________ if you first demonstrate it to her.

　　　(a) boots

　　　(b) footprints

　　　(c) behind

　　　(d) suit

15. A : Honey, you should discuss the problem with me before taking any measures.

　　B: Stop ___________. Our discussion always ends up in a bitter quarrel.

　　　(a) fussing around

　　　(b) pampering yourself

　　　(c) spoiling the game

　　　(d) blowing it wide open

16. A: It costs too much money to ship these by truck.

    B: There's more than one way to ____________ a cat. Let's check with the railroad.

       (a) skin

       (b) grab

       (c) kill

       (d) catch

17. A: Were you able to see the face of the person who broke into your house last night?

    B: No, I was just able to ____________ a figure in the dark.

       (a) make out

       (b) make in

       (c) make through

       (d) make up

18. A: I hear that Mr. Kim has a good command of English.

    B: Indeed. His British accent is excellent! He'd ____________ an Englishman anytime.

       (a) pass over

       (b) pass off

       (c) pass out

       (d) pass for

19. A: When filing your complaint, you must follow the chain of command.

    B: I already attended the orientation and was educated about the company ____________.

       (a) precedent

       (b) contrivance

       (c) protocol

       (d) brunt

20. A: What did the consultant say about your mental state?

    B: She told me I need to correct my habit of spitting ____________.

       (a) joust

       (b) crash

       (c) tacks

       (d) stifle

21. A: Do you think there is a possibility of Alex getting the job?

    B: No need to worry. According to his talent and ability, it's a(n) ___________ conclusion.

      (a) muddled

      (b) foregone

      (c) outmoded

      (d) absolute

22. A: I learned from the lecture, in order to be successful one has to be ___________ about the flow of money.

    B: I agree, I think the richer someone is, the more uptight they are about with dealing money.

      (a) savvy

      (b) suave

      (c) sagging

      (d) salubrious

23. A: What happened to Major John Watson of the Marine Corps who was involved in the murder case?

    B: It's pretty obvious. He got ___________ of his position as a result of his misconduct.

      (a) struck

      (b) entitled

      (c) served

      (d) stripped

24. A: What happened to the people who lost their houses due to the flood damage?

    B: Nothing ___________, they all started working on restoring their residential district.

      (a) inquired

      (b) daunted

      (c) compelled

      (d) inducted

25. A: Look how ___________ they look after the news on Maria's successful pregnancy.

    B: They must be pretty rapturous after a long, depressing 5 years of infertility.

      (a) erratic

      (b) ecstatic

      (c) enigmatic

      (d) eclectic

Part II **Questions 26-50**
Choose the best answer for the blank.

26. We voted on how to handle it before we spoke ____________ words.

(a) another

(b) rather

(c) such

(d) enough

27. The lawyer ____________ his brains to find decisive evidence that the opponent was bought off through bribery.

(a) pushed

(b) squeezed

(c) beat

(d) tied

28. Regarding the vitality of this matter, please make sure you ____________ up all the consequences before reporting the final draft to the boss.

(a) depose

(b) repose

(c) draw

(d) weigh

29. After Jake got dismissed, he immediately went to government offices in search of a job but he always got ____________.

(a) the sack

(b) the show on the road

(c) the run-around

(d) the picture

30. The whole world is worried sick about the little kids who are living in ____________ conditions, which leave them exposed to all sorts of diseases.

(a) binary

(b) respective

(c) sordid

(d) gratifying

31. What you are saying is perfectly ___________, but I have a somewhat doubtful feeling.

    (a) viable

    (b) vivid

    (c) vital

    (d) vial

32. After a week I neglected boss's unreasonable demand, I was given the ___________.

    (a) boot

    (b) slip

    (c) layoff

    (d) fire

33. The steel house is so ___________ that only a few people lived without inconvenience.

    (a) cramped

    (b) curbed

    (c) cozy

    (d) curfewed

34. The journal reported the unprecedented number of ___________ deaths at age one or younger.

    (a) griping

    (b) crippling

    (c) grasping

    (d) crib

35. Many new words that are used these days were ___________ from what teenagers started using as slang.

    (a) supplied

    (b) related

    (c) ditched

    (d) coined

36. To gain more support, you must get rid of your ___________ attitude and try to be more modest.

(a) haughty

(b) cordial

(c) residual

(d) transitory

37. He seemed to seek a compromise, so he suggested to ___________ in for gas.

(a) give

(b) chip

(c) rake

(d) take

38. A: I am afraid you ___________ the wrong person.
B: Sorry. My mistake.

(a) have

(b) get

(c) lose

(d) put

39. I am not aiming for a ___________ of awards and honors from people, in other words, I do not expect anything in return.

(a) demoted

(b) exhumed

(c) morose

(d) myriad

40. When I heard the news about a sex offender's continuous crime, I was filled with ___________ and was sick to my stomach.

(a) aberration

(b) revulsion

(c) volition

(d) extenuation

41. In case the participants of the conference are absent, the ____________ for every session will be provided for them.

(a) processes

(b) proceedings

(c) proceeds

(d) procedures

42. The reason why drugs are especially ____________ to teenagers is because they are not old enough to make rational decisions.

(a) fastidious

(b) repressive

(c) pernicious

(d) irksome

43. Devastated by war and natural disasters, the city was ____________ and in desperate need of assistance.

(a) destitute

(b) affluent

(c) exquisite

(d) indulgent

44. Food aid to impoverished regions will be guaranteed if you promise the ____________ of developing nuclear weapons.

(a) circulation

(b) cessation

(c) continuation

(d) convergence

45. By the time the pull-out was decided, the United Nation's premises were already _________, destroyed, and burnt.

(a) dispersed

(b) feigned

(c) probed

(d) looted

46. In Yosep's furniture shop, you will see the cozy ___________.

(a) device

(b) sectional

(c) tool

(d) typo

47. I just got done with the ___________ classes in business and now I am planning on taking more intense courses.

(a) selective

(b) formative

(c) rudimentary

(d) perpendicular

48. This year I want to run a marathon come ___________ or high water.

(a) sun

(b) hell

(c) flood

(d) snow

49. I was ___________ when I got the phone call that a close friend of mine ended his life by hanging himself.

(a) dissuaded

(b) frantic

(c) meditative

(d) gratified

50. We are planning on renovating this run-down cultural property to make sure it can ________ the storm that is coming soon.

(a) maintain

(b) stop

(c) persist

(d) weather

고난도
Actual Training
09

실제 TEPS 시험의 문항수와 동일하게 구성된 고난도 Actual Training을

제한 시간 15분 내에 모두 풀 수 있도록 노력해 보세요!

1. A: I am not ___________ about what's going on. I just trust their actions.

B: No. You think it's none of your business.

   (a) alloted

   (b) abated

   (c) nonchalant

   (d) augmented

2. A: What do you think of homosexual couples' adoption?

B: Sorry. I didn't ___________ over that matter.

   (a) ponder

   (b) brood

   (c) maul

   (d) unravel

3. A: How do the students evaluate her course?

B: Most of them think she gives quite a ___________ explanation and therefore are able to understand easily and precisely.

   (a) docile

   (b) ferocious

   (c) frugal

   (d) lucid

4. A: I don't agree with our company's staffing freeze because we are short of skilled people while there is too much work to deal with.

B: Yeah, I know the company is in financial difficuly but ___________ in staffing is going to aggravate the situation.

   (a) gulf   (b) gaps

   (c) lack   (d) shortage

5. A: Nothing can ever seem to beat this product's practicality.

B: I don't think so. There are so many different features that come in ___________ out in the market that we missed.

   (a) favor   (b) handy

   (c) flocks   (d) sight

6. A: How is everything going for you?

B: Nothing has changed, I am still up a ______________ without a paddle.

    (a) storm

    (b) island

    (c) cloud

    (d) creek

7. A: I heard on the news that a container coming from China was filled with ______________ goods such as imitations of high brands.

B: Why do people struggle so much to earn money by smuggling products that are prohibited?

    (a) contraband

    (b) cornerstone

    (c) deference

    (d) infidelity

8. A: I was with Jack the whole time to console him upon his sudden ______________.

B: I'm so sorry to hear that. I did know that his mom was struggling with cancer for quite a while.

    (a) trespass

    (b) loiter

    (c) bereavement

    (d) imposture

9. A: He lacks sportsmanship when we play golf with him.

B: What he really needs is the ability to enjoy the game and accept the result even if it is a(n) ______________ defeat.

    (a) turbulent

    (b) derivative

    (c) sleuth

    (d) ignominious

10. A: What did the famous comedian get accused of?

B: He made a remark that accidently ______________ one company's name on last week's show.

    (a) forestalled

    (b) corroborated

    (c) slandered

    (d) reared

11. A: What do you think of our company's policy of salary being _______________ with one's experience in the field?

   B: I think it is fair since more experience means they are more precise in what they do.

   (a) in a quandary

   (b) commensurate

   (c) flaunting

   (d) exuded

12. A: It makes me really mad that so many girls have to be sacrificed because of some people who are not wise and sane enough.

   B: Yeah, I heard the news. I really _______________ with the victims who were wounded both mentally and physically.

   (a) commiserate

   (b) stricken

   (c) disclaim

   (d) back out

13. A: Statistical data are _______________ for people who wish to see the constant rate of change at a glance.

   B: You're right. Statistics are crucial and useful in many fields.

   (a) fraught

   (b) lopsided

   (c) lenient

   (d) salutary

14. A: I am sorry that he was given his walking papers.

   B: He's so upset about it! I guess that he is so reserved that he'll never _______________.

   (a) have a ball

   (b) come down hard on

   (c) live it down

   (d) be loaded for bear

15. A: How did she manage to persuade the fastidious contractors from India?

   B: She is famous for being _______________ at handling delicate situations and people.

   (a) adroit

   (b) cumbersome

   (c) gratuitous

   (d) embellished

16. A: I can't believe I made such a stupid mistake. Who would trust me now?

B: Shanna, you don't have to ______________ yourself too much for failing. Everyone makes stupid mistakes from time to time.

(a) fabricate

(b) berate

(c) venerate

(d) hiatus

17. A: We all have been educated since we were little to ______________ feminity.

B: You sound like a total feminist.

(a) devour

(b) placate

(c) emulate

(d) disparage

18. A: As a result of your analyzing, what did you come up with?

B: So far we all know that apes and human beings are genetically very much alike and I am trying to find the ______________ between them and us.

(a) compatibility

(b) prodigy

(c) anatomies

(d) discernment

19. A: My indecisive attitude really seems to degrade me both inside and outside of work.

B: It is quite important to be ______________ as you grow up, so try to reduce other factors that confuse you and replace them with your thoughts.

(a) evenhanded   (b) insolvent

(c) unwavering   (d) endearing

20. A: Do you know about anyone historically famous enough to be printed on American currency?

B: I learned that one of the most ______________ faces engraved on American currency is a brave Native American woman named Sacagawea.

(a) subservient

(b) noteworthy

(c) strenuous

(d) pensive

21. A: Do you think it's better to read one book several times or instead spend that time reading several other books?

B: I personally think repetitively reading a single book will mean merely an accumulation of ______________ knowledge, the burdensome accumulation of information without real value.

(a) significant   (b) obvious

(c) superficial   (d) profound

22. A: As an educator, I really struggle with the issue of how to create a classroom of similarly adept students.

B: Same here, I guess it's because at any given grade level, there may be wide ______________ in the academic abilities of the students.

(a) discrepancies   (b) margin

(c) variation   (d) gap

23. A: Making students take the test and letting those who pass the exam graduate and those who don't stay another year at school is not very wise.

B: It is quite a ______________ approach , but we have no other choice.

(a) back and forth

(b) top and tail

(c) black and white

(d) head and toe

24. A: I realized that nobody in the West asks or knows about the relationship between blood type and personality.

B: Well that's because in this country, asking an ______________ for his blood type is somewhat bizarre.

(a) ancillary   (b) aberrance

(c) adversary   (d) acquaintance

25. A: Why is it convenient?

B: Because the shoulder ______________ for the bag is adjustable for the user's body size.

(a) strap

(b) line

(c) lane

(d) stream

Part II Questions 26-50

Choose the best answer for the blank.

26. Scientists studying cells often encounter the same _____________ problem: it is difficult to examine live specimens under a microscope.

(a) hampering

(b) pervasive

(c) emulating

(d) credulous

27. The _____________ of Senator El Lore from the party was a cruel blow to the prime minister.

(a) defection

(b) migration

(c) transformation

(d) outgoings

28. Cab drivers _____________ at such a thought, denouncing the system as an infringement of privacy.

(a) cringe

(b) vaporize

(c) disconsolate

(d) promulgate

29. Poe's _____________ stories are sometimes too morbid for reading in bed, that's why I do not recommend his works for the night.

(a) clement

(b) coalescent

(c) chimerical

(d) credulous

30. Loss of vision is not _____________, and there is no reason why the human eyes cannot maintain good vision beyond the age of 80.

(a) unprecedented

(b) inevitable

(c) impeccable

(d) embraceable

31. 10 minutes later your skin would be ______________ and cracked as all the natural oils in it would have been washed away.

(a) parched

(b) fetched

(c) patched

(d) wretched

32. In a considerable number of households, the level of waste is too high, ______________ a significant danger for those with respiratory conditions.

(a) posing

(b) bewailing

(c) disparaging

(d) infringing

33. Individuals ______________ with Alzheimer's disease ultimately forget who they are.

(a) infringed

(b) infirm

(c) infused

(d) inflicted

34. Banning alcohol would only ______________ mafia groups who would seek methods to smuggle it illegally.

(a) relapse

(b) reinvigorate

(c) remonstrate

(d) remunerate

35. Although the technology that now ______________ our modern lives can be seen as beneficial, there are some questionable aspects to it as well.

(a) obstructs

(b) relents

(c) permeates

(d) obtrudes

36. Why should only wealthy celebrities have the opportunity to have ____________ weddings?

    (a) lavish

    (b) licit

    (c) laxative

    (d) laudatory

37. Chocolate may ____________ up ideas of sweet candy bars and syrupy milkshakes, but the original chocolate was a dramatically different concoction.

    (a) illumine

    (b) grapple

    (c) garrote

    (d) conjure

38. Some people try ____________ to keep us from getting back to our land.

    (a) factiously

    (b) vehemently

    (c) bubbly

    (d) redundantly

39. Mark Twain grew as a writer to produce dark chronicles of the ____________, hypocrisies and murderous acts of humankind.

    (a) aliases

    (b) agilities

    (c) vanities

    (d) alloys

40. Students who wish to learn English by ____________ themselves abroad had better realize that there is more to English-speaking countries than just the language.

    (a) immersing

    (b) agonizing

    (c) grieving

    (d) resonating

41. Russell encountered a very _____________ environment in jail, but he still managed to author a book at the time.

(a) manageable

(b) conventional

(c) sophisticated

(d) adverse

42. Dewey was an early _____________ of the philosophy that people must link new experiences to old experiences.

(a) assonance

(b) proponent

(c) consonant

(d) transplant

43. Adult male lemurs allow females priority and display _____________ when eating, grooming, and going to sleep.

(a) dominance

(b) submissiveness

(c) coherence

(d) rage

44. Those insects are not sexually _____________, meaning that there is no significant difference between the females and the males.

(a) reconciled

(b) inherent

(c) dimorphic

(d) versatile

45. A new study has _____________ the popular theory that moderate wine consumption lowers the chances of developing heart disease, thus accepting the last conception.

(a) validated

(b) famished

(c) desponded

(d) rebutted

46. Kim doesn't deserve to ______________ the position because he was connected with the corruption.

    (a) secure

    (b) lock

    (c) reach

    (d) place

47. Hoping to give its young citizens a(n) __________ in the global economy, many governments have begun subsidizing early education programs.

    (a) cipher

    (b) edge

    (c) handicap

    (d) damnification

48. When learning becomes a(n) ____________, many students lose the motivation to study.

    (a) excitement

    (b) abstraction

    (c) extravaganza

    (d) bacchanal

49. I believe that the realization of our ambition is merely one of many factors in our _________ for fulfillment.

    (a) adequacy

    (b) research

    (c) quest

    (d) abundance

50. Heart disease is a serious health problem across the globe, and without aggressive prevention measures, problems will only become more serious later ____________.

    (a) down the road

    (b) for now

    (c) in the meantime

    (d) without care

고난도
Actual
Training

10

실제 TEPS 시험의 문항수와 동일하게 구성된 고난도 Actual Training을
제한 시간 15분 내에 모두 풀 수 있도록 노력해 보세요!

1. A: What kind of assignments would I have if I get this opportunity?

B: __________ mostly. Nothing too demanding, but it isn't the most interesting work either.

(a) Clerical

(b) Intricate

(c) Arduous

(d) Judicial

2. A: I guess I need to choose one country and compare several factors for the one country.

B: Or if you want to compare several countries, you probably need to __________ one factor.

(a) zero in on

(b) rub it in

(c) lay it off

(d) act it out

3. A: How was the interview?

B: It certainly was spontaneous in the sense that it happened very quickly and the answers that I gave were __________ responses.

(a) off limited

(b) split second

(c) wasted trips

(d) storm-prone

4. A: You can just stop by during my office hours and maybe I can give you some references, or at least I can be a __________.

B: Thank you so much for being a great help!

(a) sounding board   (b) curriculum vitae

(c) pilot test   (d) draft-dodger

5. A: If you are really serious about that lab assistant position, I can give you some information about that when I see you.

B: I can't thank you __________.

(a) so much   (b) enough

(c) little   (d) a lot

6. A: Is anything wrong?

B: I have no idea why your volunteer work was not recorded. It might have been a computer

___________.

(a) glitch

(b) velocity

(c) crouch

(d) docility

7. A: How did your slides in PowerPoint help in your presentation?

B: Some of the titles ___________ my memory.

(a) extracted

(b) parched

(c) jogged

(d) suffused

8. A: Can I tell you something? I'm embarrassed to ask you questions.

B: Why in the ___________ would that be?

(a) globe

(b) road

(c) string

(d) world

9. A: I'm having a hard time following what we've been discussing the past week.

B: If you've taken the ___________ for my class, then you shouldn't be having any problem.

(a) complacencies

(b) repulsions

(c) notorieties

(d) prerequisites

10. A: Whose fault do you think it was?

B: Beats me. I merely saw the accident from the ___________ of my eye.

(a) verge

(b) corner

(c) edge

(d) mercy

11. A: I suppose it'll be hard to get a reservation.

    B: The peak season for tennis is over. It should be ___________ to get a reservation.

      (a) a cinch

      (b) off base

      (c) out of bounds

      (d) in hot water

12. A: How would you define noise?

    B: It can even have psychological and social ___________ because it affects people's quality of life.

      (a) accommodations

      (b) applications

      (c) implications

      (d) declaration

13. A: Hey, Susan. I heard that Tim had a crush on you at first sight.

    B: I don't believe you. You're ___________. I saw him dating with Jessica yesterday.

      (a) pushing me out

      (b) pushing it

      (c) pulling my leg

      (d) pulling me up

14. A: Is there an extra cup I can use?

    B: I'm afraid not. There is a ___________ one that you can use.

      (a) derivable

      (b) discarded

      (c) disposable

      (d) decayed

15. A: You do not look so good.

    B: Yesterday, I drank until I got drunk and now I have a severe ___________.

      (a) malady

      (b) disorder

      (c) hangover

      (d) intoxication

16. A: There are not enough souvenirs to _____________ to all participants.

    B: There are more in the other box.

      (a) brush up

      (b) go around

      (c) play sick

      (d) head over heels

17. A: Are you going to work with John for this team project?

    B: Never! He _____________ for the whole session and does not participate.

      (a) fiddles about

      (b) breaks a leg

      (c) flares up

      (d) gets an inkling

18. A: What do I have to do in order to get a good grade in the writing class?

    B: The professor will like very _____________ and persuasive writing.

      (a) cohesive

      (b) creepy

      (c) dispatched

      (d) classified

19. A: Do you want to do extra work for a better grade?

    B: Since I have an 18-unit course load and I don't think I can _____________ a paper like that.

      (a) sound off

      (b) go off

      (c) touch on

      (d) squeeze in

20. A: He is not patient enough to _____________ for an hour.

    B: I guess so. He doesn't like being bored.

      (a) lay through

      (b) sit through

      (c) skim through

      (d) cut through

21. A: What we have to do today is to clean up our room and do the laundry and ventilate our room.

B: Sorry. I didn't ___________ the last part. What was it again?

   (a) get

   (b) see

   (c) retrieve

   (d) catch

22. A: I don't like Tom's rash behavior.

B: Neither do I. He ___________ about our surprise party for Samantha in front of all the others.

   (a) mouthed off

   (b) cut the mouth

   (c) put a cork in it

   (d) spread out

23. A: I'm going on a holiday to the beach.

B: You need to get into ___________ if I am to go with you.

   (a) health

   (b) shape

   (c) condition

   (d) mind

24. A: Sam, how do you like your new roommate, Chris?

B: Well, he's quite dirty and freaky. I cannot really ___________ him.

   (a) keep away from

   (b) swear off

   (c) take with

   (d) hit it off with

25. A: Park Ji Sung was dominant among the players in the Korean National Soccer Team.

B: He ___________ in the World Cup.

   (a) was a Triton among minnows

   (b) passed with flying colors

   (c) stood us up

   (d) walked on air

Part II
Questions 26-50
Choose the best answer for the blank.

26. Most people have two trillion platelets in them and they work to help the blood to _________, which means to stop bleeding.

(a) clot

(b) flourish

(c) thrive

(d) perish

27. The diagram on the next page in your text shows a ___________ match with no clumping.

(a) permeating

(b) compatible

(c) ephemeral

(d) flaunting

28. Many minor reactions can occur like fever or chills, but some reactions are so severe that they lead to a(n) ___________ destruction of the red blood cells from the donor and that can result in shock or even death.

(a) eternal

(b) tampering

(c) spontaneous

(d) overrated

29. You can do this because so much of a written text is ___________ which means that there's a lot of repetition, so quite a few words can be skipped without losing the meaning.

(a) lifelike

(b) unabated

(c) reluctant

(d) redundant

30. Although California currently leads the US in ___________ wind power, there are several other areas that also hold considerable potential for increased production.

(a) abdicating

(b) harnessing

(c) abstaining

(d) abominating

31. When musicians were not creating pieces for religious occasions and performing at church functions, they were playing in the chambers of _____________ homes of nobility.

(a) secure

(b) stately

(c) heartfelt

(d) convinced

32. As agricultural land is sold for development, hydroponics has become a _____________ alternative for almost every country in the world.

(a) viable

(b) gnawing

(c) tortuous

(d) devouring

33. In the past, it was considered adequate for a building not to collapse during an earthquake, now insurance companies and even clients are demanding buildings that will be able to maintain their structural _____________ through an earthquake and remain sound after the earthquake.

(a) inspection

(b) utility

(c) integrity

(d) inhibition

34. The wind in Texas is so _____________ that wind power alone would be unreliable as a primary source of continuous energy.

(a) aboriginal

(b) ambiguous

(c) variable

(d) puissant

35. It's true that some species of bacteria do cause diseases, but for most part, bacteria are _____________.

(a) benign

(b) virulent

(c) avid

(d) lethal

36. After extensive debate, representatives of the thirteen political bodies eventually __________ the Constitution of the United States of America, a document that represented a compromise between the rights of the states and the need for a strong centralized system of governance.

(a) ratified

(b) acknowledged

(c) reversed

(d) contended

37. Frontier home design in the US was greatly influenced by the __________ of the Homestead Act of 1862.

(a) provisions

(b) footnote

(c) manifestation

(d) denomination

38. Remote areas, especially islands, and other regions at a distance from electrical __________ are vigorously exploring wind options.

(a) transfusions

(b) irritation

(c) rhetoric

(d) grids

39. Although there are three major classifications, within these basic groups there are virtually hundreds of variations that make them somewhat more difficult to identify and classify than the rather __________ specimens.

(a) laidback

(b) tempted

(c) straightforward

(d) crossed

40. The frontier settlers had __________ the hardships of their first five years, and they'd received their claims.

(a) tolerated

(b) inflamed

(c) dissolved

(d) defamed

41. The expansion and shrinking of icebergs is caused by freezing and ____________.
   (a) sprinkling
   (b) thawing
   (c) adversing
   (d) improvising

42. Some types of depression appear to be genetically inherited, but often there's no family history of depression, or, ____________ a person with a family history may never develop a depressive disorder.
   (a) comparably
   (b) conversely
   (c) impassionately
   (d) congenially

43. All of these conditions have converged to ____________ an enormous number of species at the same time, which is mass extinction.
   (a) hamper
   (b) extirpate
   (c) foster
   (d) defy

44. Studies indicate that gang behavior is probably caused by normal ____________.
   (a) nonaggression pact
   (b) motion sickness
   (c) illiteracy rate
   (d) adolescent insecurities

45. The signal causes the gland to suppress the ____________ of a hormone called melatonin.
   (a) secretion
   (b) direction
   (c) correlation
   (d) commotion

46. It appears that there are long periods in which not very much change occurs; then _________ periods in which there are mass extinctions of species followed by diversification of the groups that survived.

(a) sporadic

(b) humiliated

(c) diversified

(d) incidental

47. The theory is that a decrease in light during the long winter months may be responsible for triggering a chemical imbalance that in turn may cause depression among those people with a ___________ to depression.

(a) mediator

(b) hideout

(c) gimmick

(d) predisposition

48. About 75 percent of those developing seasonal affective disorder are women, with a typical age of ___________ about thirty years old.

(a) onset

(b) smattering

(c) agitation

(d) deference

49. Defenders of the climate change theory say the droughts sparked a chain of events that eventually led to the ___________ of the Maya.

(a) barren

(b) demise

(c) frugality

(d) hindrance

50. This group is larger, called the "social group" and it's made up of co-workers, ___________ and so on.

(a) condolences

(b) acquaintances

(c) venerations

(d) acquisitions

고난도 Point Final Check

최근에 출제된 문제들을 분석하여 추린 최고 난도에 해당하는 어휘 내용입니다.
빈칸 채워 넣기를 통해서 자신의 내공을 평가해 보세요.

1 It is your responsibility to <u>abort</u> if you feel any physical pain.

신체적 고통을 느낄 경우 ＿＿＿＿＿＿ 것은 여러분의 몫입니다.

2 When learning becomes an <u>abstraction</u>, then many students loses the motivation to study.

학습이 ＿＿＿＿＿＿ 버리면 많은 학생들이 공부할 동기를 잃을 것이다.

3 Asking an <u>acquaintance</u> for his blood type is somewhat bizarre.

＿＿＿＿＿＿ 에게 혈액형이 무엇이냐고 묻는 것은 조금 이상하다.

4 How would you like to be <u>addressed</u>?

어떻게 ＿＿＿＿＿＿ 드릴까요?

5 She is famous for being <u>adroit</u> at handling the delicate situations and people.

그녀는 민감한 상황과 사람들을 다루는 데에 ＿＿＿＿＿＿ 하기로 유명하다.

6 My whole family is Catholic but I am still an <u>agnostic</u>.

우리 가족은 다 천주교인데 난 아직은 ＿＿＿＿＿＿ 야.

7 He responded with <u>alacrity</u>

그는 ＿＿＿＿＿＿ 하게 반응했다.

8 Who have you met recently among our <u>alumni</u>?

우리 ＿＿＿＿＿＿ 중 최근에 누구 만났어?

9 Oh, I'm sure they do have an <u>altercation</u> once in a while.

아, 그래도 두 사람 어쩌다 한 번씩 약간의 ＿＿＿＿＿＿ 은 할 거야.

10 The oral presentation was <u>ambiguous</u>.

구두 발표 내용은 ＿＿＿＿＿＿.

Answers

11 Political situation was <u>ancillary</u> to the cause of the conflict.

정치적 상황은 갈등의 ____________ 원인이었다.

12 Widespread <u>apathy</u> towards public order and morality among teenagers today is becoming a serious issue.

요즘 청소년들 사이에 팽배해 있는 공중도덕과 도덕성에 대한 ____________은 심각한 문제가 되고 있다.

13 Not everyone is <u>averse</u> to snakes.

모든 사람이 뱀을 ____________ 것은 아니다.

14 Does anybody know whether there is any home remedy to <u>beat</u> anemia?

빈혈증을 ____________ 민간요법이 있는지 누구 아는 사람 있어요?

15 For most part, bacteria are <u>benign</u>.

대부분 박테리아는 ____________ 이다.

16 You don't have to <u>berate</u> yourself too much for failing.

실패에 대해서 너 자신을 그렇게 ____________ 필요 없어.

17 I was with Jack the whole time to console him upon his sudden <u>bereavement</u>.

나는 갑작스러운 ____________을 당한 Jack을 위로하려고 내내 같이 있었다.

18 I'd like to have this white T-shirt <u>bleached</u>.

이 흰색 티셔츠를 ____________ 주세요.

19 The neighbors complained that we were so <u>boisterous</u> that they couldn't turn in.

이웃사람들이 우리가 너무 ____________ 잠을 잘 수 없다고 했어.

20 The company started its biggest sale, targeting at raising funds to <u>bolster</u> its bid for cellular phone licences.

그 회사는 차세대 휴대폰 면허를 위한 입찰권을 ____________ 위한 자금을 모으려는 목적으로 최대 규모의 할인 판매를 시작했다.

Answers

11. 부차적인 12. 무관심 13. 싫어하는 14. 치료하는 15. 양성 16. 질책할 17. 사별 18. 표백해 19. 시끄러워 20. 확보하기

21 The international organization was created not to wait on <u>bondage</u>.

그 국제 조직은 _______________ 을 하도록 만들어진 것이 아니다.

22 My check <u>bounced</u>.

내 수표가 _______________.

23 We also consider the <u>brevity</u>.

우리 역시 _______________ 을 고려한다.

24 Why is the road to the West so <u>bumpy</u>?

어째서 서방으로 가는 길은 _______________?

25 <u>Captions</u> are the words showed at the bottom of a moving picture expounding what it is all about.

_______________은 영상 아래쪽에 상황을 설명하는 글을 말한다.

26 I do not want to <u>castigate</u> Bryan for this accident.

Bryan을 _______________ 싶진 않다.

27 It's almost impossible with any degree of <u>certitude</u>.

_______________ 예상하는 것은 거의 불가능해.

28 Food aid to impoverished regions will be guaranteed if you promise the <u>cessation</u> of developing nuclear weapons.

핵무기 개발 _______________을 약속한다면 가난한 지역에 식량 지원을 할 것을 보장하겠다.

29 They don't have <u>chemistry</u> with each other.

그들은 서로 _______________이 전혀 맞지 않는다.

30 Poe's <u>chimerical</u> stories are sometimes too morbid.

Poe의 _______________한 이야기들은 가끔씩은 너무 병적이다.

31 I hope Ms. Roosevelt won't notice the <u>chipped</u> cup.
나는 루즈벨트 부인이 ＿＿＿＿＿＿＿＿ 컵을 알아채지 못했으면 좋겠어.

32 It should be a <u>cinch</u> to get a reservation.
예약하는 건 ＿＿＿＿＿＿＿＿일 거예요.

33 It's <u>clerical</u> mostly.
주로 ＿＿＿＿＿＿＿＿입니다.

34 Most people have two trillion of platelets in them and they work to help the blood to <u>clot</u>.
대부분의 사람들에게는 2조 개의 혈소판이 있어서 혈관의 벽에 있는 구멍을 치료하고 혈액이 ＿＿＿＿＿＿＿＿ 도와준다.

35 The professor will like very <u>cohesive</u> and persuasive writing.
교수님은 아주 설득력 있고 ＿＿＿＿＿＿＿＿ 글을 좋아할 겁니다.

36 Many new words that are used these days were <u>coined</u> from what teenagers started using as slang.
요즘 쓰이고 있는 많은 신조어들은 청소년들이 유행어로 쓰기 시작했던 단어들에서 ＿＿＿＿＿＿＿＿ 것이다.

37 What do you think of our company's policy of salary being <u>commensurate</u> with one's experience in the field?
그 분야에서 그 사람의 경험에 ＿＿＿＿＿＿＿＿ 월급에 대한 회사의 정책에 대해서 어떻게 생각해?

38 I really <u>commiserate</u> with the victims who were wounded.
상처 입은 피해자들이 정말 ＿＿＿＿＿＿＿＿.

39 I am trying to find the <u>compatibility</u> between them and us.
나는 그들과 우리 사이에 ＿＿＿＿＿＿＿＿을 알아내려고 노력하고 있어.

40 There is no room to be <u>complacent</u>.
＿＿＿＿＿＿＿＿하고 있을 여유가 없어.

41 A container coming from China was filled with <u>contraband</u> goods such as imitations of high brands.

중국에서 들어오는 컨테이너에 명품 모조품과 같은 _______________들이 가득했다.

42 This material <u>contract</u> when you wash it.

이 옷감은 세탁하면 _______________.

43 It is no use for you to be <u>contrite</u> after you have committed such a cruel crime.

그토록 잔인한 범행을 저질러 놓은 후에 _______________ 소용없어요.

44 <u>Conversely</u>, a person with a family history may never develop a depressive disorder.

_______________, 가족력이 있는 사람은 결코 우울증을 겪지 않을 것이다.

45 The brochure is too <u>convoluted</u>.

설명서가 너무 _______________.

46 The steel house is so <u>cramped</u> that only a few people lived without inconvenience.

그 철로 된 집은 너무 _______________ 단지 몇 사람만이 불편함 없이 살았다.

47 All the passengers were <u>cranky</u> after the 20-hour flight.

모든 승객들은 20시간의 긴 비행 끝에 _______________ 있었다.

48 Cab drivers <u>cringe</u> at such a thought, denouncing the systems.

택시 운전자들은 그 생각이 사생활을 침해하는 시스템이라며 _______________.

49 The party was <u>curtailed</u> by an electrical power cut.

그 파티는 정전으로 인해 _______________.

50 The <u>defection</u> of Senator El Lore from the party was a cruel blow to the prime minister.

El Lore 상원의원의 _______________ 은 수상에게 치명타였다.

51 Police found some inappropriate actions between the two <u>defunct</u> companies.
경찰이 _____________ 두 회사 사이에서 부적절한 행동들을 발견했다.

52 The droughts sparked a chain of events that eventually led to the <u>demise</u> of the Maya.
가뭄은 결과적으로 마야 문명의 _____________으로 이끈 일련의 사건들을 촉발했다.

53 If he didn't brush his teeth well, his teeth would get infirm, contributing to <u>dentures</u>.
이를 잘 닦지 않으면 이가 약해질 것이고 그 결과 _____________를 하게 될 것이다.

54 Although that church stood <u>derelict</u> for decades, some features still remained.
저 교회는 몇 십 년간 _____________ 채 있었지만, 몇몇 특징들이 남아있다.

55 The city was <u>destitute</u> and in desperate need of recover.
그 도시는 매우 _____________ 복구가 절박했다.

56 Politician being <u>dichotomy</u> between what they say and what they actually do usually raise people's frustration.
정치인들이 말하는 것과 실제로 행동하는 것의 _____________는 대개 사람들의 짜증을 불러일으킨다.

57 Those insects are not sexually <u>dimorphic</u>.
그 곤충들은 성적으로 _____________을 갖추고 있지 않다.

58 I guess it's because at any given grade level, there may be wide <u>discrepancies</u> in the academic abilities of the students.
내 생각엔 어느 학년의 경우라도 학생들의 학력에는 큰 _____________가 있기 마련이어서 그런 것 같다.

59 We all have been educated since we were little to <u>disparage</u> feminity.
우리는 모두 어렸을 때부터 여자라는 점을 _____________ 교육받았다.

60 There is a <u>disposable</u> one that you can use.
_____________은 쓸 수 있어요.

61   You've finally done your <u>dissertation</u>.
마침내 _____________을 마무리 지었군요.

62   It's a <u>diversion</u> from my daily life.
일상을 벗어나 _____________이 돼요.

63   Mr. Baker was cautious to dodge from the topic of marriage.
Baker씨는 결혼이라는 화제를 _____________ 조심했다.

64   We played to a <u>draw</u>.
우리는 _____________를 기록했어.

65   I'd prefer not to see your <u>drooling</u> my share.
내 몫에 네가 _____________ 말았음 해.

66   Many governments hope to give its young citizens an <u>edge</u> in a global economy.
많은 정부들은 국제 경제에서 자국 아이들에게 _____________를 제공하길 희망한다.

67   M.M.S.'s bad behavior was unusually <u>egregious</u>.
M.M.S.의 나쁜 행동은 이례적으로 _____________ 것이었습니다.

68   The chairperson has been charged with <u>embezzlement</u> of dividend from his corporation.
회장은 회사의 배당금을 _____________ 한 혐의로 기소되었다.

69   No, it may seem <u>ephemeral</u>.
아니, _____________ 보일 수도 있어.

70   He <u>eschewed</u> explanation.
그는 해명을 _____________.

71 The war <u>exacerbated</u> racial tensions.
전쟁은 인종간의 긴장을 ＿＿＿＿＿＿＿.

72 I want to <u>extend</u> the term of overseas training.
나는 해외연수 기간을 ＿＿＿＿＿＿＿ 싶다.

73 All of these conditions have converged to <u>extirpate</u> an enormous number of species.
이 모든 조건들이 모여 결국 수많은 종들을 ＿＿＿＿＿＿＿.

74 He kept on talking about topics <u>extraneous</u> to the issue at hand.
그는 계속 쟁점과는 ＿＿＿＿＿＿＿ 이야기만 계속 했다.

75 Purchasing such a costly automobile is a bit <u>extravagant</u> for a woman of her income.
그런 비싼 자동차를 구입하는 것은 그녀의 수입으로는 좀 ＿＿＿＿＿＿＿ 것이다.

76 The chair is so <u>fastidious</u>.
그 의자는 너무 ＿＿＿＿＿＿＿.

77 The voice was so <u>feeble</u>.
목소리가 너무 ＿＿＿＿＿＿＿.

78 Jack <u>forged</u> his parents signature.
Jack은 그의 부모님의 서명을 ＿＿＿＿＿＿＿.

79 What do you think is the most <u>formidable</u> obstacle?
가장 ＿＿＿＿＿＿＿ 걸림돌이 무엇이라고 생각하십니까?

80 The control of the small island has finally <u>foundered</u>.
그 작은 섬에 대한 타협은 결국 ＿＿＿＿＿＿＿.

Answers
71. 악화시켰다 72. 연장하고 73. 전멸시켰다 74. 거리가 먼 75. 사치스러운 76. 까다롭다 77. 약했다 78. 위조했다 79. 큰 80. 무산되었다

81 I was <u>frantic</u> when I got the phone call.

전화를 받았을 때 난 ______________.

82 You need to be more serious at your work than giving <u>frivolous</u> opinions during the meeting.

회의 중에 ______________ 의견을 내뱉지 않고 일에 더 진지할 필요가 있다.

83 <u>Gaps</u> in staffing is going to aggravate the situation.

직원의 ______________은 상황을 더욱 악화시킬 거예요.

84 I <u>gather</u> that the Congress should enact the law.

나는 의회가 그 법을 제정해야 한다고 ______________.

85 They were hardly <u>germane</u> to what I am looking for.

그것들은 내가 찾는 것과는 ______________이 거의 없었다.

86 It might have been a computer <u>glitch</u>.

컴퓨터 ______________인 거 같아요.

87 She is very <u>gregarious</u>.

그녀는 굉장히 ______________.

88 I have a severe <u>hangover</u>.

심한 ______________가 있네요.

89 You must get rid of your <u>haughty</u> attitude.

너는 너의 ______________ 태도를 버려야 해.

90 Do you think <u>hedonic</u> people are irresponsible?

넌 ______________ 사람들이 무책임하다고 생각하니?

91 The man got accused for <u>harboring</u> a convicted felon.
남자가 중범죄 인을 _____________ 죄로 구속되었다.

92 California currently leads the US in <u>harnessing</u> wind power.
캘리포니아가 현재 미국의 풍력의 _____________을 이끌고 있다.

93 History is not just a list of events arranged in a careless order like a <u>heap</u> of things.
역사는 물건 _____________처럼 아무렇게나 정리한 사건 더미가 아니다.

94 The film was so <u>hilarious</u>.
그 영화는 매우 _____________.

95 An example of <u>hyperbole</u> is "You told me that story a thousand times"!
"_____________의 한 예로는 "너 그 얘기 나한테 몇 천 번을 했어!"이다.

96 Matt resolved to be <u>hypnotized</u> to remember it.
Matt는 그것을 기억해내려고 _____________로 결심했다.

97 What he really need is the ability to accept the result even if it was an <u>ignominious</u> defeat.
그가 정말 필요한 건 아무리 _____________ 패배라 해도 결과를 받아들이는 능력이야.

98 In order to resolve the <u>impasse</u> over North Korea's nuclear weapons program diplomats from six nations gathered at the table.
북한의 핵무기 프로그램을 둘러싼 _____________를 해결하기 위해 6개국 대표단들이 한 곳에 모였다.

99 He is <u>impertinent</u>.
그는 _____________.

100 I just don't like his <u>impish</u> grin.
난 그냥 저 _____________ 웃음이 싫어.

101 True, it is particularly true of its <u>incarceration</u> policy.
맞아, _____________ 정책이 특히 그래.

102 Have you ever got a <u>inkling</u> of someone hiding something from you?
누가 너한테 뭘 숨기고 있다는 _____________를 알아챈 적 있어?

103 We should help those who are <u>indignant</u>.
우리는 _____________ 사람들을 도와야 해.

104 Individuals <u>inflicted</u> with Alzheimer's disease ultimately forget who they are.
알츠하이머병으로 _____________ 사람들은 결국 자신이 누군지조차 잊게 된다.

105 Insurance companies are demanding buildings that will be able to maintain their structural <u>integrity</u>.
보험사들은 지진이 일어난 후에 빌딩이 구조적으로 _____________를 유지할 수 있어야 한다고 요구하고 있다.

106 It was imprudent of you to <u>interrupt</u> the get-together.
네가 그 모임을 _____________니 신중하지 못했어.

107 He <u>jaywalked</u> despite my warning.
내가 말리는데도 그는 _____________을 했다.

108 Why should only wealthy celebrities have the opportunity to have <u>lavish</u> weddings?
왜 부유한 연예인들에게만 _____________ 결혼식을 할 기회가 주어져야 하지?

109 There's a 30-minute <u>layover</u> in Tokyo along the way.
가는 도중에 도쿄에서 30분 정도 _____________합니다.

110 The judge was <u>lenient</u> with that sex offender.
판사는 그 성범죄자에 대해 _____________.

111 Investment banks took on obscene amounts of <u>leverage</u>.
투자은행들은 엄청난 양의 _______________을 받아들였다.

112 I paid too much for a <u>lemon</u>.
_______________에 너무 많이 돈을 썼어요.

113 Our company lacks people who are <u>literate</u> in computer usage.
우리 회사는 컴퓨터 사용에 _______________ 사람이 부족하다.

114 UN's premises were already <u>looted</u>, destroyed, and burnt.
UN의 공관들이 _______________ 파괴되고 또 불에 탔다.

115 It is <u>ludicrous</u> to think that the plan could succeed.
그 계획이 성공할 수 있을 거라 생각한 것은 _______________ 것이다.

116 I always try to be <u>meticulous</u> in keeping the records up to date.
나는 기록을 가장 최근 것으로 _______________ 정리해 두려고 항상 노력한다.

117 Government's <u>myopic</u> plan will threat the country's social security system.
정부의 _______________ 계획은 국가의 사회보장제도를 위협할 거야.

118 I'm not aiming for <u>a myriad of</u> awards and honors from people.
내 목적은 사람들로부터 _______________ 상과 존경을 받는 것이 아니다.

119 They are the most <u>nefarious</u> corporation I've ever heard of.
그 기업은 내가 들은 것 중 가장 _______________이야.

120 It <u>negated</u> the possibility of economic recession.
그것은 경제 침체의 가능성을 _______________.

121 I am not <u>nonchalant</u> about what's going on.
일어나는 일들에 대해 ＿＿＿＿＿＿ 게 아니야.

122 The presidential election results were <u>nullified</u>.
대통령 선거 결과는 ＿＿＿＿＿＿가 되었다.

123 Many reporters were striving to find more information about the president's assassination to write the <u>obituary</u>.
많은 기자들이 대통령의 암살에 대한 ＿＿＿＿＿＿를 쓰기 위해 더 많은 정보를 얻으려 애쓰고 있었다.

124 The ocean basin will be <u>obliterated</u> due to natural hazard.
해양분지는 자연 재해로 인해 ＿＿＿＿＿＿ 것이다.

125 The meat is so delicious that they are <u>oblivious</u> to everything else.
그 고기는 너무 맛있어서 둘이 먹다가 하나가 죽어도 ＿＿＿＿＿＿.

126 A typical age of <u>onset</u> of seasonal affective disorder is about thirty years old.
계절적 정서 장애의 전형적 ＿＿＿＿＿＿ 연령은 30살이다.

127 The <u>ostensible</u> reason for their presence is to keep the peace.
그들이 존재하는 ＿＿＿＿＿＿ 이유는 평화를 지키기 위해서이다.

128 She wanted to meet with a proficient <u>obstetrician</u>.
그녀는 숙련된 ＿＿＿＿＿＿를 만나기를 원했다.

129 Professor Goethe <u>officiated</u> at the wedding.
괴테 교수님이 결혼식 ＿＿＿＿＿＿.

130 The clouds look so <u>ominous</u>.
구름이 매우 ＿＿＿＿＿＿ 보여.

131 It's pretty <u>onerous</u> but I am going to try my best.
꽤 _____________되지만 난 최선을 다할 거야.

132 They won't <u>outlive</u> any of their children.
그들은 자식들보다 _____________ 않을 것이다.

133 You had a sickly <u>pallor</u>.
너 아픈 사람처럼 _____________했어.

134 Your skin would be <u>parched</u> and cracked.
당신의 피부는 _____________ 갈라질 것이다.

135 He has received <u>payoffs</u> from contractors, taking advantages of his position.
그는 직위를 이용해서 건설업자들한테 _____________을 받아왔다.

136 The rain really <u>pelted</u>.
비가 매우 _____________.

137 They will sooner or later develop a nasty <u>penchant</u> for committing a crime.
머지않아 범죄를 저지르는 추악한 _____________이 그들에게 다시 나타날 것입니다.

138 It comes with nice <u>perks</u>.
_____________이 짭짤하잖아요.

139 The technology that <u>permeates</u> our lives can be seen as beneficial.
우리 삶에 _____________ 기술이 유익해 보일 수 있다.

140 The reason why drugs are especially <u>pernicious</u> to teenagers is because they are not old enough to make rational decisions.
마약이 청소년들에게 특히 _____________ 이유는 그들은 이성적인 판단을 내릴 수 있을 만큼의 나이가 되지 않았기 때문이다.

Answers

131. 부담 132. 오래 살지 133. 창백 134. 메마르고 135. 뇌물 136. 심하게 왔다 137. 성향 138. 부수입 139. 스며든 140. 치명적인

141 Poverty is <u>perpetuated</u> to the next generation.
가난은 다음 세대로 ____________.

142 I will give you another copy of our contract for you to <u>peruse</u> after the meeting.
회의가 끝난 후 ____________ 수 있도록 계약서 한 부를 드릴게요.

143 It's a <u>pinnacle</u> of my career.
내 경력의 ____________이다.

144 I'll really make a <u>pitch</u> for its success.
성공을 위해 ____________을 올리겠습니다.

145 I didn't <u>ponder</u> over that matter.
난 그 문제에 대해서는 ____________ 적이 없어.

146 Would you stop <u>poking</u> me please?
나 좀 그만 ____________?

147 The higher level of waste <u>poses</u> a significant danger for those with respiratory conditions.
쓰레기의 양이 더 많아져서 호흡기 질환이 있는 사람들에게 큰 위협을 ____________.

148 I am <u>possessed</u> with a resolution to succeed.
난 성공할 거라는 다짐에 ____________ 있다.

149 We must get rid of any <u>preconceived notion</u>.
우리는 어떠한 ____________도 없애야 한다.

150 A decrease in light may cause depression among those people with a <u>predisposition</u> to depression.
빛의 감소는 우울증에 걸리기 쉬운 ____________이 있는 사람들에게 우울증을 일으킬 수 있다.

151 How did the <u>preliminary</u> meeting for the concert go?
콘서트에 대비한 ______________ 회의는 어땠어?

152 The <u>proceedings</u> for every session will be provided for them.
매 회의에 대한 ______________이 그들에게 제공될 것이다.

153 Dewey was an early an early <u>proponent</u> of the philosophy.
듀이는 그 철학의 초기 ______________였다.

154 I already attended the orientation and was educated about the company <u>protocol</u>.
이미 예비교육에 참가하여 회사 ______________ 에 대해 교육을 받았습니다.

155 Frontier home design in the US was greatly influenced by the <u>provisions</u> of the Homestead Act of 1862.
미국의 국경지역 건축 디자인은 1862년 주택법 ______________에 의해 영향을 많이 받았다.

156 The <u>psychiatrist</u> prescribed some drugs.
그 ______________는 몇 가지 약을 처방했다.

157 No one expected him to be <u>pugnacious</u>.
그가 ______________ 거라고 아무도 예측하지 못했다.

158 The <u>pundits</u> seem to dislike me.
______________은 나를 싫어하는 것 같다.

159 The realization of our ambition is merely one of many factors in our <u>quest</u> for fulfillment.
우리 야망을 실현시키는 것은 우리를 만족시키는데 ______________ 여러 요인 중 단지 하나일 뿐이다.

160 <u>Rancid</u> odor comes into our house.
______________ 냄새가 저희 집으로 들어와요.

161 The patient who suffered a stroke did not <u>recuperate</u> as rapidly as he anticipated.
뇌졸중에 걸린 그 환자는 그가 예상했던 것만큼 빠르게 ＿＿＿＿＿＿＿ 않았다.

162 So much of a written text is <u>redundant</u>.
글의 많은 부분이 ＿＿＿＿＿＿＿.

163 Would-be employees should provide the <u>references</u>.
예비 직원들은 ＿＿＿＿＿＿＿의 이름과 주소를 제공해야 한다.

164 Banning alcohol would only <u>reinvigorate</u> the Mafia groups.
술을 금지시키는 것은 마피아 집단에게 ＿＿＿＿＿＿＿만 할 것이다.

165 He will <u>reprimand</u> me for my inexcusable behavior.
그는 변명의 여지없는 나의 행동에 대해 ＿＿＿＿＿＿＿ 것이다.

166 From many aspects, we first want them to be <u>resolute</u> in making decisions.
수많은 면들 중에서 우리는 우선 그들이 결정을 내릴 때에 ＿＿＿＿＿＿＿ 바랍니다.

167 It's very concise but <u>resonate</u> with such complex and deep expressions.
정말 간결한데 참 복잡하고 심오한 표현들로 ＿＿＿＿＿＿＿.

168 I was filled with <u>revulsion</u> and was sick to my stomach.
나는 ＿＿＿＿＿＿＿이 차올라서 몹시 화가 났다.

169 These apples are <u>tree-rippened</u>.
이 사과는 ＿＿＿＿＿＿＿ 것들이다.

170 I got done with the <u>rudimentary</u> classes in business.
나는 ＿＿＿＿＿＿＿ 비즈니스 수업들을 다 미쳤다.

171 He always gets the <u>runaround</u>.
그는 항상 _______________를 듣는다.

172 Global warming is an elaborate <u>ruse</u>.
지구온난화는 정교한 _______________이다.

173 The religious leaders banned the practice as <u>sacrilegious</u>.
종교 지도자들은 그 관행을 _______________ 것으로 금지했다.

174 Could you clearly point out the <u>salient</u> feature of the idea?
아이디어의 _______________을 좀 분명히 짚어주시겠어요?

175 Statistical data are <u>salutary</u> for people who wish to see the constant change.
통계자료는 지속적인 변화를 한눈에 보고 싶은 사람들에게 _______________.

176 Everyone started to doubt the former owner's <u>sanity</u>.
모두가 전 사장이 _______________인지 의심하기 시작했다.

177 One has to be <u>savvy</u> about the flow of money.
돈의 흐름에 대해 _______________ 해.

178 You will see the cozy <u>sectional</u> in furniture shop.
가구점에서 아늑한 _______________를 보시게 될 것입니다.

179 The signal causes the gland to suppress the <u>secretion</u> of a hormone.
그 신호는 분기기관이 호르몬 _______________를 억제시키는 원인이다.

180 She has <u>sizable</u> company holdings.
그녀는 _______________ 회사 주식을 소유하고 있다.

181 The skirmish would be ironed out.
_______________은 해소될 것이다.

182 Why do people struggle so much to earn money by smuggling proucts that are prohibited?
왜 사람들은 금지된 제품을 _______________ 돈을 벌려고 그토록 애쓰는 거지?

183 I shouldn't have snoozed.
제가 _______________ 말았어야 했는데.

184 The new boy in my class was so snobbish.
우리 반에 새로 온 아이는 너무 _______________했다.

185 The whole world is worried sick about the kids who are living in sordid conditions
_______________ 환경에서 살고 있는 아이들을 온 세계가 굉장히 걱정하고 있다.

186 They lead to a spontaneous destruction of the red blood cells from the donor.
그것은 적혈구 세포의 _______________ 파괴로 이어질 수 있다.

187 Sporadic periods in which there are mass extinctions of species followed by diversification of the groups that survived.
_______________ 기간에는 종의 대량 멸종이 일어나고 그 이후에 생존하는 종이 변형된다.

188 How can we squander those natural resources?
어떻게 그런 천연자원을 _______________ 수 있는 겁니까?

189 Few know exactly how to make a lot of money from speculation.
_______________로 많은 돈을 버는 방법을 정확히 아는 사람은 거의 없다.

190 The workers were too standoffish.
직원들은 너무 _______________.

191 There are <u>stark</u> differences between the East and the West.
동서양 간에 ＿＿＿＿＿＿＿ 차이가 있다.

192. The technology has never been improved or made as <u>state-of-the-art</u> as expected.
그 기술은 결코 향상되지도 기대만큼 ＿＿＿＿＿＿＿ 것으로 만들어지지도 않았다.

193. I gather that there's some <u>static</u> on the line.
전파 ＿＿＿＿＿＿＿가 있는 거 같아요.

194 They were playing in the chambers of <u>stately</u> homes of nobility.
그들은 귀족의 ＿＿＿＿＿＿＿ 집에서 연주하였다.

195 Every step forward will meet with more impediments if we are bent on maintaining the <u>status quo</u>.
우리가 ＿＿＿＿＿＿＿에 급급해한다면 앞으로의 모든 단계에서 더 많은 방해물을 만나게 될 것이다.

196 Two Congressional <u>statutes</u> have brought the jurisdictional and normative dimensions.
2개의 의회 ＿＿＿＿＿＿＿은 사법적이고 규범적 차원을 부각시켰다.

197 The President proclaimed yesterday a plan to create one million new jobs in an attempt to <u>staunch</u> his fall in popularity.
대통령은 인기가 ＿＿＿＿＿＿＿ 것을 막기 위한 시도로서 새로운 일자리 백만 개를 창출할 계획을 발표했다.

198 Adult male lemurs allow females priority and express <u>submissiveness</u>.
다 큰 수컷 여우 원숭이들은 암컷에 대해 우선권을 주며 ＿＿＿＿＿＿＿를 보인다.

199 Repetitively reading a single book mean merely an accumulation of <u>superficial</u> knowledge.
한 권을 반복적으로 읽는 것은 단지 ＿＿＿＿＿＿＿ 지식만 축적한다는 것을 의미한다.

200 Women seem to be more <u>susceptible</u> than men to the adverse effects of alcohol.
여성이 남성보다 술의 부작용에 더 ＿＿＿＿＿＿＿ 것 같다.

201 Tom is so <u>taciturn</u>.
톰은 매우 _____________이야.

202 The expansion and shrinkings of icebergs is caused by freezing and <u>thawing</u>.
빙하의 확장과 수축은 얼고 _____________ 때문에 생긴다.

203 The authors <u>treasured</u> the secret society.
작가들은 비밀 결사를 _____________.

204 The <u>unanticipated</u> arrival of his girlfriend from abroad lifted his sagging spirits.
해외에 있던 여자친구의 _____________ 방문으로 축 처져 있던 그의 기분이 좋아졌다.

205 Teacher praised the student as he is <u>unassuming</u>.
선생님은 그 학생이 _____________ 칭찬했다.

206 He <u>unfolded</u> his plan to me.
그는 자신의 계획을 내게 _____________.

207 You must try not to be <u>unheeding</u>.
_____________ 않도록 노력해야 해.

208 It has been so <u>unnerving</u>.
그것은 너무나 맥 _____________ 일이었다.

209 It is quite important to be <u>unwavering</u> as you grow up.
성장하면서 _____________ 것은 꽤 중요하지.

210 A new study has <u>validated</u> the popular theory.
새로운 연구가 유명한 가설을 _____________.

211 Mark Twain grew as a writer to produce dark chronicles of the <u>vanity</u>.
Mark Twain은 인간의 ____________ 에 대한 어두운 이야기를 쓰는 작가로 성장했다.

212 The essay was <u>vapid</u> and colorless.
그 에세이는 ____________ 개성이 없다.

213 Some people try <u>vehemently</u> to keep us from getting back to our land.
어떤 이들은 우리가 우리 땅으로 다시 돌아가는 것을 막기 위해 ____________ 노력을 한다.

214 Tell me the time and the <u>venue</u> of the meeting.
회의 ____________ 와 시간 좀 알려줘.

215 Jade was very well <u>versed</u> in manners.
Jade는 예의에 매우 ____________ .

216 Hydroponics has become a <u>viable</u> potion.
수경재배는 ____________ 대안이 되었다.

217 Process of which <u>vigorous</u> cancer cells multiply has not been fully understood by the experts yet.
____________ 암세포가 증식하는 과정은 전문가들에 의해 아직 완전히 밝혀지지 않았다.

218 She used to be so joyful and <u>vivacious</u>.
그녀는 예전에 무척 즐겁고 ____________ 모습이었다.

219 We can <u>weather</u> the storm that is coming soon.
우리는 다가오는 폭풍을 ____________ 수 있다.

220 The plants that listen to classical music are likely to be better able to <u>withstand</u> disease.
클래식 음악을 들려준 식물은 질병에 더 잘 ____________ 경향이 있다.

동사+명사

221 Mr. President ac_____________ the cheers of the people on the street.
대통령은 길거리의 사람들의 인사에 답례하여 손을 흔들었다.

222 Smith had ad_____________ himself to the issue.
Smith는 그 문제에 전념했다.

223 Yes, it's awful that they had to am_____________ his leg to get him out.
예, 그를 빼내기 위해서 다리를 절단해야 했다니 아주 끔찍해요.

224 They an_____________ my name.
그들은 나의 이름을 불렀다.

225 This site is intriguing and interactive to help children ap_____________ astronomy.
이 사이트는 흥미롭고 쌍방향적이어서 아이들이 천문학을 올바르게 이해하도록 도와준다.

226 The drug will at_____________ the virus.
약이 바이러스를 약화시킬 것이다.

227 She will b_____________ the expenses of lunch.
그녀가 점심비용을 부담할 거야.

228 The explosion b_____________ home the point that safety rules ought to be abided by.
그 폭발사고는 안전규칙을 꼭 지켜야 한다는 것을 뼈저리게 느끼게 했다.

229 I didn't c_____________ the last part.
마지막 부분을 못 들었어요.

230 Some say keeping their c_____________ is not that important if they use the protection.
어떤 이들은 피임을 한다면 순결을 지키는 것은 그다지 중요하지 않다고 한다.

231 It contributes to _c___________ children's creativity.
그것은 아이들의 창의성을 제한하는 원인이 된다.

232 Susan and Johnson met with a travel agent and _c___________ airline tickets.
Susan과 Johnson은 여행사 직원을 만나서 비행기 티켓을 받았다.

233. I don't give _c___________ to anything he says.
나는 그가 하는 말은 전부 믿지 않아.

234 We reached _c___________ altitude.
우리는 순항고도에 진입했다.

235 The greatest concern of Obama was that many of the hard-core supporters would rather lose the election than _c___________ the vote.
Obama의 가장 큰 걱정은 그들의 많은 핵심 지지자들이 표를 모으기는커녕 선거에서 패할 것이라는 것이었다.

236. The central bank's policy of zero interest rates _d___________ the currency.
중앙은행의 제로 금리 정책은 화폐 가치를 떨어뜨렸다.

237 The ethnic minorities were generally _d___________ the opportunity of education.
소수 민족에게는 일반적으로 교육의 기회가 제공되지 않았다.

238 Look how _e___________ they look after the news.
그 소식 후에 그들이 얼마나 기뻐하는지 좀 봐.

239 The residents _en___________ a compromise.
주민들은 절충안을 고려하였다.

240 You're going to _ex___________ your cold if you work in such bad weather out.
이런 험한 날씨에 밖에서 일하면 감기가 심해질 것이다.

241 People can ex______________ the right to remain silent.
사람들은 묵비권을 행사할 수 있다.

242 Angelina i______________ a suit against her manager.
Angelina는 매니저에 대해 소송을 제기하였다.

243 Some of the titles i______________ my memory.
제목들이 제 기억들을 되살렸어요.

244 He is just m______________ time.
그 아이는 그냥 허송세월을 하고 있어요.

245 He does not m______________ his words.
그는 조심스럽게 돌려서 말하지 않아.

246 Plenty of professors at the university have been warned not to p______________ other peer scholars' thesis.
대학의 많은 교수들은 다른 동료 학자들의 논문을 표절하지 말라고 경고받았다.

247 The workers p______________ the factory gates.
노동자들은 공장 출입구에서 피켓 시위를 했다.

248 The defendant p______________ guilty to the crime.
피고는 범행에 대해 유죄를 인정했다.

249 If you've taken the p______________ for my class, then you shouldn't be having any problem.
만약에 선수과목을 들었다면 너는 전혀 문제가 없을 것이다.

250 The other day the prosecution in the International Court of Justice announced that it would p______________ charges against the war criminals.
일전에 국제사법재판소[ICJ]는 검찰 측이 전쟁 범죄자에 대해 기소할 것이라고 발표했다.

251 The financial expert has been p_____________ a 20% consumer price surge for the entire year.
그 재무 전문가는 한 해를 통틀어 소비자 물가지수가 20퍼센트 폭등할 것이라고 예측해왔다.

252 Representatives of the thirteen political bodies r_____________ the Constitution of the United States of America.
13개 정치단체의 대표들은 미국 헌법을 비준하였다.

253 A host of Ireland-born novelists have been writing plenty of literary works r___________ the tale of an impoverished Irish peasant.
아일랜드 출신의 많은 소설가들은 가난한 아일랜드 농부이야기에 관한 수많은 문학작품을 써왔다.

254 You can just r___________ the money.
그냥 송금해주면 돼.

255 The school resolved to r___________ the rules.
그 학교는 그 규칙을 폐기했다.

256 I hope you will find a job you can s___________ your teeth into.
나는 네가 푹 빠져서 할 수 있는 일을 찾았으면 좋겠다.

257 He made a remark that accidently _____________ one company's name.
저번 주 쇼에서 그의 발언이 뜻하지 않게 어떤 회사의 명예를 훼손했다.

258 The U.S. government s___________ sanctions on four people.
미국 정부는 네 명에 대한 제재를 가하였다.

259 Everyone was very impressed by the information provided and thought the content really hit the s___________.
모든 사람들이 제공된 정보에 굉장히 감명을 받았으며 내용이 아주 만족럽다고 생각했다.

260 I also had a s___________.
나도 말더듬었는데.

261 His sister will follow s____________.
그의 동생이 선례를 따를 것이다.

262 Stop t____________ yourself.
너무 자책하지 마라.

263 Hurricane Katrina u____________ plenty of trees.
허리케인 카트리나가 수많은 나무를 뿌리째 뽑았다.

264 We cannot w____________ two wars at once.
우리는 동시에 2개의 전쟁을 수행할 수 없다.

265 Please make sure you w____________ all the consequences.
모든 결과를 신중히 고려해주세요.

형용사+명사

266 The president announced that he would focus on solving the ____________ poverty.
대통령은 극빈을 해결하기 위해 집중적으로 힘쓰겠다고 발표하였다.

267 Studies indicate that gang behavior is probably caused by normal __________ insecurities.
연구결과는 패거리행동이 단순한 사춘기의 불안정이 원인이라는 것을 알려준다.

268 Regrettably, nobody in her class is supporting her due to her ____________ character.
유감스럽게도, 그녀의 호전적 성격 때문에 반에서 누구도 그녀를 지지하지 않았다.

269 I had a close c____________ when a school bus nearly hit me.
학교 버스에 거의 치일 뻔했는데 구사일생했다.

270 He's tall and has c____________ features.
키도 크고 조각 같은 얼굴을 하고 있어.

271 This is a c___________ document.
이것은 비밀문서이다.

272 Most of them are born with c___________ talents.
그들 대부분은 선천적인 끼를 가지고 태어났다.

273 Owing to c___________ technology, our lives have become more and more convenient.
첨단 기술 덕택에 우리의 삶은 더욱더 편리해졌다.

274 A d___________ charge of $20 will be paid by the purchaser.
연체료 20달러를 구매자가 지불하게 될 것이다.

275 Your d___________ tactics may compel me to call off the contract.
당신의 지연작전은 나로 하여금 계약을 취소하게 만들 수도 있어요.

276 Yes, it does. From people who practice what's called the d___________ science.
예, 그렇습니다. 암울한 과학이라고 불리는 것을 업으로 삼는 사람들의 관점에서는요.

277 Economic d___________ had been brought about by the surge of oil prices.
경기침체는 유가 폭등에 의한 결과였다.

278 I have such e___________ taste.
나는 대단한 미식가이다.

279 She also gave us an equ___________ answer.
그녀 역시 우리에게 애매모호한 대답을 해주었다.

280 E-mail coming from the development of computer technology is virtually a f___________ way of giving and taking information.
컴퓨터 발달의 부산물인 이메일은 정보를 실질적으로 주고받는 아주 쉬운 방법이다.

281 It's a f___________ conclusion.
이미 따 놓은 당상이야.

282 I guess he has cleaned up small f___________ from his business.
짐작건대, 그는 사업으로 상당한 돈을 벌었을 것이다.

283 I prefer simple designs over inattentive and g___________ interior designs.
나는 산만하고 화려한 인테리어 디자인보다는 심플한 디자인을 더 좋아한다.

284 Because they offer such g___________ portions, I treasure it.
양을 많이 주기 때문에 마음에 든다.

285 Remote areas and other regions at a distance from electrical g___________ are vigorously exploring wind options.
오지나 전기시설에서 멀리 떨어진 지역은 풍력을 강력히 탐구하고 있다.

286 Simba the Lion appeared with an im___________ timing and he helped her.
사자 심바가 아주 절묘한 순간에 나타나서 그녀를 도왔다.

287 We are just im___________ enemies.
우린 화해할 수 없는 적이다.

288 It can even have psychological and social im___________.
심리적 · 사회적 영향이 있을 것이다.

289 Most of them think she gives quite a l___________ explanation.
대부분의 학생들은 그녀가 명쾌한 설명을 해준다고 생각한다.

290 Doctor found a m___________ tumor in my breast.
의사가 내 가슴에서 악성 종양을 발견했다.

291 It acquired a n___________ reputation in the industry.
그것은 업계에서 악명 높은 평판을 얻었다.

292 She is in a n___________ situation at the moment.
그녀는 지금 매우 어려운 상황이야.

293 The company had to go through a p___________ loss.
회사는 재정적 손실을 겪어야만 했다.

294 How did the p___________ meeting for the concert go?
콘서트에 대비한 예비 회의 어땠어?

295 I think it desirable that we await a more p___________ occasion.
더 좋은 시기를 기다리는 게 바람직하다고 생각해.

296 Eight q___________ doctors who used licenses from real doctors were taken into custody.
진짜 의사로부터 구한 자격증을 사용한 여덟 명의 돌팔이 의사가 구속되었다.

297 Export of U.S beef angers Korean p___________ .
미국의 쇠고기 수출이 한국의 축산업자들을 분노하게 했다.

298 The unanticipated arrival of his girl friend from abroad lifted his s___________ spirits.
해외에 사는 여자 친구의 예상치 못한 방문으로 그의 축 처졌던 기분이 나아졌다.

299 It was a s___________ hit.
대성공이었어.

300 It makes them more difficult to identify and classify than the rather s___________ specimens.
그 때문에 비교적 간단한 표본들보다 그것들을 분류하고 확인하는 게 더 어렵다.

301 Smoking could do s____________ damage to your brain.
흡연이 당신의 뇌에 상당한 손상을 입힐 수 있다.

302 He left his parents at the t____________ age of thirteen.
그는 13세라는 어린 나이에 부모를 떠났다.

303 I guess he seems to have an u____________ ability to talk people into buying things.
내 생각엔 그가 사람들을 설득해서 물건을 사게 하는 신기한 능력이 있는 것 같아요.

304 It was a u____________ failure in Japan.
일본에서는 완전한 실패작이었다.

305 He's a real v____________ eater.
그는 정말 게걸스럽게 먹어.

306 When a rape takes place, the police have a tight security c____________ around the building.
성폭행이 발생했을 때, 경찰은 빌딩 주위에 삼엄한 비상 경계선을 구축했다.

307 The journal reported the unprecedent number of the c____________ deaths at age one or younger.
그 잡지는 한 살 이하에서 전례 없는 영아 사망자 수에 대해서 기사화했다.

308 Do you want me to lend you ski g____________?
너는 내가 스키 장비를 빌려주었으면 하는 거니?

309 It might have been a compute g____________.
컴퓨터 오류인 것 같아요.

310 It is necessary to use mouth-to-nose r____________.
구강 대 비강 인공호흡법을 사용하는 것이 필수입니다.

Answers

301. substantial 302. tender 303. uncanny 304. utter 305. voracious 306. cordon 307. crib 308. gear 309. glitch
310. resuscitation

311 The shoulder s____________ was adjustable for the user's body size.
그 가방의 어깨끈은 사용자의 체형에 맞출 수 있는 것이었다.

312 People making the world green are called t____________.
세상을 푸르게 만드는 사람들을 "나무를 끌어안는 사람(환경운동가)"이라고 부른다.

전치사+명사

313 It is out of b____________ to wear inappropriate clothes.
부적절한 옷을 입고 오는 것은 금지되어 있습니다.

⬈ 중요 2어 동사   다음 2어 동사의 의미를 쓰시오.

314 I shouldn't have <u>asked it out</u> on her.
내가 그녀에게 ____________ 하지 말았어야 했는데.

315 That news really <u>brings me down</u>.
그 소식을 들으니 정말 ____________.

316 He <u>brought that upon</u> himself.
____________이에요.

317 <u>Bundle up</u> if you are to go out.
외출하려면 ____________.

318. Their attempts to <u>buy off</u> the opposition were failed.
경쟁사를 ____________ 그들의 시도는 실패했다.

319 He was <u>cast adrift</u> in the English Channel.
그는 영국해협에서 ____________했다.

320 Doubts were <u>cast upon</u> the verity of the suspect.
그 용의자의 진실성에 대해 몇 가지 의문점이 ____________.

321 Chocolate may <u>conjure up</u> ideas of sweet candy bars and syrupy milkshakes.
초콜릿은 단 초콜릿 과자와 시럽이 든 셰이크를 ＿＿＿＿＿＿ 있다.

322 <u>Chew over</u> everything before you make up your mind.
무엇을 해야 할지 결정하기 전에 모든 것을 ＿＿＿＿＿＿.

323 He suggested to <u>chip in</u> for gas.
그가 기름 값을 ＿＿＿＿＿＿하자고 제안했다.

324 She didn't <u>come up to</u> my expectations.
그녀는 내 기대에 ＿＿＿＿＿＿ 못했지.

325 Bad habits <u>creep up</u> on us while we are not conscious of them.
나쁜 버릇은 무의식중에 ＿＿＿＿＿＿.

326 The electricity was <u>cut off</u> for hours.
전기가 몇 시간 동안 ＿＿＿＿＿＿.

327 Julia was <u>enrolled in</u> that class.
줄리아가 그 반에 ＿＿＿＿＿＿.

328 They did to <u>ferret out</u> some useful information.
그들은 유용한 정보를 ＿＿＿＿＿＿ 위해서 그랬어.

329 You should not have <u>flared up</u>.
넌 ＿＿＿＿＿＿ 말아야 했어.

330 How can I get my mail <u>forward</u>?
제 우편물은 어떻게 ＿＿＿＿＿＿ 하나요?

331 Stop <u>fussing around</u>!
____________ 좀 그만해요!

332 She <u>got sacked</u> without any prior notification.
그녀는 아무런 사전통지도 없이 ____________.

333 The boss <u>gave her a crack</u>.
상사가 그녀에게 ____________.

334 I have not the vaguest idea what she was trying to <u>get across</u>.
그녀가 뭘 ____________ 하는지 전혀 모르겠다.

335 The spokesperson made a clever attempt to <u>gloss over</u> the many failures of his company.
그 대변인은 회사의 많은 실수들을 ____________ 위한 교활한 시도를 했다.

336 There is not enough souvenirs to <u>go around to</u> all participants.
기념품이 모든 참가자들에게 다 안 ____________ 것 같아요.

337 I will never <u>go back on</u> my word again.
다시는 약속을 ____________ 않겠다.

338 He <u>fiddles about</u> for the whole session.
그는 회의 내내 ____________.

339 There are rumors <u>going around</u> about him.
그에 관해 ____________ 소문이 있어.

340 Poor nutrition can <u>hold back</u> adult growth.
충분한 영양이 공급되지 않으면 어른으로 성장하는 것을 ____________ 수 있다.

341 It's just <u>holding up</u> for a moment.

잠시 _____________ 일 뿐이래.

342 Workers were <u>incensed against</u> the company's owner for excessive amount of workload.

노동자들은 과도한 노동량으로 인해 사장에 _____________ 하였다.

343 He ought not to have <u>interfere with</u> the meeting.

그가 모임을 _____________ 말았어야 해.

344 The government has decided to <u>kick off</u> a program of radical reform.

정부가 조만간 근본적인 개혁 프로그램을 _____________ 로 결정했다.

345 We can <u>knock off</u> five percent.

5퍼센트 _____________ 수 있습니다.

346 When the class <u>let out,</u> it was late compared to the usual time.

수업이 _____________ 때, 평상시에 비해 늦은 시각이었다.

347 I guess that he is so reserved that he'll never <u>live it down</u>.

내 생각에 그는 내성적이어서 결코 _____________ 어려울 거야.

348 He <u>made off</u> the final exam.

그는 기말고사를 _____________ .

349 I'm going to have to <u>make do with</u> what I have.

내가 가지고 있는 것을 가지고 _____________ 야 할 거야.

350 He <u>mouthed off</u> about our surprise party for Samantha in front of all the others.

그는 우리가 Samantha를 위해 준비한 깜짝 파티를 모두들 앞에서 _____________ .

351 I <u>owe it to</u> your assistance.
당신의 도움에 _______________.

352 You'd <u>pass for</u> an Englishman anytime.
당신은 언제라도 영국 사람으로 _______________.

353 I have made it a rule to <u>punch in</u> at 8:00 a.m.
아침 8시에 _______________하는 것을 규칙으로 삼고 있다.

354 He has no choice but to <u>put in</u> a piece of metal to hold the bones together.
그의 뼈를 붙어 있게 하려면 금속조각을 _______________ 않으면 안 된다.

355 Could you <u>refer me to</u> a good attorney.
좋은 변호사를 한 사람 _______________ 줄 수 있나요?

356 One of our customers <u>reneged on</u> the contract.
고객 중 한 명이 계약을 _______________.

357 The newly released cars these days <u>replete with</u> the latest technology.
새로이 출시되는 차들은 최신 기술을 _______________.

358 The aircraft tried to <u>swerve away</u> from the runway.
항공기가 활주로로부터 _______________ 시도했다.

359 My boy, are you ready to <u>set off</u>?
얘야, _______________ 준비 됐니?

360 I believe that I have to <u>shop around</u> for others.
다른 보험을 _______________ 할 것 같아요.

361 Their benefits had <u>slipped through</u> their fingers.

그들의 이익금이 순식간에 _____________.

362 It took a while to <u>sink in</u> the implication.

그 암시를 _____________ 한참 걸렸어.

363 He is not patient enough to <u>sit through</u> for an hour.

한 시간 동안 _____________ 참을성이 있지 않아요.

364 I don't think I can <u>squeeze in</u> a paper like that.

그 과제를 _____________ 없을 것 같아요.

365 She <u>stood up to</u> them.

그녀는 그들_____________했다.

366 How are you <u>taking along with</u> David?

당신은 David와 얼마나 _____________ 있나요?

367 I can't <u>thank you enough</u>.

정말 _____________!

368 Can you <u>tuck me in</u>?

이불 좀 _____________?

369 Plagiarism will not be able to <u>go uncensured</u>.

표절은 _____________ 못할 것이다.

370 Why don't you <u>work out</u> more often at the gym?

체육관에서 더 자주 _____________ 게 어때?

371 You probably need to <u>zero in on</u> one factor.

당신은 한 가지 요소에 _____________ 할 것이다.

372　We must hold our president _____________ for economic recession.
우리는 경기 불황에 대해 대통령에게 책임을 물어야 한다.

373　The brand tried to keep it _____________ by recruiting innovative and creative designers.
그 브랜드는 혁신적이고 창조적인 디자이너들을 영입함으로써 활기를 유지하려고 노력했다.

374　We decided how to deal with it before we spoke _____________ words.
우리는 그 일을 어떻게 처리할지 즉석에서 결정했다.

375　It occurred _____________ the beginning of the graduation ceremony.
졸업식이 시작할 때 발생했어.

376　The lawyer _____________ his brains to find decisive evidence.
변호사는 명백한 증거를 찾기 위해 머리를 짜냈다.

377　He was saved by the _____________.
그는 간신히 곤경을 면했다.

378　All I have to do is _____________ my time.
내가 해야 할 일은 참고 기다리는 것뿐이다.

379　I was given the a _____________ after the strike.
나는 파업 후에 해고 통지서를 받았다.

380　It is worthless and for the _____________.
무익하고 형편없다.

381 It is quite a _____________ and white approach.
좀 흑백논리이긴 하다.

382 Park has hit five goals this season in the U.K but drew _____________ in his country's opening two World Cup qualifiers.
박 선수는 영국에서 이번 시즌에 5골을 넣었지만, 정작 자국에서 치른 두번의 월드컵 예선에서는 죽을 쑤었다.

383 The manager says that Tom will get the _____________.
지배인이 Tom을 해고하겠대.

384 Plenty of investment companies tend to _____________ the probability of legal action for the wrongdoings of their employees.
많은 투자회사들은 직원들의 비리에 대해 법적 조치를 취할 가능성에 대비하는 경향이 있다.

385 I have money to _____________.
나는 돈이 엄청나게 많다.

386 She is a _____________ off the old brick.
그녀는 아빠를 꼭 닮았다.

387 I merely saw the accident from the _____________ of my eye.
나는 단지 우연히 그 사건을 목격했을 뿐이다.

388 They were arrested at the scene while trying to sell illegal drugs under the _____________.
그들은 불법 약을 비밀리에 판매하려는 다 현장에서 체포되었다.

389 I guess you really need to take a day off before you _____________ under the strain.
당신 무리해서 아프기 전에 정말 휴식을 취해야 할 것 같아요.

390 I am still up a _____________ without a paddle.
난 아직도 곤경에 빠져서 헤어 나오질 못하고 있어.

391 You'd better _____________ to the chase.
바로 본론으로 들어가는 게 낫겠어요.

392 I'm afraid we will just have to make _____________ with something at home.
우리 오늘은 그냥 집에서 그런대로 때워야 할 것 같구나.

393 Problems will only become more serious later _____________ the road.
미래에는 문제가 더 심각해질 것이다.

394 The world _____________ South Korea to the skies.
세계가 남한을 극구 칭찬하였다.

395 It was impressive to see how Cindy coped with her new work considering she up to her _____________ in her work.
일에 몰두하고 있는 것을 볼때 Cindy가 새로운 직장에서 얼마나 잘 해나가고 있는지 알 수 있어서 인상적이었다.

396 I always try to sit on the _____________ and try to settle things down.
나는 항상 중립을 지키면서 상황을 진정시키기 위해 노력한다.

397 What do usually you do to keep yourself as fit as a _____________?
당신은 건강을 유지하기 위해 보통 무엇을 합니까?

398 This case is something we don't want to make a big _____________ about.
이 일은 우리가 침소봉대하고 싶지 않은 일이다.

399 Educator's job is to _____________ their students into life.
교육자가 할 일은 학생들에게 활력을 불어넣어 주는 것이다.

400 Don't meet trouble _____________.
지레 걱정부터 하지 마.

Answers

391. cut 392. do 393. down 394. extolled 395. eyes 396. fence 397. fiddle 398. fuss 399. galvanize 400. halfway

401 There are so many different features that come in ______________ out in the market that missed.

지금 시중에 나와 있는 특징 중 우리가 모르고 지나쳤지만 쓸모 있는 것들이 정말 많아.

402 The reason is that he is the man who's ______________ responsible when something goes awry.

그 이유는 무언가 일이 잘못되었을 때 그가 책임을 져야 하는 사람이기 때문이야.

403 In spite of the low attendance, the party went on without a ____________.

참석률이 저조했지만 파티는 지체 없이 잘 진행되었다.

404 You don't have to blow your ____________.

너는 자화자찬할 필요 없다.

405 Politicians really need to hold their ______________ and discuss the matters thoughtfully rather than make a violent scene.

정치가들은 폭력적인 상황을 만들기보다 진정하고 문제들을 진지하게 토론해야 한다.

406 She brought down the ____________.

그녀는 관객으로부터 만장의 박수갈채를 받았다.

407 Students wish to learn English by ____________ themselves abroad.

학생들은 외국에 나가 영어를 공부하고 싶어 한다.

408 I'm most ____________ to Mr. Watson.

나는 Watson씨에게 가장 큰 신세를 졌다.

409 I want to know all the ____________ of the case.

나는 그 사건의 내막을 모두 알고 싶다.

410 I was so upset when you ____________ the gun.

당신이 다짜고짜 화를 낼 때 정말 저도 속상했어요.

411 I want to keep my life on an even ______________ from now on.
앞으로는 안정적인 삶을 원해.

412 She ______________ a stiff upper lip.
그녀는 꿋꿋이 잘 버티고 있어.

413 If we don't get the ______________ out, we'll miss the last bus.
우리가 서두르지 않으면 마지막 버스를 놓칠 거야.

414 Do not try to hand me a ______________.
나를 속이려고 들지 마.

415 The government's aim is to make all the companies compete on a ______________ playing field.
정부의 목표는 모든 회사들이 공평한 경쟁의 장에서 경쟁하도록 만드는 것입니다.

416 I only call her once in a blue ______________.
아주 가끔씩만 전화합니다.

417 What about doing a little ______________ and tuck on your beer belly?
당신의 술배에 지방제거 수술을 받는 거 어때요?

418 After a little heated discussion, the chair called the meeting to ______________.
다소 열띤 토론 후에 의장은 정숙할 것을 당부했다.

419 Today's lecture was also as ______________ as day.
오늘 강의 역시 일목요연했다.

420 I finally decided to take the ______________.
드디어 모험을 하기로 결정했다.

421 I guess they are lying on the _______________ of protecting the country.
그들은 나라를 보호한다는 구실에서 거짓말하고 있는 것 같아.

422 The law firm _____________ out of the deal.
그 법률회사는 거래에서 손을 뗐다.

423 We must keep suspicious patients in _____________ from others.
우린 의심 가는 환자들을 다른 사람들로부터 격리시켜야 한다.

424 Her sharp words still cut me to the _____________.
그녀의 날카로운 말은 여전히 마음에 사무친다.

425 It finally hit the _____________!
그게 드디어 성과를 거뒀어!

426 The food was delicious, not to _____________ cheap.
음식이 참 맛있더라, 싸기도 하고.

427 Even when he was beset with something irritating, he used to be calm and_____________.
그는 무언가 짜증나게 하는 것이 있어도, 조용하고 침착했다.

428 You need to get into _____________.
너 몸 만들어야겠다.

429 The judge dropped the other _____________.
판사는 끝마무리를 했다.

430 I can give you some references or at least I can be a _____________ board.
내가 자료를 주기니 최소한 무슨 말인지 들어줄 수는 있어.

431 My irresponsible brother-in-law seems to always stay ____________ financially.
나의 무책임한 매형은 늘 재정적으로 곤란한 지경에 있는 것 같다.

432 It happened very quickly and the answers that I gave were ____________ second response.
그 일은 아주 빠르게 진행되었고 나는 짧은 순간에 대답을 해야 했다.

433 She told me I need to correct my habit of spitting ____________.
그녀는 나에게 화내는 버릇을 고쳐야 된다고 말했다.

434 I cannot ____________ it off with him.
그와는 잘 지낼 수가 없다.

435 You must feel ____________ advantage of.
이용 당한 느낌이겠네요.

436 I make mental ____________ of what I buy whenever I shop.
나는 쇼핑할 때마다 내가 사는 것을 마음속으로 계산하면서 산다.

437 He takes modern guys to ____________ for using Facebook as a "X-rated version of amateur porn."
그는 페이스북을 아마추어 포르노의 엑스 등급[성인용]으로 이용한다는 이유로 현대인들을 몹시 비난한다.

438 He was a ____________ among minnows in the World Cup.
그는 월드컵에서 군계일학이었다.

439 This apple pie is out of this ____________.
이 애플파이 맛은 환상적이야.

440 The moment the prodigal son got back home, his mother ____________ her arms around him.
방탕한 아들이 집에 돌아오자, 어머니는 팔로 감싸 안아주었다.

441 nothing daunted

____

442 Act like you belong.

____

443 come hell or high water

____

444 Kevin and Anna, they are history.

____

445 I am afraid you have the wrong person.

____

446 Are you decent?

____

447 Welcome to the club.

____

448 That'll be the day!

____

449 No offense (is meant).

____

450 There's more than one way to skin a cat.

____

Answers
441. 전혀 굴하지 않고 442. 태연하게 행동해. 443. 어떠한 고난이 있어도 444. Kevin과 Anna는 끝난 사이다.
445. 사람을 잘못 보신 것 같습니다. 446. 들어가도 돼?(남의 방을 출입할 때) 447. 나도 같은 입장이야. 448. 믿을 수가 없어!
449. 악의는 없었다. 450. 문제를 해결하는 데는 여러 가지 방법이 있다.

고난도 TEPS in TEPS 어휘 TEST BooK

고득점을 위한 point를 정확히 알려주는 학습서

TEPS 고득점을 위한 Actual Training!

고만고만한 빈출 문제만으로는 자신의 한계를 극복할 수 없다. 실전에서 경쟁력을 높일 수 있는 고난도 문제들만이 정체된 성적을 올릴 수 있다.

흐렸던 기억이 또렷해지는 Final Check!

어휘 학습의 기본은 반복! Final Check를 적극 활용하여 Actual Training에서 다룬 핵심 어휘들을 확실히 흡수할 수 있다.

고난도 문제의 핵심을 꿰뚫는 해설!

아무리 어려운 문제라도 질문의 point를 정확히 알면 문제없다. 고난도 문제의 출제 의도를 정확히 분석한 해설로 TEPS 어휘력을 높일 수 있다.

ISBN 978-89-6049-241-7 13740
978-89-6049-239-4(세트)

₩16000

고난도 TEPS in TEPS

박기혁 · 정구영 지음

어휘
ANSWER
BooK

Vocabulary

Actual Training 10회분 & Final check & 해설

사람in

Answers & Explanations

1. (c)	2. (c)	3. (a)	4. (c)	5. (c)	6. (d)	7. (c)	8. (c)	9. (d)	10. (c)
11. (c)	12. (b)	13. (c)	14. (d)	15. (c)	16. (d)	17. (d)	18. (b)	19. (c)	20. (d)
21. (d)	22. (c)	23. (d)	24. (b)	25. (b)	26. (b)	27. (b)	28. (b)	29. (d)	30. (c)
31. (b)	32. (b)	33. (d)	34. (b)	35. (d)	36. (c)	37. (b)	38. (b)	39. (c)	40. (d)
41. (d)	42. (a)	43. (d)	44. (b)	45. (c)	46. (c)	47. (b)	48. (b)	49. (d)	50. (a)

Part I Questions 1-25

1 유형 고난도 어휘

A: Does money buy happiness?

B: Yes, it does. From people who practice what's called the ___________ science. For when economists tackled the question, they started from the observation that when people put something up for sale they try to get as much for it as they can.

(a) cognitive

(b) histrionic

(c) dismal

(d) convalescent

해석 A: 돈으로 행복을 살 수 있어요?
B: 네, 그래요. 경제학이라는 것을 업으로 삼는 사람들의 관점에서는 그렇죠. 왜냐하면 경제학자들이 그 문제와 씨름할 때, 사람들은 무언가를 팔려고 내놓을 때 그것으로 가능한 한 많이 얻어 내려고 애를 쓴다는 관찰에서 출발하니까요.

해설 물건을 사고파는 것과 관련된 학문은 경제학이며 그런 의미의 단어로 dismal science(우울한 과학; 경제학의 별칭)가 쓰이고 있다.

어휘 cognitive 인지의 histrionic 꾸민 듯한
dismal 암울한 convalescent 회복기의

2 유형 2어 동사

A: Does your brother stand on his own two feet?

B: I hope so, but he is still ___________ my parents.

(a) living it up

(b) coalesce into

(c) living off

(d) squaring up to

해석 A: 네 남동생 자립했니?
B: 그러길 바라는데 아직도 부모님 밑에 얹혀 살아.

해설 coalesce는 '통합하여 하나가 되다'라는 뜻이다.

어휘 live it up 흥청망청 살다, 즐기다
live off 기식하다, 얹혀 살다
square up to 용감히 저항하다

3 유형 고난도 어휘

A: You know what? Some scientists, trying to muzzle dissenting voices, have fervently spreaded their opinion on conservative blogs. I believe these opinions have fueled widespread suspicion that global warming is an elaborate ___________.

B: It was shocking to hear the news. I wonder what the truth is.

(a) ruse
(b) distraction
(c) candor
(d) spate

해석 A: 있잖아. 일부 기후학자들이 반대파의 목소리를 막으려고 보수적인 블로그에 자신들의 견해를 열심히 퍼뜨렸대. 지구온난화가 잘 짜인 정교한 속임수라는 널리 퍼져 있는 의심에 그들의 견해가 기름을 붙는 격이 된 것 같아.

B: 그 소식은 충격적이었어. 진실이 무엇인지 궁금해.

해설 지구온난화에 대한 부정적 의미의 말이 들어가야 하므로 '잘 짜인 속임수, 계략'이라는 의미인 ruse가 들어간다.

어휘 ruse 속임수 distraction 방심, 심란 candor 솔직함 spate 홍수, 범람

4 유형 고난도 어휘

A: What do you think about the future of carbon?

B: The cap-and-dividend would set a price on carbon, thus giving Americans a powerful ___________ to burn less filthy fuel.

(a) paucity
(b) plethora
(c) incentive
(d) instinct

해석 A: 탄소의 미래에 대해 어떻게 생각하십니까?

B: 배출총량 규제·환급제 탄소에 가격을 매기는 것인데, 그러면 미국인들에게 강력한 동기를 부여하여 더러운 연료를 덜 쓰게 만들 겁니다.

해설 빈칸은 미국인들에게 행동하도록 하는 것이므로 문맥상 어울리는 단어는 '자극, 동기'를 뜻하는 incentive이다.

어휘 filthy fuel 공해 연료(석탄, 석유 등 오염물질을 방출하는 연료) paucity 소량, 결핍 plethora 적혈구 과다증 incentive 동기 instinct 본능

5 유형 고난도 어휘

A: Do you know what Mr. Knox says?

B: Yes I do. He does not ___________ his words. He describes Bush's legacy as dishonest wars, stolen wars, and economic collapse.

(a) expound
(b) mark
(c) mince
(d) abominate

해석 A: 너는 Knox씨가 무슨 말하는지 아니?

B: 알지. 그는 조심스럽게 돌려서 말하지 않아. 그는 부시 대통령의 유산을 부정직한 전쟁, 훔친 전쟁, 경제적 몰락이라고 규정하고 있어.

해설 빈칸 뒷문장의 내용이 직접적인 비난을 하는 것이므로 빈칸에 들어갈 단어는 말을 돌려서 하지 않는다는 의미의 mince가 적절하다.

어휘 legacy 유산 expound 설명하다 mark 표시하다 mince 조심스럽게[완곡하게] 말하다 abominate 혐오하다

6 유형 의미상 혼동 어휘

A: The criminal justice system is in need of an overhaul.

B: True, it is particularly true of its ___________ policies. Too many people are being put behind bars who do not need to be there.

(a) probation
(b) apprehension
(c) inquisition
(d) incarceration

해석 A: 사법 시스템을 완전히 새롭게 해야 할 필요가 있어.
B: 맞아, 투옥에 관해선 특히 그래. 너무나 많은 사람들이 그럴 필요가 없는데도 감옥에 갇혀 있어.

해설 감옥에 가두어둔다는 내용이 뒷문장에 나오므로 그것을 대신하는 말은 incarceration이다.

어휘 overhaul (전면적인) 점검, 정비 probation 집행유예 apprehension 우려, 체포 inquisition 심문 incarceration 투옥, 감금

7 유형 연어

A: As an expert in the economy, what are your prospects for our future?

B: The central bank's policy of zero interest rates, the large stimulus and ensuing deficits would, by some iron law of economics, ___________ the currency and boost the government's long-term borrowing costs.

(a) appreciate
(b) undergird
(c) debase
(d) fiddle

해석 A: 경제 전문가로서 우리의 미래에 대한 전망은 어떤가요?
B: 중앙은행의 제로 금리 정책과 대규모 경기부양책과 뒤이은 적자들이 경제학의 철칙에 따라 화폐 가치를 떨어뜨려서 장기적으로 정부의 차입비용을 증가시킬 것입니다.

해설 빈칸에는 문맥상 부정적 의미의 단어가 들어가야 하며 화폐가치를 떨어뜨린다는 의미로 debase가 쓰이는 것이 적절하다.

어휘 appreciate 평가하다, 감사하다
undergird 단단히 묶다, 보강하다(= bolster)
debase 가치를 떨어뜨리다 fiddle 장난치다, 조작하다

8 유형 이디엄

A: What do you think about the American television program?

B: I guess it is worthless and ___________.

(a) for kicks
(b) diamond in the rough
(c) for the birds
(d) in there pitching

해석 A: 미국 TV 프로그램에 대해 어떻게 생각하세요?
B: 제 생각엔 무가치하고 형편없다고 봅니다.

해설 부정적 의미의 말이 빈칸에 필요하다. for the birds가 적절하다.

어휘 for kicks 재미로
diamond in the rough 겉은 투박하지만 속은 꽉 찬 것
for the birds 시시한, 형편없는
in there pitching 열심히 노력하는

9 유형 형태상 혼동 어휘

A: In what situation is the Parliament?

B: Two Congressional ___________ arising out of the war on terror have brought the jurisdictional and normative dimensions of the Great Writ of habeas corpus into sharp relief.

(a) statues

(b) status

(c) statures

(d) statutes

해석 A: 의회는 어떤 상황에 있나요?
B: 대 테러 전쟁에서 나온 2개의 의회 법령이 인신 보호 영장의 사법적이고 규범적 차원을 날카롭게 부각시켰어요.

해설 혼동 어휘 문제인데 의회와 어울릴 만한 단어는 법령이므로 (d) statutes가 적절하다.

어휘 writ of habeas corpus 인신 보호 영장(이유 없는 구금이나 장기간 구류를 막기 위한 법률)
jurisdictional 사법권의 normative 규범적인
statue 동상 status 지위 stature 키, 신장
statute 법령

10 유형 의미상 혼동 어휘

A: Do you know what *Double X* contributor Amanda Marcotte tries to say?

B: He takes modern guys to ___________ for using Facebook as a "X-rated version of amateur porn."

(a) job

(b) occupation

(c) task

(d) employment

해석 A: 당신은 〈더블엑스〉에 기고한 Amanda Marcotte가 무엇을 말하려는지 알아요?
B: 그는 페이스북을 성인용 아마추어 포르노로 이용한다는 이유로 현대인을 신랄하게 비난하고 있어요.

해설 take ~ to task가 '신랄하게 비난하다'라는 의미로 쓰인다는 것을 알아두자.

어휘 contributor (잡지의) 기고[투고]자
porn 포르노(pornography) occupation 직업

11 유형 의미상 혼동 어휘

A: I was impressed with Nicholas regarding his patience.

B: I thought so too. Even when he was beset with something irritating, he used to be calm and ___________.

(a) restive

(b) infuriating

(c) poised

(d) sinewy

해석 A: 나는 Nicholas의 인내심에 감명받았어.
B: 나도 그렇게 생각했어. 그는 짜증나는 일에 시달려도 조용하고 침착했지.

해설 calm and poised는 자주 쓰이는 표현이므로 통으로 암기하도록 한다.

어휘 restive 침착성이 없는, 들떠 있는
infuriating 열받게 하는 poised 침착한
sinewy 기골이 장대한

12 유형 연어

A: How can home appliances operate?

B: They can get electricity from either a battery unit which is sold in convenience stores or from a wall ___________.

  (a) consent

  (b) outlet

  (c) merchandise

  (d) vent

해석　A: 가전제품은 어떻게 작동되나요?
B: 편의점에서 파는 건전지나 벽의 콘센트에서 전력을 쓸 수 있습니다.

해설　outlet은 '배출구'의 의미도 있지만 전기 콘센트를 의미하기도 한다. 그런 점에서 답을 (a)로 착각하지 않기를 바란다.

어휘　consent 동의 outlet 배출구, 전기 콘센트
merchandise 상품 vent 통풍구

13 유형 고난도 어휘

A: How come the students alienate the young professor?

B: He ___________ expanation after he made some blunders in grading process.

  (a) construed

  (b) bereaved

  (c) eschewed

  (d) stipulated

해석　A: 왜 학생들이 그 젊은 교수를 따돌리는 거야?
B: 성적평가 과정에서 실수를 해놓고 해명을 회피했거든.

해설　문맥상 '(일부러) 피하다'의 의미가 필요하므로 (c)가 적절하다.

어휘　construe 해석하다 bereave 빼앗아가다
eschew 피하다 stipulate 규정하다, 약정하다

14 유형 형태상 혼동 어휘

A: Why does the Danish boy look so gloomy?

B: He was alarmed to hear that he could not inherit the family estate on the grounds that he was an ___________ child, born to his father's mistress.

  (a) illegal

  (b) illiterate

  (c) lawless

  (d) illegitimate

해석　A: 그 덴마크 소년은 왜 그렇게 우울해 보일까?
B: 자기가 아버지의 정부에게서 태어난 서자라는 것 때문에 가족의 토지를 물려받을 수 없다는 얘기를 듣고 놀라서 그래.

해설　문맥상 '사생아'라는 의미의 연어이므로 illegitimate이 적절하다.

어휘　alarmed 깜짝놀란 inherit 물려받다
mistress 애인, 정부 illegal 불법적인
illiterate 읽고 쓸 줄 모르는, 문맹의
lawless 무법의 illegitimate 서출의, 사생아의

15 유형 연어

A: Do you remember when *Harry Potter* came out first?

B: Of course, I do. It was a(n) ___________ hit.

  (a) irascible

  (b) piqued

  (c) smash

  (d) triggering

해석　A: 〈해리포터〉가 처음 출간되었을 때 기억나니?
B: 물론이지. 대성공이었잖아.

해설　엄청난 성공을 말할 때 쓰는 연어적 표현을 묻는 문제이다. a smash hit은 '대성공'이라는 의미.

어휘　irascible 화를 잘 내는, 성급한 piqued 화난
triggering 야기시키는

16 유형 전치사

A: When did the bombing take place?

B: It occurred ___________ the beginning of the graduation ceremony.

(a) to

(b) in

(c) for

(d) at

해석 A: 폭발이 언제 일어났지?
B: 졸업식이 시작할 때 발생했어.

해설 작은 시점을 말할 때는 전치사 at을 사용한다. 사소한 부분에서도 점수를 잃지 않도록 한다. 이런 문제들도 은근히 틀리기 쉬워서 애를 먹인다.

어휘 bombing 폭발 graduation ceremony 졸업식

17 유형 연어

A: Do you remember the physician that ___________ her injuries following the accident?

B: I'm not certain, but I guess it was Dr. Garner.

(a) cared

(b) cured

(c) redeemed

(d) treated

해석 A: 사고 후에 그녀의 상처를 치료해준 의사를 기억하니?
B: 확실히 모르겠지만 Garner 박사인 것 같아.

해설 치료를 한다는 의미에서는 (b)도 답이 될 수 있어 보인다. 그러나, 여기에서의 치료는 완치보다는 환자를 치료하기 위해 의학적인 도움을 준다는 의미가 강하기에 정답은 (d)가 되어야 한다.

어휘 care 돌보다, 신경 쓰다 cure (병을) 고치다, 치유하다
redeem 회복하다
treat 치료하다(의사가 행하는 일체의 의료행위)

18 유형 연어

A: How come you are fond of the restaurant so much?

B: Because they offer such ___________ portions, I treasure it.

(a) general

(b) generous

(c) magnificent

(d) voracious

해석 A: 왜 당신은 그 식당을 그렇게 좋아해요?
B: 양을 많이 주기 때문에 그게 마음에 들어요.

해설 음식의 '양'을 말하는 portion과 어울리는 단어로는 '관대한, 후한'이라는 의미의 generous가 적절하다.

어휘 generous 관대한, 후한
magnificent 참으로 아름다운 voracious 게걸스러운

19 유형 이디엄

A: This apple pie is ___________.

B: I just made it myself. Isn't it fantastic?

(a) white elephant

(b) black sheep

(c) out of this world

(d) skeleton in the closet

해석 A: 이 애플파이 최고야.
B: 내가 방금 만들었어. 환상적이지 않니?

해설 idiom 문제이다. out of this world(세상에 없는, 최고의)라는 표현을 암기하자.

어휘 fantastic 기막히게 좋은, 환상적인
white elephant 애물단지 black sheep 말썽꾼
out of this world 세상에 없는, 최고의
skeleton in the closet 숨기고 싶은 비밀

20 유형 의미상 혼동 어휘

A: It was imprudent of you to ___________ the get-together.

B: I didn't mean to bother, but it was urgently needed. I couldn't help it.

　(a) interfere

　(b) hurl

　(c) overhaul

　(d) interrupt

해석 A: 모임을 방해하다니 신중하지 못했어요.
　　B: 그럴 의도는 아니었는데 너무 다급해서 어쩔 수 없었어요.

해설 남의 일에 끼어드는 것처럼 추상적인 의미의 방해를 의미할 때는 interfere를 쓰지만, 말이나 행동을 방해하거나 무엇을 잠깐 중단시키는 상황에서처럼 물리적인 방해를 말할 때는 interrupt가 타당하다.

어휘 interfere 방해하다, 간섭하다　hurl 던지다
　　overhaul 철저히 점검하다　interrupt 방해하다

---

21 유형 형태상 혼동 어휘

A: I suppose meeting the deadline is not easy.

B: You mean you want to ___________, don't you?

　(a) elongate

　(b) expand

　(c) expend

　(d) extend

해석 A: 마감시한을 맞추는 것은 쉽지 않다고 생각합니다.
　　B: 마감시한을 연장해달라는 거죠, 그렇죠?

해설 '늘리다/연장하다/확장하다'의 의미를 가지는 말들 중에서도 extend는 기한을 연장할 때 쓰인다.

어휘 elongate (혀를) 길게 늘어뜨리다
　　expand 팽창하다　expend 소비하다
　　extend (길이 등을) 연장하다, 늘리다

---

22 유형 형태상 혼동 어휘

A: What do you do as a coast guard?

B: In case of emergency on the beach, I use mouth-to-nose ___________.

　(a) rehabilitation

　(b) regurgitation

　(c) resuscitation

　(d) resurrection

해석 A: 해안 경비대원으로서 무슨 일을 하나요?
　　B: 해변에서 비상사태가 일어났을 때, 구강 대 비강 인공호흡법을 사용합니다.

해설 resuscitation은 같은 재활의 의미 중에서도 생명을 소생시키는 인공호흡법을 말한다. 신체적 기능의 재활은 (a)를 쓴다는 것에 주의해야 한다.

어휘 rehabilitation 재활　regurgitation 먹은 것을 토하는 것
　　resurrection 부활

---

23 유형 고난도 어휘

A: Can you tell me who helped you while you were writing this article?

B: Of course. I'm most ___________ to Mr. Watson.

　(a) accustomed

　(b) opposed

　(c) qualified

　(d) indebted

해석 A: 네가 이 기사를 쓸 때 누가 도와주었는지 말해줄 수 있니?
　　B: 물론. Watson 씨에게 신세를 가장 많이 졌어.

해설 문맥상 필요한 것은 indebted(신세를 진, 은혜를 입은)이다.

어휘 accustomed to ~에 익숙한　opposed to ~에 반대하는
　　qualified 자격을 갖춘
　　indebted to ~에 신세를 진, 은혜를 입은

24 유형 2어 동사

A: I'm so overweight nowadays.

B: Why don't you ___________ more often?

   (a) walk out

   (b) work out

   (c) set about

   (d) set back

해석 A: 나 요즘 살이 너무 많이 쪘어.
B: 좀 더 자주 운동을 하는 게 어때?

해설 문맥상 운동을 더 하라는 충고가 들어가야 하므로 (b)가 정답이다.

어휘 walk out 파업하다 work out 운동하다
set about 시작하다 set back 후퇴하다

25 유형 고난도 어휘

A: The morning walk every day after breakfast is lively and ___________, isn't it?

B: Yes, I think so, too.

   (a) mediocre

   (b) salubrious

   (c) mortal

   (d) peripheral

해석 A: 매일 아침 식사 후 걷는 것은 활기차고 건강에 좋죠, 그렇죠?
B: 예, 저도 그렇게 생각해요.

해설 문맥상 '건강에 좋은'이라는 의미의 salubrious가 어울린다.

어휘 mediocre 평범한, 보통의
salubrious 살기 좋은, 건강에 좋은
mortal 죽을 운명의 peripheral 주변부의

Part Ⅱ Questions 26-50

26 유형 2어 동사

Plenty of investment companies tend to ___________ the probability of legal action for the wrongdoings of their employees.

   (a) get over

   (b) brace for

   (c) give in

   (d) let up

해석 많은 투자회사들은 그들의 직원들의 비리에 대해 법적조치를 취할 가능성을 대비하는 경향이 있다.

해설 문맥상 '준비하다, 대비하다'가 적절하므로 (b)가 알맞다.

어휘 wrongdoing 범법[부정] 행위, 죄 get over 극복하다
brace for 준비하다 give in 굴복하다
let up (비 등이) 그치다

27 유형 고난도 어휘

Historically speaking, a host of tiny island countries have ___________ become a hub for smuggling drugs. In other words, they went bad without any knowledge of it.

- (a) methodically
- **(b) inadvertently**
- (c) pugnaciously
- (d) ferociously

해석 역사적으로 말하자면 많은 섬나라 국가들은 우연히 마약밀매의 중심지가 되었다. 즉 자신들도 모르는 사이에 상황이 악화된 것이다.

해설 without any knowledge of it에서 빈칸에 '우연하게, 자신도 모르게'의 의미를 갖는 부사가 필요함을 알 수 있다.

어휘 smuggling 밀수, 밀반입
methodically 주도면밀하게
inadvertently 무심코, 자기도 모르게, 우연히
pugnaciously 호전적으로 ferociously 사납게

28 유형 연어

David has argued that the economic ___________ were brought about by the surge of oil prices.

- (a) recess
- **(b) doldrums**
- (c) libel
- (d) graft

해석 David은 경제침체가 유가 폭등에 의해 야기되었다고 주장해왔다.

해설 '경제의'라는 단어와 결합하여 유가 폭등에 어울리는 단어는 doldrums이다. 원래는 적도의 무풍지대를 의미하는 단어이다.

어휘 surge 폭등 recess 휴식 doldrums 침체 libel 비방
graft 접목, 접붙이기

29 유형 고난도 어휘

Barring unanticipated events, the ___________ would be ironed out sooner or later.

- (a) conservation
- (b) assortment
- (c) sanitation
- **(d) skirmish**

해석 예상치 못한 사건만 일어나지 않는다면 충돌은 조만간 해소될 것이다.

해설 문맥상 iron out이라는 표현이 쓰이기 위해서는 부정적 의미가 와야 하고, 그 부정적 의미가 오기 위해서는 (d)가 가정 적절하다.

어휘 conservation 보존, 보호 assortment 모음, 조합
sanitation 위생 skirmish 충돌

30 유형 고난도 어휘

Purchasing such a costly automobile is a bit ___________ for a woman of her income.

- (a) perspicacious
- (b) scathing
- **(c) extravagant**
- (d) frugal

해석 그런 비싼 자동차를 구입하는 것은 그녀의 수입으로는 다소 사치스런 것이다.

해설 정답인 (c) 자체는 크게 어렵게 느껴지지 않더라도 (a)와 같은 어휘로 인해 답을 확신하지 못해 틀릴 수 있는 문제이다.

어휘 perspicacious 명민한, 통찰력 있는
scathing 냉혹한, 가차 없는 extravagant 사치스런
frugal 검소한

31 유형 고난도 어휘

The technology has never been improved or made as ___________ as expected.

(a) scrupulous
(b) state-of-the-art
(c) ludicrous
(d) intangible

해석 그 기술은 기대한 만큼 향상되지도 않았고 최신식의 것도 아니었다.

해설 일반적 기술이 아니라 특정 기술에 대한 언급이라는 것에 주목하지 않으면 오류를 범할 수 있다. 앞의 improved와 어울릴 만한 의미를 찾으면 정답은 (b)가 된다.

어휘 scrupulous 양심적인 state-of-the-art 최신식의 ludicrous 우스꽝스런 intangible 만질 수 없는

32 유형 고난도 어휘

Few know exactly how to make a lot of money from investment or ___________.

(a) stipend
(b) speculation
(c) conjecture
(d) approbation

해석 투자나 투기로 많은 돈을 버는 방법을 정확히 아는 사람은 거의 없다.

해설 돈에 관련된 보기 stipend, speculation 중 많은 돈을 번다는 문장에 더욱 적합한 단어는 봉급보다는 투기이다. 따라서 정답은 (b).

어휘 stipend (목사 등의) 봉급, 장학금 speculation 투기 conjecture 어림짐작, 추측 approbation 칭찬

33 유형 고난도 어휘

This site is intriguing and interactive to help children ___________ astronomy.

(a) estrange
(b) unearth
(c) aggravate
(d) appreciate

해석 이 사이트는 재미있고 쌍방향적이어서 아이들이 천문학을 올바르게 이해하도록 도와준다.

해설 appreciate가 '평가하다' 외에 '이해하다'는 의미가 있다는 것을 알아두도록 한다.

어휘 estrange 소원하게 하다 unearth 발굴하다 aggravate 악화시키다 appreciate 올바르게 이해하다

34 유형 고난도 어휘

The financial expert has been ___________ a 20% consumer price surge for the entire year.

(a) protracting
(b) projecting
(c) imploding
(d) condoning

해석 그 재무 전문가는 소비자 물가지수가 한 해를 통틀어 20퍼센트 상승할 것이라고 예측해왔다.

해설 project는 보통 '계획하다'라는 뜻으로 쓰이지만, 이 문제에서처럼 간혹 '예측하다' 의 의미로 쓰이기도 한다는 것에 유의해야 한다.

어휘 protract 오래 끌다 project 예측하다 implode 내파하다 condone 용서하다

35 형태상 혼동 어휘

People in ethnic minorities are generally __________ economic and educational opportunity, and therefore they often lack self-esteem.

   (a) delayed
   (b) degenerated
   (c) dissembled
   (d) denied

해석 소수 민족집단 사람들은 일반적으로 경제적 · 교육적인 기회를 받지 못하고, 그에 따라 자존감이 부족한 경우가 많다.

해설 deny는 not give(주지 않다)의 의미이다. 즉 단순하게 '거부하다'의 의미 이상으로 쓰임을 알아야 한다.

어휘 self-esteem 자존감, 자부심 degenerate 퇴보하다
dissemble 속이다, 가장하다

36 의미상 혼동 어휘

The President __________ the cheers of the people on the street, waving his hands.

   (a) booked
   (b) conserved
   (c) acknowledged
   (d) salvaged

해석 대통령은 거리에 나온 사람들의 환호에 답례하여 손을 흔들었다.

해설 acknowledge는 '인정하다' 이외에 '(경례에) 답하다, 사례하다' 등의 뜻이 있다.

어휘 book 예약하다 conserve 보존하다 salvage 인양하다

37 연어

As a well-known political scientist, he has __________ the problems of politics throughout his book.

   (a) bewitched
   (b) addressed
   (c) withdrew
   (d) retreated

해석 유명한 정치학자로서 그는 그의 책을 통해서 정치의 문제점을 다루어왔다.

해설 address the problem는 '문제를 다루다'의 의미로 TEPS에서 아주 자주 출제된다.

어휘 bewitch 마법을 걸다 address 다루다(= tackle)
withdraw 예금을 인출하다 retreat 후퇴하다

38 연어

Susan and John met with a travel agent and __________ airline tickets.

   (a) gathered
   (b) collected
   (c) contained
   (d) comprised

해석 Susan과 John은 여행사 직원을 만나서 항공기 티켓을 받아왔다.

해설 '받기로 한 것을 받다'의 의미로 collect가 정답이다.

어휘 gather (아무 기준 없이) 모으다
collect 가지러 가다, 가져오다
contain 포함하다, 억제하다
comprise 포함하다, 구성되다

39 유형 고난도 어휘

Plenty of professors at the university have been warned not to ___________ other peer scholars' thesis.

(a) capsize

(b) rebate

(c) plagiarize

(d) stack

해석 대학의 많은 교수들이 다른 동료 학자들의 논문을 표절하지 말라는 경고를 받았다.

해설 문맥상 적절한 단어는 '표절한다'는 의미이므로 정답은 (c)이다.

어휘 thesis 논문 capsize 전복되다, 뒤집어지다
rebate 환불하다 plagiarize 표절하다
stack 쌓아올리다; 더미

40 유형 고난도 어휘

The chairperson has been charged with ___________ of dividends from his corporation.

(a) supplements

(b) decrial

(c) latch

(d) appropriation

해석 회장은 회사의 배당금을 유용한 혐의로 기소되었다.

해설 문맥상 회사의 공적인 돈을 사용하는 것이므로 (d)가 정답이다.

어휘 dividend 배당금 decrial 비난, 매도
latch 빗장, 걸쇠
appropriation 유용(남의 돈을 적당히 자기가 사용하는 것)

41 유형 고난도 어휘

Generally speaking, women seem to be more ___________ than men to the adverse effects of alcohol.

(a) specious

(b) sprightly

(c) suspended

(d) susceptible

해석 일반적으로 말해서, 여자들은 술의 많은 부작용에 대해서 남자들보다 더 취약한 것처럼 보인다.

해설 '~에 취약하다'의 표현은 be susceptible to, be vulnerable to 등이 있다.

어휘 adverse effect 역효과, 부작용
specious 겉만 번지르르한, 남을 속이는
sprightly 활발한, 씩씩한 suspended 중단된, 연기된
susceptible to ~에 취약한

42 유형 형태상 혼동 어휘

The artist was not a loser. After all, his works were ___________ in a famous gallery.

(a) exhibited

(b) encased

(c) embittered

(d) entranced

해석 그 미술가는 실패자가 아니었다. 결국 그의 작품들은 유명한 미술관에서 전시되었다.

해설 선택지에 함께 제시된 단어들은 다소 어렵지만 내용상 찾기 어려운 문제는 아니다.

어휘 exhibit 전시하다 encase 싸다 embittered 고된
entrance 도취시키다

43 유형 연어

Owing to ___________ technology, our lives have become more and more convenient.

    (a) astute

    (b) discrete

    (c) rudimentary

    (d) cutting-edge

> 해석 첨단 기술 덕택에 우리의 삶은 더욱 더 편리해졌다.
>
> 해설 우리의 삶이 편리해지려면 '첨단의'라는 의미가 필요할 것이고 cutting-edge가 그런 단어이다.
>
> 어휘 astute 명민한 discrete 개별의, 분리된 rudimentary 기초적인 cutting-edge 첨단의

44 유형 형태상 혼동 어휘

Many passengers got completely ___________ after the 20-hour flight.

    (a) dilapidated

    (b) cranky

    (c) destitute

    (d) decrepit

> 해석 많은 승객들은 20시간의 장시간 비행을 한 후 몹시 짜증이 나 있었다.
>
> 해설 긴 여행을 한 승객들의 상태를 나타내기에 가장 적합한 단어는 cranky이다. 따라서 정답은 (b).
>
> 어휘 dilapidated 황폐한 cranky 짜증이 난 destitute 가난한 decrepit 노쇠한

45 유형 의미상 혼동 어휘

Regrettably, nobody in her class is supporting her due to her ___________ character.

    (a) grudging

    (b) grimacing

    (c) bellicose

    (d) filthy

> 해석 유감스럽게도, 그녀의 호전적인 성격 때문에 그녀의 학급에서 누구도 그녀를 편들어주지 않는다.
>
> 해설 bellicose는 싸우기 좋아하는 성격이나 행동을 가리키는 말이다. (d)는 사람의 성격 묘사에 어울리지 않는다.
>
> 어휘 grudging 앙심을 품은 grimacing 얼굴 찌푸리는 bellicose 호전적인 filthy 더러운

46 유형 고난도 어휘

Mr. Baker was cautious to ___________ from the topic of marriage as Susan had just broken up with her boyfriend.

    (a) align

    (b) quench

    (c) dodge

    (d) stifle

> 해석 Baker씨는 Susan이 남자친구와 헤어진 지 얼마 안됐기 때문에 결혼을 화제로 올리지 않도록 조심했다.
>
> 해설 상대가 겪은 안 좋은 경험을 떠올리지 않게 하기 위하여 취하려는 행동이 답인데 결혼이라는 화제를 억제한다는 것보다 회피한다는 것이 문맥상 자연스럽다. 정답은 (c).
>
> 어휘 align 정렬시키다 quench (갈증을) 해소하다 dodge 회피하다 stifle 억제하다

47 유형 형태상 혼동 어휘

Park has hit five goals this season in the UK but drew
___________ in his country's opening two World
Cup qualifiers.

 (a) breaks

 (b) blanks

 (c) brinks

 (d) blinks

해석 박 선수는 영국에서 이번 시즌에 5골을 넣었지만, 정작 자국에서 치른 두 차례의 월드컵 예선에서는 죽을 쑤었다.

해설 draw blanks라고 하면 '죽을 쑤다, 실패하다'의 의미를 나타낸다.

어휘 qualifier 예선전, 예선 경기 break 휴식시간
brink 중대한 국면, 가장자리
blink (눈을) 깜박거림, 일순간

48 유형 의미상 혼동 어휘

The other day the prosecution in the International Court
of Justice announced that it would ___________ charges
against the war criminals.

 (a) convict

 (b) press

 (c) accuse

 (d) blame

해석 일전에 국제사법재판소(ICJ)의 검찰은 전쟁 범죄자들을 기소할 것이라고 발표했다.

해설 '기소하다'에 해당하는 다양한 표현들을 잘 알아둬야 한다.

어휘 convict 유죄를 확정하다 press charges 기소하다
accuse 비난하다, 고소하다 blame 비난하다

49 유형 형태상 혼동 어휘

In 1994, the Korean Scholastic Aptitude Test was first
___________ to high school students.

 (a) arranged

 (b) braced

 (c) brewed

 (d) administered

해석 1994년에 한국의 대학수학능력시험이 고등학생들에게 처음으로 시행되었다.

해설 administer a test에서 administer가 시험 등을 시행한다는 의미로 쓰임을 주지해야 한다.

어휘 arrange 정돈하다 brace 준비하다 brew (일을) 꾸미다

50 유형 고난도 어휘

Two days ago, Hurricane Katrina ___________
plenty of trees and telephone poles in New Mexico.

 (a) uprooted

 (b) foamed

 (c) berated

 (d) saturated

해석 이틀 전에 허리케인 카트리나가 뉴멕시코의 많은 나무들과 전신주들을 뿌리째 뽑았다.

해설 단순하게 생각하면 물과 관련하여 연상되는 효과 때문에 (d)가 답이 될 것이라고 생각할 수 있다. 그러나 나무와 전신주를 뽑았다는 의미가 되어야 하기에 정답은 (a)가 된다.

어휘 uproot 뿌리째 뽑다 foam 거품이 일게 하다
berate 비난하다 saturate 흠뻑 적시다

1. (d)	2. (b)	3. (c)	4. (d)	5. (b)	6. (d)	7. (a)	8. (c)	9. (d)	10. (d)
11. (a)	12. (c)	13. (c)	14. (d)	15. (c)	16. (a)	17. (b)	18. (c)	19. (d)	20. (d)
21. (c)	22. (b)	23. (b)	24. (b)	25. (c)	26. (c)	27. (b)	28. (b)	29. (b)	30. (d)
31. (c)	32. (c)	33. (a)	34. (d)	35. (b)	36. (c)	37. (b)	38. (c)	39. (b)	40. (d)
41. (a)	42. (a)	43. (b)	44. (b)	45. (d)	46. (c)	47. (d)	48. (c)	49. (c)	50. (d)

Part I Questions 1-25

1 유형 형태상 혼동 어휘

A: Did you get any new items today?

B: No. It seems that I'm going to have to __________
what I have.

(a) make believe
(b) make up for
(c) make for
(d) make do with

해석 A: 당신은 오늘 새로운 아이템을 얻었나요?
B: 아니요. 가지고 있는 것을 가지고 그럭저럭 해나가야
할 것 같아요.

해설 선택지를 꼼꼼하게 읽지 않으면, 정답이 (b)가 된다고 생
각하기 쉽다. 그러나 여기서는 문맥상 '그럭저럭 해나가다'
의 의미가 되어야 한다. 따라서, (d)가 정답이 된다.

어휘 make believe ~인 체하다 make up for 보충하다
make for ~로 향하다 make do with ~으로 때우다

2 유형 2어 동사

A: Did the Bakers quarrel again?

B: Yes, you know, most married couples __________
with each other over money.

(a) fall back
(b) fall out
(c) get away
(d) hold out

해석 A: Baker 씨 부부는 또 싸웠나요?
B: 네, 대부분의 부부들은 돈 문제로 서로 싸우잖아요.

해설 문맥상 싸운다는 의미의 어구가 들어가야 하는데 그런 의
미를 지닌 것은 (b)이다.

어휘 fall back (on) 의지하다 fall out 싸우다
get away 용케 피하다 hold out 저항하다

3 유형 고난도 어휘

A: It was a bad accident, wasn't it?

B: Yes, it's awful that they had to ___________ his leg to get him out. There simply wasn't any other option.

(a) forsake

(b) hoodwink

(c) amputate

(d) palter

해석 A: 끔찍한 사고였어요, 그렇지 않아요?

B: 예, 그를 빼내기 위해서 다리를 잘라내야 했다니 끔찍해요. 다른 방법이 없었거든요.

해설 구조를 위해 어떤 방법을 써야 했기에 끔찍하다는 것인지를 생각하면 (c)가 정답임을 알 수 있다.

어휘 forsake 버리다 hoodwink 눈가림하다, 속이다
amputate 절단하다 palter 말끝을 흐리다, 얼버무리다

4 유형 연어

A: How did the bird manage to run away?

B: Simba the Lion appeared with ___________ timing and he helped her.

(a) hefty

(b) apocryphal

(c) unaffected

(d) impeccable

해석 A: 그 새는 어떻게 도망갈 수 있었지?

B: 사자 심바가 아주 절묘한 순간에 나타나서 그 새를 도와줬어.

해설 impeccable은 원래 '결점이 없는' 의 의미를 가진다. 우리도 일상생활에서 "완벽한 타이밍이야"라는 말을 자주 사용하듯이, '절묘한 순간'이라고 할 때는 impeccable timing 이라는 표현을 사용한다.

어휘 hefty 거대한 apocryphal 가짜의
unaffected 꾸밈없는, 가식의
impeccable 절묘한, 완벽한

5 유형 고난도 어휘

A: The new boy in my class was so ___________ that he didn't even talk to other students.

B: You said it, he has his nose in the air all the time.

(a) hale

(b) snobbish

(c) irresistible

(d) compelling

해석 A: 우리 반에 새로 온 아이는 너무 잘난 척을 해서 다른 학생들에게 말도 안 걸어.

B: 네 말이 맞아, 걘 항상 거드름을 피워.

해설 snob은 원래 '속물'이라는 뜻이다. 즉 거드름 피우고 젠체하는 사람을 가리킬 때 주로 쓰는 말이다. 그래서 snobbish 라고 하면 '거드름을 피우는'이라는 의미가 된다.

어휘 hale (노인이) 건강한, 정정한
snobbish 거드름 피우는, 우쭐대는
irresistible (거부할 수 없이) 유혹적인
compelling 설득력 있는, 매력적인

6 유형 고난도 어휘

A: If you work in such bad weather, you're going to ___________ your cold.

B: I appreciate your concern.

(a) ameliorate

(b) prostrate

(c) coddle

(d) exacerbate

해석 A: 그런 악천후에 밖에서 일하면 감기가 심해질 거예요.

B: 염려해주셔서 감사합니다.

해설 날씨가 안 좋을 때 밖에 나가면 감기가 악화될 것을 예상할 수 있으므로 적합한 선택지는 (d).

어휘 ameliorate 개선하다
prostrate 엎드리게 하다, 굴복시키다
coddle 버릇없이 키우다, 귀여워하다
exacerbate 악화시키다

7 유형 고난도 어휘

A: Where and how was Admiral Nelson's funeral held?

B: It was conducted by means of ___________ in England.

  (a) cremation

  (b) incarceration

  (c) bogeyman

  (d) knoll

[해석] A: Nelson 제독의 장례식은 어디에서 어떻게 치러졌나요?
B: 잉글랜드에서 화장 방식으로 치렀습니다.

[해설] 장례 방법을 묻고 있으므로 문맥상 cremation이 적절하다.

[어휘] conduct 치르다 cremation 화장(火葬)
incarceration 투옥, 감금 bogeyman 망령, 귀신
knoll 작고 둥근 언덕

8 유형 이디엄

A: Elizabeth said to me that she ___________ your father into attending her birthday party.

B: Yeah, she has a way with words.

  (a) took

  (b) told

  (c) talked

  (d) spoke

[해석] A: Elizabeth가 그러는데 걔가 너의 아버지를 설득해서 자기 생일파티에 참석하도록 했다던데.
B: 응, 걘 말재주가 있어.

[해설] have a way with words는 '말재주가 있다'는 뜻의 표현이다. 원래 have a way라고 하면 '재주 있다'를 뜻하기 때문이다. 따라서, 빈칸에는 말을 듣는 대상으로 하여금 설득을 시켜서 어떤 행동을 하게 했다는 표현이 들어가야 하기에 정답은 (c)가 된다.

[어휘] talk ~ into -ing ~설득하여 ~하게 하다

9 유형 2어 동사

A: My boy, are you ready to ___________?

B: Yes sir, except for the fact that I should buy things for camping.

  (a) put out

  (b) put off

  (c) take off

  (d) set off

[해석] A: 애야, 출발 준비 됐니?
B: 예, 캠핑때 쓸 물건을 사야 한다는 것만 빼면요.

[해설] 필요한 물건을 사는 것을 빼고 출발 준비가 되었다고 했기에 다소 희화적인 내용이 될 수도 있으나, '출발을 하다'는 표현은 set off가 된다.

[어휘] put out 불을 끄다 put off 연기하다
take off 이륙하다; 옷을 벗다 set off 출발하다

10 유형 연어

A: My brother-in-law has ___________ a great deal of money after selling his cosmetics business.

B: It is astounding that he has become a billionaire.

  (a) dislocated

  (b) dislodged

  (c) concocted

  (d) accrued

[해석] A: 내 처남은 화장품 회사를 매각한 후 대단히 많은 돈을 모았어.
B: 그가 억만장자가 되었다니 놀랍군요.

[해설] 보통 '돈을 모으다'라고 하면 make money 등을 쓰지만, 오랜 기간에 걸쳐 돈과 부를 축적한다고 할 때는 accrue money를 쓴다는 점이 고난도 출제사항이다.

[어휘] dislocate 탈구시키다 dislodge 이동시키다
concoct 조리하다 accrue (돈이나 부를) 축적하다

11 유형 의미상 혼동 어휘

A: He should not have ___________ with the board meeting.

B: I've heard that it was an emergency. He couldn't avoid it.

   (a) interfered

   (b) interrupted

   (c) perpetrated

   (d) bothered

해석 A: 그는 이사회 회의를 방해하지 말았어야 했어.
B: 긴급 상황이었다라고 들었어. 그도 어쩔 수 없었어.

해설 interfere는 with와 같이 쓰여야 한다. 그렇지 않으면 interrupt를 사용.

어휘 perpetrate 죄를 범하다

12 유형 의미상 혼동 어휘/ 2어 동사

A: I discovered that Julia is ___________ in that class.

B: Yes, she will start in a few days.

   (a) registering

   (b) getting

   (c) enrolling

   (d) signing

해석 A: Julia가 그 강의에 등록할 거라는 것을 알게 되었어.
B: 응, 며칠 있으면 듣기 시작할 거야.

해설 '수업에 등록하다'라는 의미로 사용되는 어휘를 정확히 알아두자. register for, sign up for, take the class, enroll in 모두 '수강 신청을 하다'의 의미를 가진다. 따라서 제시된 in을 감안해서 정답은 (c)가 된다.

어휘 discover 발견하다, 알다 register 등록하다

13 유형 이디엄

A: Did you watch the final round yesterday?

B: Certainly. It was thrilling. There was a score ___________.

   (a) sitting on a gold mine

   (b) leaving no stone unturned

   (c) at the eleventh hour

   (d) in the hole

해석 A: 어제 결승전 봤니?
B: 물론이지. 손에 땀을 쥐게 했지. 마지막 순간에 득점이 있었어.

해설 at the eleventh hour 마지막 순간에

어휘 sitting on a gold mine 돈이 많은
leaving no stone unturned 모든 수단을 동원한
in the hole 빚진 상태에 있는

14 유형 의미상 혼동 어휘

A: The bookcase that matches these books seems a little too large. Do you have any ___________?

B: I'm sorry, we don't have other items.

   (a) substitutes

   (b) altercations

   (c) garment

   (d) alternatives

해석 A: 이 책들에 어울리는 책장은 좀 커 보이네요. 다른 것은 없나요?
B: 미안합니다만 다른 제품은 없습니다.

해설 alternative는 같은 종류로서 대신할 수 있는 것을 말하고, substitute는 같은 기능을 하는 다른 물건, 예를 들어서 밥을 라면으로 때우는 경우에 해당한다.

어휘 altercation 분규 garment 의복

15 유형 고난도 어휘

A: If my memory serves me right, it's not my signature on the check!

B: Do you mean that somebody ___________ it?

(a) plagiarized
(b) drew
(c) forged
(d) spared

 A: 내 기억이 맞다면 수표에 있는 서명은 내가 한 게 아니야!

B: 누군가가 그것을 위조했다는 말이니?

 문맥상 가장 적절한 것은 다른 사람이 위조했다는 의미이므로 (c)가 정답이다.

 plagiarize 표절하다 forge 위조하다
spare 따로 떼어두다, 아껴두다

---

16 유형 연어

A: I believe that the vice president was going on too much about our mistakes at the meeting.

B: The reason is that he is the man who's ___________ responsible when something goes awry.

(a) held
(b) been
(c) taken
(d) gone

 A: 부통령이 우리가 한 실수에 대해 회의 때 너무 지나쳤다는 생각이 들어.

B: 그렇게 한 이유는 무슨 일이 잘못되면 그가 책임을 져야 하는 사람이기 때문이야.

 hold someone responsible for(~에게 책임을 지우다)의 수동태 구문이다. 그래서 더 어렵게 느껴지는 문제이다.

 go awry 실패하다, (일이) 틀어지다

---

17 유형 의미상 혼동 어휘

A: Have you noticed Professor Kim's hair is ___________?

B: Yes, you can tell he is going bald.

(a) shortening
(b) thinning
(c) slimming
(d) belittling

 A: 김 교수의 머리숱이 적어지고 있는 것 알았니?
B: 예, 그는 대머리가 되어가고 있어요.

 머리숱이 적어지는 것을 hair is thining이라고 한다.

 shorten 줄이다 slim 가늘어지다
belittle 무시하다

---

18 유형 연어

A: Never forget this is a ___________ document.

B: I'll keep that in mind. I mean I'll make sure that no one can see it.

(a) confident
(b) diffident
(c) confidential
(d) draconian

 A: 이것이 비밀문서라는 것을 잊지 말아요.
B: 명심하겠습니다. 아무도 볼 수 없게 확실히 하겠습니다.

 비밀문서는 confidential document이다. document를 생략하고도 쓸 수 있다.

 confident 확신하는 diffident 소심한
confidential 비밀의 draconian 가혹한

19 유형 고난도 어휘

A: When you were in law school, did you do your utmost?

B: No. I ___________ to not doing my best.

   (a) mean
   (b) remember
   (c) chide
   (d) confess

해석 A: 너 로스쿨에 다닐 때, 최선을 다했니?
B: 아니, 솔직히 고백하는데 최선을 다하지 못했어.

해설 confess to -ing를 알아두자. 즉 마음속에 있는 말을 할 때 자주 쓰는 말인데, 특히 여기서는 to와 어울려서 나온다는 점도 기억해야 한다.

어휘 chide 비난하다, 혼내다 confess 고백하다

20 유형 고난도 어휘

A: How could the city official own such a luxurious house with his modest salary?

B: It is likely that he has received ___________ from contractors, taking advantage of his position.

   (a) doldrums
   (b) setbacks
   (c) alimony
   (d) payoffs

해석 A: 그 시청 공무원 말야, 얼마 되지도 않는 수입으로 어떻게 그런 고급주택을 갖고 있는 거지?
B: 아마 직위를 이용해서 건설업자들한테 뇌물을 받아왔겠지.

해설 많지 않은 수입으로 고급주택을 살 수 있었던 이유로, B는 직위를 이용해 뇌물을 받았을 것이라는 추측을 내놓고 있다. payoff는 주로 특정 직위에 있는 사람에게 부정한 대가를 바라고 주는 돈, 즉 '뇌물'을 뜻한다.

어휘 doldrums 침체 setbacks 실패, 좌절 alimony 위자료 payoff 뇌물

21 유형 이디엄

A: Why do you go home so early?

B: If I don't get home on time, my parents will jump down my ___________.

   (a) mind
   (b) heart
   (c) throat
   (d) obloquy

해석 A: 왜 그렇게 일찍 집으로 돌아가니?
B: 시간에 맞춰서 집에 가지 않으면 부모님이 심하게 야단치시거든.

해설 jump down one's throat는 '찍소리 못하게 하다, 심하게 꾸짖다'의 의미이다.

어휘 obloquy 비방, 불명예

22 유형 의미상 혼동 어휘

A: Do you know his father-in-law is in the hospital?

B: Yeah, the old man's bones are so ___________ that he broke his legs after falling.

   (a) infirm
   (b) fragile
   (c) flimsy
   (d) feeble

해석 A: 그의 장인어른이 병원에 입원하신 것 알고 있니?
B: 응, 연로하신 그분의 뼈가 너무 약해서 넘어진 후에 다리가 부러졌대.

해설 제시된 단어들이 다 '약함'을 의미하는 단어들이지만, 이 중에서 fragile이 '깨지기 쉬운, (뼈 등이) 부러지기 쉬운'이라는 의미를 갖고 있다. infirm은 신체적으로 허약한 것을 나타내고, flimsy는 근거나 변명 등이 얄팍한 것, feeble은 심성이나 기력이 약한 것을 의미한다.

어휘 infirm 마음약한 flimsy 얇은, 얄팍한
feeble 기력이 없는

23 유형 2어 동사

A: Have you heard the news?

B: Yes, I have. They say that the government has decided to ___________ a program of radical reform sooner or later.

  (a) go back on

  (b) kick off

  (c) let on

  (d) wipe out

해설 A: 그 소식 들었어요?
    B: 네, 들었어요. 정부가 조만간 근본적인 개혁 프로그램을 실시하기로 결정했다고 하던데요.

해설 kick off는 off가 주는 어감 때문에 파괴 등의 부정적 내용을 가지는 어구가 될 수 있으나, '시작하다'라는 뜻이다.

어휘 go back on 어기다 kick off 시작하다
let on (비밀을) 누설하다 wipe out 파괴하다

24 유형 고난도 어휘

A: Please hand in your ___________ of expenses before you leave.

B: Okay. I'll have submitted it by the time I call it a day.

  (a) measure

  (b) estimate

  (c) endorsement

  (d) defile

해석 A: 떠나기 전에 비용 견적서를 제출해 주세요.
    B: 예. 일과를 끝낼 때까지 제출하겠습니다.

해설 estimate는 동사로는 '어림잡다', 명사로는 '견적서'를 의미하는 말이다. 단어 자체는 크게 어렵게 느껴지지 않더라도 묻고 있는 상황의 파악이 금방 되지 않아서 힘든 문제이다.

어휘 measure 측정법 endorsement 이서, 지지
defile 좁은 길, 1열 종대 행진

25 유형 고난도 어휘

A: What was the result of your team last weekend?

B: To our disappointment, we played to a _________, but our opponent was last season's champion.

  (a) landslide

  (b) venture

  (c) draw

  (d) neck

해석 A: 지난 주말 너희 팀 결과는 어땠니?
    B: 실망스럽게도 무승부를 기록했어. 그렇지만 상대는 지난 시즌 챔피언이었어.

해설 '무승부'라는 의미로 draw가 쓰인다는 것을 알아두자.

어휘 landslide 산사태, 압도적 승리
venture (사업상의) 모험, 투기 draw 무승부
neck and neck 막상막하의

Part Ⅱ Questions 26-50

26 유형 의미상 혼동 어휘

According to the weather forecast, there will be a lot of thick morning fog, which will cause poor ___________.

(a) spectrum
(b) spectacle
(c) visibility
(d) vision

해석 일기예보에 따르면 아침 안개가 짙게 낄 것이고, 그로 인해 시계가 불안정할 것입니다.

해설 제시된 선택지들이 전부 시각에 관계된 말들이다. 이 중에서 '눈으로 볼 수 있는 범위'를 의미하는 것은 (c)이다.

어휘 spectacle 광경 visibility 시계[視界]
vision 비전, 환상

27 유형 형태상 혼동 어휘

Because neither company could come to an agreement, compromise over the control of the small island has finally ___________.

(a) found
(b) foundered
(c) founded
(d) flinched

해석 어떠한 회사도 합의에 이를 수 없었기 때문에 그 작은 섬의 통제를 둘러싼 타협은 결국 무산되었다.

해설 합의에 이를 수 없다면 당연히 최종적 결과는 와해될 수밖에 없을 것이다. 따라서, 정답은 (b)가 된다. 특히 founder는 found(설립하다)와 스펠링 차이가 크지 않은데도 전혀 다른 뜻임을 유의해야 한다.

어휘 found 설립하다 founder 실패하다, 와해되다
flinch 움찔하다, 겁먹다

28 유형 고난도 어휘

Both heavy drinking and smoking could do ___________ damage to your brain.

(a) transient
(b) substantial
(c) meticulous
(d) astute

해석 과도한 음주와 흡연은 둘 다 당신의 뇌에 상당히 큰 손상을 입힐 수 있습니다.

해설 흡연과 과음이 가져올 수 있는 뇌 손상의 정도를 말하는 문장이므로 '대단한, 상당한'이라는 의미를 지닌 단어가 빈칸에 들어가는 것이 적절하다.

어휘 transient 일시적인 substantial 상당한
meticulous 꼼꼼한 astute 명민한

29 유형 2어 동사

Poor nutrition in the early stages of infancy can ___________ adult growth.

(a) hold up
(b) hold back
(c) get at
(d) get away

해석 유아기 초기에 영양이 결핍되면 성인으로 성장하는 과정이 저해될 수 있다.

해설 문맥상 '막는다'는 의미가 필요하므로 (b)가 답이다.

어휘 hold up 강탈하다, 지지하다 hold back 억제하다
get at 도달하다, 암시하다 get away 달아나다

30 유형 연어

Your ___________ tactics may compel me to call off the contract because the job must be finished on time.

    (a) deferential
    (b) nefarious
    (c) genteel
    (d) dilatory

해석 당신의 지연작전 때문에 제가 계약을 취소할 수밖에 없게 될 수도 있어요. 일은 제시간에 끝내야 하니까요.

해설 dilatory tactics는 '지연작전'이라는 의미의 연어이다. 제시간에 끝내지 못할 경우의 결과를 말하고 있으므로 문맥상 그것의 원인이 되는 표현이 빈칸에 와야 합당하다.

어휘 deferential 정중한, 예의 바른 nefarious 악명 높은 genteel 상류사회의, 품위 있는

31 유형 고난도 어휘

M.M.S.'s bad behavior was unusually ___________, but it's hard to think of a recent catastrophe in the business world that wasn't abetted by inept regulation.

    (a) extraneous
    (b) innocuous
    (c) egregious
    (d) decorous

해석 M.M.S.의 나쁜 행동은 이례적으로 지나친 것이었다. 그러나 최근 경제계에서 일어난 대참사가 부적절한 규정으로 방조된 것이 아니라고 생각하기는 어렵다.

해설 특히 it's hard라는 부분과 wasn't가 결합해서 일종의 이중 부정적 문장이 되어 해석이 쉽지 않기 때문에 더 고난도의 느낌을 주는 문제이다.

어휘 abet 부추기다, 사주하다 inept 부적절한, 서투른 extraneous 무관한, 이질적인 innocuous 무해한 egregious 지나친, 극악한 decorous 예의 바른

32 유형 고난도 어휘

The Stock Exchange Commission failed to spot the frauds at Enron and decided to let investment banks take on obscene amounts of ___________.

    (a) viceroy
    (b) trumping
    (c) leverage
    (d) indemnity

해석 증권거래 위원회는 엔론사의 사기 건을 찾아내는 데 실패하고 투자은행들이 엄청난 양의 차입금을 받아들이도록 결정했다.

해설 금융 전문 용어로서 leverage는 '지렛대'라는 기본적 의미 외에 '차입금'이라는 뜻이 있다.

어휘 obscene 엄청난 viceroy 총독 trump (상대를) 누르다, 능가하다 leverage 차입금 indemnity 손해배상

33 유형 이디엄

Robert strived to act carefree although he had been laid off, but I don't believe anybody was taken in ___________ how he really felt.

    (a) as to
    (b) as for
    (c) as of
    (d) as with

해석 Robert는 정리해고되었지만 아무렇지 않게 행동하려고 애썼다. 그러나 난 그가 정말 어떤 기분일지에 관해서는 그 누구도 속지 않았다고 생각한다.

해설 as와 관련된 단어를 잘 구별해두자.

어휘 as to ~에 관하여 as of ~부로
cf. as of today 오늘부로

34 유형 연어

The explosion accident at the rubber factory really ____________ home the point that safety rules ought to be abided by.

- (a) made
- (b) got
- (c) ran
- **(d) brought**

해석 고무공장에서 일어난 폭발사고는 안전규칙을 꼭 지켜야 한다는 것을 뼈저리게 느끼게 하는 것이었다.

해설 '~을 뼈에 사무치게 하다'라는 표현은 bring ~ home, drive ~ home 을 쓴다.

어휘 explosion 폭발 safety 안전 abide by 준수하다

35 유형 이디엄

If you think that unemployment issue could be swept ____________, it would be self-deception.

- (a) under the weather
- **(b) under the rug**
- (c) over the cover
- (d) below the roof

해석 실업문제를 감출 수 있을 것이라고 생각한다면 그것은 자기 기만일 것이다.

해설 sweep ~ under the rug는 문제나 어려움 등을 '눈 가리고 아웅하는 식으로 숨긴다'는 것을 뜻한다.

어휘 under the weather 컨디션이 좋지 않은

36 유형 연어

In retrospect, Samuelson said that he left his parents behind in their hometown at the ____________ age of thirteen and made for Chicago so as to pursue his dream.

- (a) small
- (b) beginner
- **(c) tender**
- (d) unassuming

해석 돌이켜 생각해보니, Samuelson은 자신이 13세라는 어린 나이에 고향의 부모를 떠나 꿈을 좇아 시카고로 향했다고 했다.

해설 at the tender age of 는 '~라는 어린 나이에'라는 의미이다.

어휘 in retrospect 돌이켜 생각해보면
unassuming 주제넘지 않은, 겸손한

37 유형 이디엄

The renowned law firm ____________ out of the deal after the terrible scandal.

- (a) pushed
- **(b) pulled**
- (c) kept
- (d) carried

해석 그 유명 법률회사는 심각한 사건이 터진 후 그 거래에서 손을 뗐다.

해설 scandal은 우리말로는 흔히 '추문'이라고 번역되지만, 실제로는 '사건'이라는 의미로 쓰인다. 그 점에 유념해서 문제를 풀어야 한다.

어휘 renowned 유명한
pull out of the deal 거래에서 손을 떼다

38 유형 연어

Mac flunked the course because he ___________ off
the final exam.

    (a) took

    (b) headed

    (c) blew

    (d) made

해석 Mac은 기말고사를 보지 않아서 그 과목을 낙제했다.

해설 off를 동반하여 출제되는 어휘의 의미를 잘 기억해야 한다. blow off는 '해야 할 일을 하지 않다, 수업을 빼먹다' 의 의미가 있다.

어휘 head off 방해하다
make off with ~을 가지고 도망가다, ~와 함께 도망가다

39 유형 형태상 혼동 어휘

Korean people usually say that Kalbi is so delicious
that they are ___________ to everything else.

    (a) obsolete

    (b) oblivious

    (c) ostentatious

    (d) obligatory

해석 한국 사람들은 대개 갈비는 너무 맛있어서 둘이 먹다가 하나가 죽어도 모른다고 말한다.

해설 oblivious to는 '~이 안중에 없는, 깨닫지 못하는'이라는 뜻이다. 그래서 둘이 먹다가 하나가 죽어도 모른다는 표현은 거기에 everything else를 덧붙인다.

어휘 obsolete 낡은 ostentatious 과시하는
obligatory 의무적인

40 유형 형태상 혼동 어휘

The patient who suffered a stroke did not ___________
as rapidly as he anticipated.

    (a) reimburse

    (b) reclaim

    (c) replenish

    (d) recuperate

해석 뇌졸중에 걸린 그 환자는 그가 예상한 만큼 빠르게 회복되지 않았다.

해설 re-가 들어가는 까다로운 단어들을 잘 외워야 한다. 문맥상 '회복되다'라는 뜻의 recuperate을 사용한다.

어휘 stroke 뇌졸중 anticipate 예상하다
reimburse 변제하다 reclaim (땅을) 간척하다
replenish 다시 채우다, 가득 채우다
recuperate 회복되다

41 유형 고난도 어휘

The residents were disappointed with the new
member of the House Representatives elected in their
___________.

    (a) constituency

    (b) electorate

    (c) civilization

    (d) court

해석 주민들은 자신들의 선거구에 뽑힌 새 국회의원에 대해서 실망했다.

해설 문맥상 '선거구'라는 지역적, 구획적 의미의 말이 와야 한다. 그것이 바로 constituency이다.

어휘 electorate 유권자 civilization 문명 court 법정, 궁정

42 유형 고난도 어휘

The essay was thorough and technically competent but ___________ and colorless; the writer seemed to have no fresh ideas about his subject.

- **(a) vapid**
- (b) estranged
- (c) adamant
- (d) complacent

해석 그 에세이는 빈틈없고 기술적으로 능숙하나 지루하고 개성이 없었다. 작가는 자신의 주제에 관해 참신한 아이디어가 없는 것 같았다.

해설 and 뒤의 단어와 호응을 이루는 것은 (a)이다.

어휘 competent 능숙한 vapid 지적이지 못한, 재미없는 estranged 소원한 adamant 단호한 complacent 자기 만족의

43 유형 이디엄

We need perseverance to succeed. All I have to do is ___________ and everything will work out.

- (a) get off the hook
- **(b) bide my time**
- (c) do justice
- (d) fall flat on my face

해석 우리는 성공하려면 인내가 필요하다. 내가 해야 할 일은 참고 기다리는 것뿐이다. 그러면 잘될 것이다.

해설 문맥상 bide one's time(참고 때를 기다리다)가 적절하다.

어휘 get off the hook 면제되다 do justice to ~을 올바르게 평가하다 fall flat on one's face 완전히 실패로 돌아가다

44 유형 의미상 혼동 어휘

The General Hospital in the decent area has ___________ for as many as two hundred patients.

- (a) affiliation
- **(b) accommodations**
- (c) embezzlement
- (d) domicile

해석 괜찮은 지역의 종합병원은 200명이나 되는 많은 환자들을 수용한다.

해설 병원은 환자를 수용하므로 accommodations가 정답이다.

어휘 affiliation 동맹 accommodations 수용시설 embezzlement (공금) 횡령 domicile 주소지, 주거

45 유형 의미상 혼동 어휘

To my disappointment, last night's farewell party was ___________ by an electrical power cut.

- (a) condensed
- (b) compressed
- (c) abbreviated
- **(d) curtailed**

해석 실망스럽게도, 지난밤의 송별회가 정전으로 인해 단축되었다.

해설 제시된 선택지가 모두 '줄어들다'라는 어감을 가지고 있지만, 일정보다 단축되었다는 의미에서는 curtail을 사용해야 한다.

어휘 condense 응축하다 compress (공기 등을) 압축하다 abbreviate 생략하다 curtail 단축하다

46 유형 2어 동사

When the class ___________, it was late compared to the usual time.

    (a) get out

    (b) lay out

    (c) let out

    (d) make out

해석 수업이 끝났을 때, 평상시와 비교해서 늦은 시간이었다.

해설 문맥상 수업이 평상시보다 늦게 끝났다는 것이므로 '(수업이) 끝나다'라는 의미의 let out이 빈칸에 적합하다.

어휘 get out 나가다　lay out 펼치다
let out (수업이) 끝나다, 파하다　make out 이해하다

47 유형 고난도 어휘

The deceitful history of the chief executive officer ___________ just after he stepped down from his position.

    (a) measured

    (b) enunciated

    (c) perused

    (d) unfolded

해석 그 최고 경영자의 더러운 과거가 그가 자리에서 물러난 직후 드러났다.

해설 문맥상 '(비밀이) 밝혀지다, 드러나다'의 의미를 지닌 단어가 나와야 한다.

어휘 deceitful 부정직한　step down from ~에서 물러나다
enunciate 명확히 밝히다　peruse 정독하다
unfold 펼쳐지다, 드러나다

48 유형 고난도 어휘

The rumor has it that his wife is so wealthy that she not only owns several houses but also has ___________ company holdings.

    (a) abject

    (b) naught

    (c) sizable

    (d) murky

해석 그의 아내가 아주 부자여서 집을 몇 채 갖고 있을 뿐 아니라 상당한 정도의 회사 주식도 가지고 있다는 소문이 있다.

해설 규모 면에서 꽤 크다는 의미로 sizable이 시사 독해에 자주 나온다.

어휘 abject 비열한, 비참한　naught 무가치한, 무익한
sizable 상당한 규모의　murky 어두운, 우울한

49 유형 연어

After closer screening, some doubt was ___________ upon the verity of the suspect.

    (a) hauled

    (b) hoisted

    (c) cast

    (d) coiled

해석 보다 자세히 조사하고 나니, 그 용의자의 진실성에 대해 몇 가지 의문점이 생겼다.

해설 cast doubt는 '의문점이 생기다'의 의미. 단순 능동형으로 출제되면 쉬운 문제지만 수동형으로 나왔을 때 더 어려운 문제가 된다.

어휘 verity 진실성　haul 조사하다　hoist 높이 올리다
coil (뱀이) 똬리를 틀다

50 유형 고난도 어휘

The unanticipated arrival of his girlfriend from abroad lifted his __________ spirits.

(a) infuriating

(b) embittered

(c) outright

(d) sagging

해석 해외에서 여자친구가 갑작스럽게 와서 축 처져 있던 그의 기분이 좋아졌다.

해설 여자 친구가 기분을 상승시키려면 그 전엔 기분이 가라앉았어야 말이 된다. sagging이 가장 적절한 표현.

어휘 infuriating 격분하게 만드는, 화나게 하는
embittered 고된 outright 노골적인, 명백한
sagging 축 처진

1. (b)	2. (c)	3. (c)	4. (d)	5. (c)	6. (b)	7. (c)	8. (d)	9. (c)	10. (d)
11. (c)	12. (b)	13. (c)	14. (d)	15. (d)	16. (a)	17. (c)	18. (c)	19. (b)	20. (d)
21. (d)	22. (c)	23. (d)	24. (a)	25. (d)	26. (b)	27. (b)	28. (c)	29. (c)	30. (b)
31. (d)	32. (c)	33. (c)	34. (b)	35. (b)	36. (a)	37. (c)	38. (b)	39. (c)	40. (d)
41. (c)	42. (d)	43. (b)	44. (c)	45. (c)	46. (b)	47. (c)	48. (d)	49. (c)	50. (b)

Part I Questions 1-25

1 유형 형태상 혼동 어휘

A: Did you understand the professor's lecture?

B: No, not a word. I seem to be ___________.

(a) unintelligible

(b) unintelligent

(c) comprehensible

(d) apprehensible

해석 A: 그 교수의 강의를 이해했니?
B: 아니, 한 마디도 모르겠어. 나는 우둔한가 봐.

해설 unintelligent는 '지적이지 못한, 우둔한'의 의미이고, unintelligible은 사물이 주어가 되어서 '이해하기 힘들게 되어 있는'이라는 뜻이다. 그러므로 상황에 맞게 잘 살펴봐야 한다. 여기서는 사람이 주어가 되고 있기에 정답은 (b)가 된다.

어휘 unintelligible (내용이) 이해되지 않는, 난해한

2 유형 2어 동사

A: You know what! Jessy played hooky again.

B: I guess that he is just ___________.

(a) malicious

(b) malfunctioning

(c) malingering

(d) malpracticing

해석 A: 있잖아! Jessy가 또 땡땡이 쳤어.
B: 내 생각에 걘 꾀병 부리는 것 같아.

해설 mal-은 부정적 의미를 가지는 어근이다. 따라서 그것이 들어가는 합성어들은 다 부정적 의미를 가지게 됨을 유의해야 한다.

어휘 play hooky 학교를 빼먹다, 땡땡이 치다
malicious 악의 있는
malfunction 제대로 작동하지 않다
malinger 꾀병 부리다

3 유형 고난도 어휘

A: Why don't you announce your plan?

B: I think it is desirable that we await a more ___________ occasion to do it.

(a) procrastinating

(b) preceding

(c) propitious

(d) provocative

해석 A: 네 계획을 발표하는 게 어때?
B: 발표하기에 더 좋은 시기를 기다리는 게 바람직하다고 생각해.

해설 어떠한 때를 기다리는 이유에 어울리는 선택지는 (c) propitious이다.

어휘 procrastinating 연기하는 preceding 선행하는
propitious 좋은 provocative 도발적인

4 유형 연어

A: What do you think about him?

B: I could see by his brazen manners that he is
___________.

   (a) impeccable

   (b) immaculate

   (c) innocuous

   (d) impertinent

해석 A: 그에 대해서 어떻게 생각하니?
B: 그의 철면피 같은 태도로 보아 뻔뻔스럽다는 걸 알겠어.

해설 brazen은 brag에서 유래한 즉, '허풍을 떠는, 철면피 같은'
이라는 의미의 말이다. 이를 근거로, 빈칸에는 뻔뻔스럽다
는 의미가 있는 말이 와야 하기에 정답은 (d)가 된다.

어휘 brazen 철면피 같은 impeccable 완벽한
immaculate 순결한, 완전히 깨끗한
innocuous 무해한 impertinent 건방진, 뻔뻔스러운

5 유형 고난도 어휘

A: What's the reason that you chose James for the top
sales manager?

B: I guess he seems to have an ___________ ability
to talk people into buying things.

   (a) giddy

   (b) stark

   (c) uncanny

   (d) emaciate

해석 A: 당신이 James를 최고의 영업 매니저로 선택한 이유는
무엇인가요?
B: 내 생각엔 그가 사람들을 설득해서 물건을 사게 하는
신기한 능력이 있는 것 같아요.

해설 uncanny는 설명하기 어렵고 이상한 것을 지칭하는 표현으
로, '초인적인, 신비한, 묘한'이라는 의미가 있다.

어휘 giddy 경솔한, 경박한 stark 가혹한
emaciate 여위게 하다

6 유형 고난도 어휘

A: I'm disappointed that Harry has been dishonest
with me all the time.

B: You said it. I don't give ___________ to anything
he says.

   (a) justice

   (b) credence

   (c) visibility

   (d) streak

해석 A: Harry가 언제나 나에게 정직하지 못해서 실망이야.
B: 네 말이 맞아. 나는 그가 뭐라고 말하든 믿지 않아.

해설 단순하게 생각하면 답이 (b)라는 것을 알 수 있는 문제이
지만, 실제 시험장에서는 문제를 풀고 나서 너무 쉬웠다는
의심으로 뜻이 불분명한 (d)를 답으로 바꾸어 틀릴 수도 있
는 문제이다.

어휘 justice 정의 credence 신뢰, 신용 visibility 시계[視界]
streak 줄(무늬)

7 유형 고난도 어휘

A: Olson is so outgoing that everybody likes him. Is
his brother Tom the same?

B: In fact, they couldn't be more different. Tom is so
___________.

   (a) extroverted

   (b) indigent

   (c) taciturn

   (d) extravagant

해석 A: Olson은 아주 외향적이어서 모두가 그를 좋아해. 그의
동생 Tom도 그러니?
B: 사실 둘은 너무 달라. Tom은 아주 과묵해.

해설 문맥을 분석하면 '내성적인'이라는 의미의 단어가 들어가야
한다. 보통은 내성적이라고 하면 introverted를 쓰는데, 여
기서는 그 단어가 없어서 당황하기 쉽지만 taciturn이 말
수가 적다는 의미에서 발전하여 '수동적인'이라는 의미가
있기에 정답이 된다.

어휘 extroverted 외향적인 indigent 궁핍한
taciturn 내성적인(=reserved) extravagant 낭비하는

8 이디엄

A: How come you didn't get the teaching job in Seattle?

B: I'm sick and tired of moving around. I want to keep my life ___________ from now on.

   (a) up in arms

   (b) in the nick of time

   (c) in the offing

   (d) on an even keel

[해석] A: 왜 시애틀에서 교직을 구하지 않았니?
B: 옮겨 다니는 데 질렸어. 앞으로는 안정적인 삶을 원해.

[해설] on an even keel은 '안정적인, 조용한'이라는 의미의 숙어이다. keel은 선박 바닥의 중앙을 받치는 큰 재목인 '용골'을 말한다.

[어휘] up in arms 화난 in the nick of time 때마침
in the offing 임박한

9 2어 동사

A: I'm concerned that my niece has a speech impediment.

B: I'm sorry, but I believe that you don't have to worry too much. When I was younger, I also had a ___________, and it's OK now.

   (a) shriek

   (b) shackle

   (c) stutter

   (d) streak

[해석] A: 내 조카딸이 언어 장애가 있어서 걱정이야.
B: 안됐구나. 하지만 너무 걱정하지 않아도 될 것 같아. 어렸을 때 나도 말을 더듬었는데 지금은 괜찮아.

[해설] 빈칸에 자신도 말을 못 했다거나 더듬거렸다는 의미가 나오면 되므로 (c)가 적절하다.

[어휘] shriek 날카로운 비명 shackle 수갑, 속박
stutter 말더듬기 streak 줄무늬, 연속

10 연어

A: Excuse me, ma'am. Does this flight go directly to LA?

B: No. There's a 30-minute ___________ in Tokyo along the way.

   (a) setback

   (b) redirection

   (c) backtrack

   (d) layover

[해석] A: 실례합니다. 이 비행기 LA 직행인가요?
B: 아니요. 가는 도중에 도쿄에서 30분 정도 기착할 겁니다.

[해설] 대화에서 직행이냐고 묻는 질문에 No라고 대답했으므로 머물렀다가 간다는 말이 뒤에 나와야 한다.

[어휘] setback 차질, 걸림돌 redirection 방향 변경
backtrack 귀로 layover 정차, 기착지

11 유형 의미상 혼동 어휘

A: Excuse me, sir. Is this the right way to the museum?

B: Yes, just keep going straight until you come to the ___________ of Abraham Lincoln at the corner there.

(a) status

(b) statute

(c) statue

(d) stature

해석 A: 실례합니다만, 이 길로 가면 박물관이 나오나요?
B: 예, 저쪽 모퉁이에서 아브라함 링컨 동상이 나올 때까지 쭉 가세요.

해설 의미상 필요한 것은 동상이며 그것은 statue이다.

어휘 status 지위 statute 법령 statue 동상 stature 키, 신장

---

12 유형 의미상 혼동 어휘/ 2어 동사

A: Hey, Joel, congratulations on being appointed the new promotions manager.

B: Thanks a million! I was so amazed when they ___________ my name.

(a) promulgated

(b) announced

(c) remitted

(d) proclaimed

해석 A: 안녕, Joel, 새로운 홍보 과장으로 임명된 거 축하해요.
B: 정말 고마워요! 제 이름이 불렸을 때 너무 놀랐어요.

해설 promulgate, proclaim은 국가적인 중대사를 발표하는 경우 등에 사용된다.

어휘 promulgate 선포하다 remit 송금하다
proclaim 공포하다

---

13 유형 이디엄

A: Now that it is hot today, let's have pork for lunch.

B: Are you serious? Don't you know that I am ___________ to meat.

(a) disposed

(b) adverse

(c) averse

(d) innocuous

해석 A: 오늘 날이 더우니까, 점심으로 돼지고기를 먹자.
B: 너 진심이야? 내가 고기라면 질색인 거 모르니?

해설 문맥상 음식(돼지고기)에 대한 호불호를 말하는 표현이 적절하다. Are you serious?라는 말에서 고기를 싫어한다는 것을 짐작할 수 있어야 한다. adverse와 averse의 형태를 혼동하지 않도록 유의한다.

어휘 be disposed to ~을 좋아하다
adverse 부정적인, 불리한
be averse to ~을 무척 싫어하다 innocuous 무해한

---

14 유형 의미상 혼동 어휘

A: How do you feel about your new laptop?

B: I can't make it out. The brochure is too ___________.

(a) confounded

(b) preposterous

(c) prodigious

(d) convoluted

해석 A: 네 새 노트북 어때?
B: 난 이해를 못 하겠어. 매뉴얼이 너무 복잡해.

해설 문맥상 이해하기 어렵고 복잡한 것을 나타내는 말이 나와야 하기에 convoluted(대단히 복잡한)가 적절하다.

어휘 confounded 혼란한 preposterous 터무니없는
prodigious 굉장한

15 유형 고난도 어휘

A: How was your birthday party last night?

B: It was too much. The neighbors complained that we were so ___________ that they couldn't turn in.

    (a) construed

    (b) ovoid

    (c) convalescent

    (d) boisterous

해석 A: 어젯밤 생일파티 어땠어?
B: 너무 심했어. 이웃사람들이 우리가 너무 시끄러워서 잠을 잘 수 없다고 했어.

해설 옆집에서 잠을 잘 수 없다고 항의했다는 것에서 파티가 어땠는지를 묘사하는 표현을 유추할 수 있다. 따라서 '난폭하고 시끄러운'이라는 의미의 boisterous가 답이다.

어휘 turn in 잠자리에 들다 construed 해석된
ovoid 계란형의 convalescent 회복기의

---

16 유형 연어

A: I shouldn't have broken up with my fiancée.

B: Don't you know "What's done is done."? Why don't you stop ___________ yourself and make a new start?

    (a) torturing

    (b) degrading

    (c) contending

    (d) ingurgitating

해석 A: 약혼녀와 헤어지지 말았어야 했는데.
B: '엎질러진 물'이라는 말 모르니? 너무 자책하지 말고 새 출발하는 게 어때?

해설 torture가 단독으로 쓰이면 순수하게 '고문하다'의 의미를 지니지만 oneself와 결합하면 '자책하다'의 의미가 된다.

어휘 degrade 품위를 떨어뜨리다 contend 경쟁하다
ingurgitate 게걸스럽게 마구 들이키다

---

17 유형 의미상 혼동 어휘

A: You did a good job on your presentation this morning.

B: I appreciate your help. I always ___________ it to your assistance.

    (a) contribute

    (b) draft

    (c) owe

    (d) trespass

해석 A: 너 오늘 아침 발표 잘했어.
B: 도와줘서 정말 고마워. 늘 네가 도와준 덕분이지.

해설 owe는 '신세지다, 빚지다'의 의미로 owe A to B의 형식으로 쓰인다. 동의어로는 attribute가 있는데, 이 문제처럼 오답으로 contribute가 제시되면 자칫 함정에 빠질 수 있으니 주의해야 한다.

어휘 assistance 도움 owe 신세를 지다
trespass 무단 침입하다

---

18 유형 연어

A: Do you give your mother a call very often?

B: No. I only call her ___________.

    (a) over the hill

    (b) until the fat lady sings

    (c) once in a blue moon

    (d) top-of-the-line

해석 A: 당신은 어머님께 전화 자주 하나요?
B: 아뇨. 아주 가끔씩만 전화합니다.

해설 once in a blue moon은 '아주 가끔'이라는 의미로 쓰인다.

어휘 over the hill 한물간
top-of-the-line 최신식의, 최고급품의

19 유형 고난도 어휘

A: Will you be serving refreshments on this flight?

B: Not this moment, but we will be giving some food after we reach ___________ altitude.

(a) flying

(b) cruising

(c) anchoring

(d) traveling

해석 A: 이 비행기에서 간식이 제공되나요?
B: 지금은 아니고요, 비행기가 순항 고도에 진입한 후에 음식을 제공할 것입니다.

해설 뒤에 오는 '고도(altitude)'에 가장 어울리는 선택지는 (b)이다.

어휘 anchor 정박하다 cruising altitude 순항 고도

20 유형 고난도 어휘

A: Do you hear me? I can't hear you well.

B: I gather that there's some ___________ on the line. I'll call you later.

(a) mix

(b) cut

(c) plight

(d) static

해석 A: 내 말 들려요? 난 잘 안 들려요.
B: 전파 방해가 있는 것 같아요. 나중에 전화할게요.

해설 상황에 가장 적절한 말을 고르는 문제이다. static은 '정전기, 전파 방해'의 의미로 사용된다.

어휘 gather 이해하다, 헤아리다 plight 곤경, 궁지

21 유형 이디엄

A: I do hope that I'll go skiing on Saturday.

B: Do you want me to lend you ski ___________?

(a) resort

(b) tool

(c) apparatus

(d) gear

해석 A: 토요일에 스키 타러 꼭 갔으면 좋겠어.
B: 내가 스키 장비 빌려줄까?

해설 스키 장비와 같은 '특수한 용도의 장비나 도구'는 gear를 사용한다.

어휘 tool (기능공 등이 사용하는 단순한) 도구

apparatus 장치

22 유형 의미상 혼동 어휘

A: I can't make up my mind whether or not to take the job.

B: Why don't you take it? The annual salary is not so great, but it comes with nice ___________.

(a) tailgate

(b) allowance

(c) perks

(d) dawdle

해석 A: 그 일자리를 잡아야 할지 말아야 할지 결정을 못 하겠어요.
B: 잡는 게 어때요? 연봉은 그리 높지 않지만 부수입이 괜찮잖아요.

해설 perks는 임직원 등이 받는 '합법적인 부수입(extra income, perquisite)'을 말한다.

어휘 tailgate 트럭의 뒷문 allowance 용돈, 수당
dawdle 빈둥거리다; 굼벵이

23 유형 2어 동사

A: How is the weather outside?

B: It's so cold that you'd better ___________ up if you are to go out.

(a) dress

(b) wear

(c) trudge

(d) bundle

해석 A: 바깥 날씨가 어때요?

B: 너무 추워서 밖에 나가려면 옷을 껴입는 게 좋을 거예요.

해설 날씨가 추울 때 외출 시 어떤 차림을 해야 할지를 생각하면 '옷을 껴입다'라는 뜻의 bundle up이 적절하다.

어휘 dress up 정장하다 trudge 터덜터덜 걷다
bundle up 옷을 껴입다

24 유형 고난도 어휘

A: The President said he's not involved in the sex scandal with the famous actress.

B: He is just trying to ___________ the eyes of the public. Everybody knows it's a big lie.

(a) pull the wool over

(b) come down with

(c) make up

(d) dwell on

해석 A: 대통령은 유명 여배우와의 섹스 스캔들과 관련이 없다고 말했어.

B: 단지 국민의 눈을 속이려고 하는 것뿐이야. 새빨간 거짓말이라는 건 누구나 알고 있어.

해설 대통령이 거짓말을 하고 있다고 B가 말하고 있으므로 이에 적절한 표현은 '~의 눈을 속이려 하다'라는 뜻의 pull the wool over the eyes of이다.

어휘 a big lie 새빨간 거짓말
pull the wool over the eyes of ~의 눈을 속이다
come down with (병에) 걸리다
make up (이야기 등을) 지어내다
dwell on ~을 깊이 생각하다

25 유형 고난도 어휘

A: Have you decided to stick with the old insurance policy?

B: No. I believe that I have to ___________ around for others.

(a) juggle

(b) dribble

(c) foam

(d) shop

해석 A: 기존의 보험을 계속 유지하기로 했어요?

B: 아니요. 다른 보험을 알아봐야 할 것 같아요.

해설 shop around(물건을 사러 여기저기 돌아다니다) 자체는 크게 어려운 표현은 아니다. 오히려 insurance policy 부분이 다소 어렵게 느껴지기에 고난도 문제가 되는 것이다. 여기에서 policy는 '정책의' 의미가 아니라, 약관이라는 말에서 유래한 '보험(증권)'의 의미이다.

어휘 dribble 똑똑 떨어지다, 침을 흘리다 foam 거품이 일다

Part II Questions 26-50

26 유형 의미상 혼동 어휘

The religious leaders who are focused on something sacred in the Catholic World banned the practice as ___________.

- (a) finicky
- **(b) sacrilegious**
- (c) proverbial
- (d) prosaic

해석 가톨릭 세계에서 신성한 것을 중시하는 종교 지도자들은 그 관행을 신성 모독한 것으로 금지했다.

해설 종교 지도자들이 특정 관행을 금지하려는 이유로 타당한 표현을 찾으면 된다. 즉, '신성 모독적인(sacrilegious)' 관행으로 여겨 금했다고 하는 것이 적절하다.

어휘 finicky 까다로운 proverbial 널리 알려진, 유명한 prosaic 단조롭고 긴, 지루한

27 유형 고난도 어휘

The chair is so ___________ about the method the conference is run that it seems impossible to please him.

- (a) nefarious
- **(b) fastidious**
- (c) menial
- (d) vicarious

해석 회의를 진행하는 방식에 대해 의장이 너무 까다로워서 그의 마음에 들기는 불가능한 것 같다.

해설 여기에서 the chair는 단순한 의자가 아니라 명사 chair가 관사 the와 결합해서 의장직을 맡은 사람(의장)을 나타내는 형식이 된다. 문맥상 의장의 성격을 가리키는 적절한 어휘는 fastidious(까다로운)가 된다.

어휘 chair 의장 nefarious 극악무도한 menial 하인의, 천한 vicarious 대리의

28 유형 고난도 어휘

Employers can require that would-be employees provide ___________ so as to verify their former work performance.

- (a) remittance
- (b) reimbursement
- **(c) references**
- (d) recommendation

해석 고용주들은 이전 직장에서의 업무 성과를 확인하기 위해 입사 희망자에게 추천서를 낼 것을 요구할 수 있다.

해설 references는 원래 '참조, 참고서적'이라는 의미이다. 거기에서 유래하여 좀 더 어려운 뜻으로 '추천서'의 의미가 도출된다.

어휘 remittance 송금 reimbursement 변제 recommendation 추천

29 유형 의미상 혼동 어휘

The grandmother's voice was so ___________ that I could hardly hear her when she died.

- (a) fragile
- (b) flimsy
- **(c) feeble**
- (d) robust

해석 할머니의 목소리가 너무 힘이 없어서 돌아가실 때 목소리를 거의 들을 수 없었다.

해설 목소리나 심장 박동 등이 약하다고 할 때는 feeble을 쓴다.

어휘 fragile (유리같이) 깨지기 쉬운 flimsy (천이나 종이 등이) 매우 얇은

30 유형 연어

The Fifth Amendment in the American Constitution ensures that people can ___________ the right to remain silent.

   (a) endow

   (b) exercise

   (c) estrange

   (d) epitomize

해석 미국 헌법 수정조항 제 5조는 묵비권을 행사할 수 있도록 보장한다.

해설 exercise에는 '권리를 행사하다, 실력을 발휘하다, 운동하다'와 같은 여러 의미가 있다.

어휘 the right to remain tranquil[silent] 묵비권
endow 부여하다, 주다
estrange 이간질하다, 소원하게 하다
epitomize 요약하다

31 유형 고난도 어휘

At length, the defendant ___________ guilty of the crime he had been charged with after a long denial.

   (a) conceived

   (b) beseeched

   (c) admitted

   (d) pleaded

해석 마침내 피고는 오랫동안 부인한 후에 기소된 범죄에 대해 유죄를 인정했다.

해설 법정에서 피고가 자신의 유무죄 여부를 인정하는 것과 관련하여 쓰이는 동사를 알아두어야 한다. plead guilty는 '죄를 인정하다', plead not guilty는 '무죄를 주장하다'의 의미.

어휘 conceive 생각을 품다, 잉태하다 beseech 간청하다
admit 인정하다, 받아들이다

32 유형 고난도 어휘

If an installment is not paid within 7 days after it is due, a ___________ charge of $20 will be paid by the purchaser.

   (a) tardy

   (b) plus

   (c) delinquent

   (d) down payment

해석 할부금이 납부일이 지난 후 7일 이내에 지불되지 않으면 구매자는 연체료 20달러를 지불해야 할 것이다.

해설 정해진 기간 내에 약속된 비용을 지불하지 않아 부과되는 것을 보통 '연체료', 즉 delinquent charge라고 한다.

어휘 installment 할부(금) purchaser 구매자 tardy 지체된
down payment 선수금, 계약금

33 유형 이디엄

Nobody is perfect and we should acknowledge the fact that all the people in the world are ___________ to make errors.

   (a) tend

   (b) infallible

   (c) liable

   (d) garrulous

해석 아무도 완벽하지 않다. 우리는 세상의 모든 사람이 실수할 수 있다는 것을 인정해야 한다.

해설 원래 liable은 '책임이 있는'이라는 뜻이다. 그러나 여기서의 의미는 '~하는 경향이 있는'이라는 의미가 된다.

어휘 acknowledge 인정하다 infallible 실수하지 않는
garrulous 말이 많은, 수다스런

34 유형 연어

I've heard that Mr. Kim was apprehended for sexual harrassment and I want to know all the ___________ of the case.

    (a) ebb and flow

    (b) ins and outs

    (c) odds and ends

    (d) part and parcel

해석 김 선생이 성희롱으로 체포되었다고 들었는데 그 사건의 내막을 모두 알고 싶다.

해설 문맥상 사건의 자세한 내용을 알고 싶다는 것이 자연스러우므로 '자세한 내막, 상세한 부분, 자초지종'을 뜻하는 ins and outs가 답이다.

어휘 apprehend 체포하다 sexual harrassment 성희롱
ebb and flow 주기적인 변화
odds and ends 잡동사니, 어중이떠중이
part and parcel 중요 부분

35 유형 이디엄

Ever since I got a job, I have made it a rule to ___________ in at 8:00 a.m. in the morning.

    (a) report

    (b) punch

    (c) roll

    (d) position

해석 나는 취직한 이후로 아침 8시에 출근하는 것을 규칙으로 삼고 있다.

해설 출근부에 펀치를 찍는 것을 전제로 해서 punch in은 '출근하다'의 의미가, 반대로 punch out은 '퇴근하다'의 의미가 된다.

어휘 *cf.* report for work 출근하다

36 유형 연어

The former President, in an attempt to ___________ his fall in popularity, proclaimed yesterday a plan to create one million new jobs in the battered domestic economy.

    (a) staunch

    (b) reclaim

    (c) spew

    (d) relinquish

해석 전직 대통령은 인기가 하락하는 것을 막기 위한 시도로서 피폐해진 국내 경제에 새로운 일자리를 백만 개 창출할 수 있는 계획을 어제 발표했다.

해설 staunch는 '멈추게 하다, 막다'의 의미이고, fall은 여기서 '하락'의 의미를 가지게 된다. 따라서 '하락을 막다'라는 표현으로는 staunch fall을 쓰면 된다.

어휘 battered 큰 타격을 입은, 박살난 reclaim 개간하다
spew 내뿜다 relinquish (권리 등을) 포기하다

37 유형 이디엄

After a little heated discussion, the chair called the meeting to ___________.

    (a) halt

    (b) end

    (c) order

    (d) beginning

해석 다소 열띤 토론 후에 의장은 정숙할 것을 당부했다.

해설 call ~ to order는 '개회를 선언하다, 회의를 시작하다, 정숙히 할 것을 명하다' 등의 의미로 쓰인다.

어휘 heated 열띤, 격한 halt 멈추다

38 유형 연어

A host of Ireland-born novelists have been writing plenty of literary works ___________ the tale of an impoverished Irish peasant.

(a) talking
(b) **relating**
(c) making
(d) speaking

해석 아일랜드 출신의 많은 소설가들은 가난한 아일랜드 농부 이야기에 대한 수많은 문학작품을 써왔다.

해설 relate에는 '관련[관계]이 있다'의 의미가 있다. '~와 관계가 있다'의 의미로는 relate A with[to] B를 쓴다.

어휘 a host of 다수의 literary 문학의
impoverished 가난한 peasant 농부

39 유형 고난도 어휘

The conductor once ___________ a famous pianist with a cynical remark that there were for him no stars except those in the universe.

(a) seconded
(b) motioned
(c) **cowed**
(d) championed

해석 그 지휘자는 우주에 있는 별을 제외하고는 그 어떠한 별도 자신에게는 존재하지 않는다는 냉소적인 말로 어느 유명 피아니스트를 주눅 들게 한 적이 있다.

해설 문맥상 부정적인 의미의 단어가 들어가야 한다.

어휘 cow 주눅 들게 하다, 겁주다 second 지지하다
motion 제안하다; 동의, 발의 champion 지지하다

40 유형 형태상 혼동 어휘

E-mail coming from the development of computer technology is virtually a ___________ way of giving and taking information from one side to another at great speed.

(a) airproof
(b) waterproof
(c) shatterproof
(d) **foolproof**

해석 컴퓨터 발달의 부산물인 이메일은 사실상 빠른 속도로 한 장소에서 다른 장소로 정보를 주고받는 아주 쉬운 방법이다.

해설 ~proof는 '~의 영향을 받지 않는, ~로부터 안전한'이라는 의미이다. foolproof는 '바보가 없는, 또는 바보로부터 안전한'의 의미가 아니라 바보도 할 수 있을 정도로 쉽다는 의미를 가지게 된다.

어휘 airproof 공기의 영향이 없는, 공기가 통하지 않는
waterproof 방수의
shatterproof (유리 따위가) 박살나지 않는

41 유형 형태상 혼동 어휘

I'm certain that every parent hopes that they won't ___________ any of their children.

(a) outgrow
(b) outline
(c) **outlive**
(d) outnumber

해석 나는 모든 부모가 자기 자식들보다 오래 살지 않기를 바란다고 확신한다.

해설 혼동 어휘문제이다. out- 단어는 타동사이다.

어휘 outgrow ~보다 더 성장하다
outlive ~보다 오래 살다
outnumber ~보다 숫자가 많다

42 유형 고난도 어휘

___________ are the words displayed underneath a moving picture expounding what it is all about.

(a) Subtexts
(b) Credits
(c) Captives
(d) Captions

해석 자막은 영상 아래쪽에 상황을 설명해주는 글자를 말한다.

해설 caption에 대한 사전적 정의는 '사진·삽화 등에 붙인 설명'이지만 '영화 자막'이라는 의미로도 쓰인다.

어휘 credit 공적 captive 포로

43 유형 이디엄

Ten months after Robert was cast ___________ in the English Channel, he returned to his native land.

(a) adroit
(b) adrift
(c) amuck
(d) awesome

해석 Robert는 영국해협에서 표류한 지 10개월 만에 고국으로 돌아갔다.

해설 '표류하다'라는 표현으로는 be cast adrift를 쓴다.

어휘 adroit 노련한 amuck 미쳐서 날뛰는

44 유형 연어

Nokia started its the biggest sale, targeting at raising funds to ___________ its bid for next-generation cellular phone licences all around the world.

(a) rebut
(b) surrogate
(c) bolster
(d) solicit

해석 노키아는 전 세계에 걸쳐 차세대 휴대폰 면허 입찰에 필요한 자금확보를 목표로, 최대 규모의 할인판매를 시작했다.

해설 '입찰권을 확실하게 얻다'라는 의미로 bolster its bid가 일종의 연어처럼 쓰인다. 나머지 선택지들은 넣어보면 뜻이 어색하다.

어휘 rebut 물리치다, 거절하다 surrogate 대리 노릇을 하다 bolster 강화하다 solicit 간청하다

45 유형 형태상 혼동 어휘

In the digital photo world, ___________ are possible: if you snap a lousy picture, then delete it and take another shot.

(a) turn-outs
(b) leftovers
(c) do-overs
(d) turn-ons

해석 디지털사진 세계에서는 사진을 다시 찍는 것이 가능하다. 즉, 사진을 잘못 찍으면 삭제하고 다시 찍으면 된다.

해설 do-over는 '어떤 일을 다시 하는 것, 여기서는 사진을 다시 찍는 것'을 말한다.

어휘 leftover(s) 남은 음식
turn-on 특별히 아끼고 좋아하는 것

46 유형 이디엄

When I was younger, I had a __________ when a school bus nearly hit me as I was crossing the street.

   (a) lion's share
   (b) close call
   (c) white elephant
   (d) black sheep

해석 나는 어렸을 때 길을 건너다가 학교 버스에 치일 뻔했는데 구사일생으로 살았다.

해설 close call은 narrow escape와 마찬가지로 '구사일생, 아슬아슬한 상황'을 뜻한다. have a close call이라고 하면 '구사일생으로 살다, 아슬아슬하게 살아남다'라는 의미.

어휘 lion's share 제일 좋은 몫, 알짜배기
white elephant 애물단지

47 유형 고난도 어휘

The champion is so nimble that when the bell sounded, he responded with __________.

   (a) albatross
   (b) gloat
   (c) alacrity
   (d) glum

해석 그 챔피언은 매우 날렵해서 벨 소리가 났을 때 민첩하게 반응했다.

해설 문맥상 nimble과 잘 어울리는 단어는 빠르게 반응하는 것이므로 (c)가 정답이다.

어휘 nimble 재빠른, 날렵한
albatross 알바트로스(새), 걱정거리 gloat 고소해 함
alacrity 민첩함, 행동이 빠름 glum 시무룩한

48 유형 고난도 어휘

The workers __________ the factory gates during the general strike, lest others should gain access to the demonstration area.

   (a) hoisted
   (b) retreated
   (c) hurled
   (d) picketed

해석 노동자들은 총파업 기간 동안에 다른 사람들이 시위지역에 접근하지 못하도록 공장 출입구에서 피켓을 들고 감시했다.

해설 picket은 노동 쟁의에서의 전문 용어로 '피켓 들고 시위하다, 둘러싸고 감시하다'의 의미가 있다. 문제를 푸는 수험자 입장에서는 정답이 (d)가 아니고 (c)가 아닐까라는 생각을 가질 수 있지만, hurl은 '던지다'라는 의미일 뿐이다.

어휘 hoist 들어 올리다 retreat 후퇴하다 hurl 던지다

49 유형 고난도 어휘

Mr. Hatoyama asked residents to __________ a compromise that would keep the base on the island while the government sought to move the Marine Corps air base elsewhere.

   (a) backtrack
   (b) stake
   (c) entertain
   (d) dislodge

해석 Hatoyama 씨는 일본 정부가 미군 해병대 기지를 다른 곳으로 옮기려고 애쓰는 동안 그 기지를 섬에 두게 될 절충안을 생각할 것을 주민들에게 요청했다.

해설 '생각을 품다, (제의를) 받아들이다'의 의미로 적절한 동사는 entertain이다.

어휘 compromise 타협안, 절충안
backtrack 지지를 철회하다, 다른 길을 택하다
stake 내기를 걸다 dislodge 몰아내다

50 유형 형태상 혼동 어휘

The international organization was created to resolve problems, not to create them; to nurture freedom, not to wait on ___________.

- (a) bond
- **(b) bondage**
- (c) bandage
- (d) boundary

해석 그 국제 조직은 문제를 만드는 것이 아니라 해결하기 위해 만들어졌고 속박을 하도록 하는 것이 아니라 자유를 신장시키기 위해 만들어졌다.

해설 문맥상 들어갈 단어는 '자유'의 반대 의미이므로 '속박'을 의미하는 bondage가 적절하다.

어휘 nurture 키우다 bond 채권, 유대관계 bandage 붕대 boundary 경계

고난도 Actual Training 04

1. (c)	2. (a)	3. (d)	4. (b)	5. (d)	6. (d)	7. (d)	8. (d)	9. (c)	10. (d)
11. (d)	12. (c)	13. (b)	14. (c)	15. (a)	16. (d)	17. (c)	18. (c)	19. (b)	20. (b)
21. (d)	22. (d)	23. (b)	24. (b)	25. (c)	26. (c)	27. (c)	28. (d)	29. (b)	30. (c)
31. (d)	32. (c)	33. (d)	34. (b)	35. (c)	36. (b)	37. (c)	38. (d)	39. (c)	40. (c)
41. (c)	42. (b)	43. (c)	44. (d)	45. (b)	46. (a)	47. (c)	48. (c)	49. (a)	50. (b)

Part I Questions 1-25

1 유형 의미상 혼동 어휘

A: Do you know the meaning of ___________?

B: Yes, I do. It is a short sentence or phrase, usually from a politician's speech, which is broadcast during a news bulletin.

(a) maxim

(b) precept

(c) soundbite

(d) quote

해석 A: 사운드바이트의 의미를 아니?

B: 응, 알아. 주로 정치인 연설에서 따온 짧은 문장이나 어구인데, 뉴스 시간에 방송되는 거야.

해설 정치가들이 자주 사용하는 짧은 문구를 soundbite라고 한다.

어휘 soundbite 정치적 연설 등의 핵심적인 내용
maxim 격언 quote 인용구, 견적 가격

2 유형 고난도 어휘

A: Did you attend Alex Gigg's wedding ceremony?

B: Yeah. I was his bestman, and Professor Goethe ___________ at the wedding.

(a) officiated

(b) tumbled

(c) notarized

(d) lubricated

해석 A: Alex Gigg의 결혼식에 참석했니?

B: 응. 내가 들러리였어. Goethe 교수님이 결혼식 주례를 서 주셨지.

해설 officiate는 '주례를 서다, (성직자가) 집전하다'의 의미로 쓰인다.

어휘 bestman 신랑 들러리 tumble 굴러 떨어지다
notarize 공증하다 lubricate 윤활유를 바르다

3 유형 2어 동사

A: Have you followed the instructor's main point?

B: No way. I am in the dark about what she was trying to ___________.

(a) play down

(b) impart to

(c) come across

(d) get across

해석 A: 강사가 말하는 요점을 알겠어?
B: 전혀 모르겠어. 무엇을 말하려는지 전혀 모르겠어.

해설 상대방에게 자신의 생각을 이해시킨다는 의미로 get across를 알아두자.

어휘 instructor 대학의 전임 강사
in the dark 아무 것도 모르는 play down 무시하다
impart 주다 come across 우연히 만나다
get across 이해시키다

4 유형 연어

A: Does anybody know whether there is any home remedy to ___________ anemia?

B: Eat chicken soup and stay in bed all day long. That works.

(a) catch

(b) beat

(c) develop

(d) contract

해석 A: 빈혈증을 치료하는 민간요법이 있는지 누구 아는 사람 있어?
B: 닭고기 수프를 먹고 하루 종일 누워있어 봐. 그거 효과 있어.

해설 beat은 '병을 물리치다, 치료하다'의 의미로 쓰인다.

어휘 catch, contract, develop (병에) 걸리다

5 유형 고난도 어휘

A: What is the best way to preserve the clean environment?

B: I ___________ that the Congress should enact the law which keeps people from incinerating any products.

(a) dilate

(b) delve

(c) garble

(d) gather

해석 A: 깨끗한 환경을 유지하기 위한 가장 좋은 방법은 무엇일까?
B: 사람들이 물건들을 불에 태우는 것을 막는 법을 의회가 제정해야 한다고 생각해.

해설 gather는 뒤에 that절이 어어질 경우 '생각하다, 믿다'의 의미로 쓰인다.

어휘 enact (법을) 제정하다 incinerate 소각하다
dilate 팽창하다 delve into 면밀히 조사하다
garble 왜곡하다

6 유형 이디엄

A: What do usually you do to keep yourself as fit as a ___________?

B: I work out on a regular basis every day.

(a) shape

(b) health

(c) fitness

(d) fiddle

해석 A: 평소 건강을 유지하기 위해서 무엇을 합니까?
B: 매일 규칙적으로 운동합니다.

해설 원래 fiddle은 바이올린을 뜻하는 단어인데, 구어에서 as fit as a fiddle이라고 하면 '매우 건강한'이라는 의미를 나타낸다.

어휘 as fit as a fiddle 건강한

7 유형 2어 동사

A: If I purchase lots of items, would you make them a little cheaper?

B: Certainly. If you buy more than 20, we can __________ five percent.

 (a) go off
 (b) come off
 (c) carry off
 (d) knock off

해석 A: 제가 물건을 다량 구매하면 좀 싸게 해 주실래요?
B: 물론이죠. 20개 이상 사시면 5퍼센트 깎아 드립니다.

해설 knock off는 '물건의 값을 깎아주다'의 의미로 쓰인다.

어휘 go off 폭발하다 come off 성공하다, 실현되다
carry off (상을) 타다, 해내다

8 유형 2어 동사

A: He has no choice but to __________ a piece of metal to hold the bones together.

B: I assume it is a very tough operation.

 (a) pull over
 (b) drive up
 (c) take out
 (d) put in

해석 A: 그의 뼈가 붙어 있게 하려면 금속조각을 집어넣는 수밖에 없어요.
B: 굉장히 어려운 수술이겠군요.

해설 2어 동사 put in 자체가 어렵다기보다는 상황을 파악하는 것이 어려워서 풀기 힘든 문제이다.

어휘 pull over 차를 세우다 take out (음식 등을) 가져가다

9 유형 이디엄

A: Did Mary obey her parents?

B: No. She __________ them when they disapproved of her marriage with Jim.

 (a) went in for
 (b) stood up for
 (c) stood up to
 (d) played up to

해석 A: Mary는 부모님 말씀에 순종했나요?
B: 아니요. 부모님이 Jim과의 결혼을 허락하지 않자 부모님에게 맞섰어요.

해설 문맥상 들어갈 말은 부정적인 의미이므로 (c)가 정답이다.

어휘 go in for ~에 관심을 가지다
stand up for ~에 지지하다, 옹호하다(= stick up for)
stand up to ~에 맞서다, 용감히 대항하다
play up to ~에 아부하다

10 유형 이디엄

A: Why don't you hurry up?

B: I see. If we don't __________, we'll miss the last bus.

 (a) get the nod
 (b) air our grievances
 (c) fill the bill
 (d) get the lead out

해석 A: 서두르는 게 어때?
B: 알았어. 서두르지 않으면 우린 마지막 버스를 놓칠 거야.

해설 문맥상 A의 말에 나오는 hurry up과 같은 의미의 표현이 필요하다. get the lead out은 '서두르다, 일에 착수하다'라는 뜻으로 쓰인다.

어휘 get the nod 선택되다 air our grievances 불평하다
fill the bill 조건[기대]에 맞다; 제값을 하다

11 유형 2어 동사

A: Your daughter looks down in the dumps.

B: She broke my favorite vase, so I blamed her for being carelessness. I shouldn't have ___________ on her.

(a) gotten it up

(b) asked it out

(c) given it away

(d) taken it out

해석 A: 네 딸 우울해 보여.
B: 걔가 내가 제일 아끼는 꽃병을 깨뜨려서 조심성 없다고 혼내줬거든. 그 애한테 화풀이하지 말았어야 했는데.

해설 문맥상 '나무라다, 혼내다'의 의미가 나와야 하므로 (d)가 정답이다.

어휘 down in the dumps 우울한, 맥없는
ask out 데이트 신청하다 give away 무료로 나누어주다
take it out on ~에게 화풀이하다

12 유형 연어

A: Ann told me that she will ___________ the expenses of lunch.

B: Again? No. I suggest that I foot the bill.

(a) claim

(b) cost

(c) bear

(d) keep

해석 A: Ann이 점심값을 내겠다고 하던데.
B: 또? 안 돼. 내가 계산할 거야.

해설 일종의 연어(collocation) 문제이다. bear the expenses of 는 '~의 비용을 부담하다'라고 할 때 쓰는 표현이다.

어휘 expense 비용 foot the bill 계산을 치르다

13 유형 의미상 혼동 어휘

A: Would it be possible for you to ___________ me to a good attorney?

B: Don't worry about it. I will fix you up with a good lawyer as soon as possible.

(a) show

(b) refer

(c) take

(d) have

해석 A: 저에게 좋은 변호사를 한 사람 소개해줄 수 있겠어요?
B: 걱정 마세요. 가능한 한 빨리 훌륭한 변호사를 소개해 드리겠습니다.

해설 refer to는 '보내다, 소개하다'의 의미가 있다.

어휘 fix up with 소개하다

14 유형 구어

A: My bosom friend broke the window, but I turned a blind eye to his mistake.

B: ___________ it. Anyway, the window had to be replaced.

(a) Put up

(b) Take away

(c) Get over

(d) Set about

해석 A: 제 단짝 친구가 창문을 깨뜨렸는데 전 그의 잘못을 눈 감아 주었어요.
B: 별일도 아닌데 뭐. 어쨌든, 창문은 갈아 끼워야 했어.

해설 별로 대수롭지 않은 일로 걱정하고 있는 사람에게 걱정 그만하고 '잊어버려'라고 말할 때 get over it을 쓴다.

어휘 bosom friend 절친한 친구 put up 세우다
take away 빼앗아가다 set about 시작하다

15 유형 **2어 동사**

A: There still remains robust opposition preventing my progress.

B: I suppose you had better __________ everything before you make up your mind what to do next.

(a) chew over

(b) catch up

(c) fix up

(d) set about

해석 A: 내 발전을 막는 강력한 반대세력이 여전히 있어.
B: 다음에 무엇을 할지 결정하기 전에 모든 것을 곰곰이 생각해보는 게 좋을 거야.

해설 결정하기 전에 해야 할 것은 곰곰이 생각하는 것이므로 (a)가 정답이다.

어휘 robust 강한 set about 시작하다
catch up 따라잡다 fix up 고치다
chew over 곰곰이 생각하다, 심사숙고하다

16 유형 **연어**

A: Janet has been in hot water since last week.

B: You can say that again. She is in a __________ at the moment.

(a) elusive circumstances

(b) delectable environment

(c) digressive one

(d) no-win situation

해석 A: Janet은 지난주 이후로 어려움을 겪고 있어.
B: 네 말이 맞아. 지금 아주 어려운 상황에 놓여 있어.

해설 no-win situation은 '승산이 없는 어려운 상황, 절망적인 상황'을 말한다.

어휘 elusive 정의하기 어려운 delectable 즐거운
digressive 중심에서 벗어난

17 유형 **구어**

A: I saw you sleep through the momentous part of the class.

B: I know. I shouldn't have __________.

(a) tossed and turned

(b) turned in

(c) snoozed

(d) been caught napping

해석 A: 네가 수업 중 중요한 부분에서 줄곧 자는 것을 봤다.
B: 알아요. 졸지 말았어야 했는데.

해설 snooze는 '꾸벅꾸벅 졸다'라는 뜻으로 doze off와 같은 의미이다. 자명종 시계가 울리면, 당장 일어나지 않고 다시 잠들려고 할 때 누르는 버튼이 바로 snooze이다.

어휘 toss and turn 잠 못 이루고 뒤척이다
turn in 잠자리에 들다 be caught napping 허를 찔리다

18 유형 **이디엄**

A: I don't like the job any more, it's just boring.

B: I hope you will find a job you can __________ your teeth into.

(a) extract

(b) subside

(c) sink

(d) bite

해석 A: 나는 그 일을 더 이상 하고 싶지 않아. 지루하기만 해.
B: 네가 푹 빠져서 할 수 있는 일을 찾았으면 좋겠어.

해설 '몰두하다, 푹 빠지다'의 의미로 쓰이는 sink one's teeth into라는 숙어 표현을 알아두자.

어휘 extract 뽑아내다 subside 가라앉다 bite 물어뜯다

19 유형 이디엄

A: Mr. Bae is running three hotels and two restaurants in total and they pay their own way.

B: I guess he has cleaned up ___________ from his businesses.

(a) good paper

(b) a small fortune

(c) dud coin

(d) petty cash

해석 A: 배씨는 총 호텔 세 곳과 식당 두 곳을 운영하고 있는데 수지가 맞대.
B: 내 생각에 그 사람 자기 사업으로 꽤 많은 돈을 벌었을 거야.

해설 배씨의 사업이 잘 되고 있다는 A의 말로 미루어 보아 B의 빈칸에 들어갈 말은 '상당한 재산(a small fortune)'이 적절하다.

어휘 pay one's own way 수지가 맞다
clean up 돈을 긁어모으다
good paper 지불이 확실한 어음
a small fortune 거금, 상당한 재산
dud coin 위조화폐 petty cash 소액 현금

20 유형 이디엄

A: I'm afraid that I won't be able to get the first prize in the piano competition.

B: Don't ___________. You never know till you try.

(a) be brash

(b) meet trouble halfway

(c) give yourself airs

(d) fall into a bias

해석 A: 피아노 콩쿠르에서 일등을 하지 못할까 봐 걱정이 돼요.
B: 지레 걱정부터 하지 마. 해보기 전에는 모르는 일이야.

해설 일등을 하지 못할 것 같다는 A의 말에 격려를 해주고 있다. 따라서 걱정하지 말라는 표현이 가장 적절하다.

어휘 be brash 자신만만하다
meet trouble halfway 지레 걱정을 하다
give oneself airs 젠체하다, 거드름 피우다
fall into a bias 편견에 빠지다

21 유형 고난도 어휘

A: How wonderful you are! You've finally done your ___________.

B: I owe you many things. I appreciate your proofreading it.

(a) letters

(b) scheme

(c) hypothesis

(d) dissertation

해석 A: 당신 정말 훌륭해요! 마침내 논문을 끝냈군요.
B: 당신에게 신세 많이 졌어요. 교정해 주신 것 감사드립니다.

해설 교정이 필요하다면 그것은 보다 전문성이 있는 내용일 것이다. 그래서 '논문'이 답이 된다.

어휘 proofread 교정하다 hypothesis 가설
dissertation 학위 논문

22 [유형] 형태상 혼동 어휘

A: I hope Ms. Roosevelt won't notice the ___________ cup.

B: Some hope! She's got eyes like a hawk.

   (a) chopped
   (b) churned
   (c) clogged
   (d) chipped

[해석] A: Roosevelt 부인이 이가 빠진 컵을 알아보지 못했으면 좋겠어.
B: 꿈도 꾸지 마! 그녀는 무엇이든 못 보고 놓치는 법이 없어.

[해설] chipped는 컵이나 그릇에서 '이가 빠진' 것을 말한다.

[어휘] pull one's leg ~를 놀리다
have eyes like a hawk 매처럼 눈이 예리하다, 무엇이든 놓치는 법이 없다 chop 잘게 썰다 churn 휘젓다 clogged 꽉 막힌

23 [유형] 2어 동사

A: Have you read James Joyce?

B: Yes, but it's not easy. The implication in his novel took a while to ___________.

   (a) stand in
   (b) sink in
   (c) sleep on
   (d) set on

[해석] A: James Joyce 책 읽어봤니?
B: 응, 그런데 쉽지 않아. 그의 소설 속에 내포된 의미를 이해하는 데 한참 걸렸어.

[해설] sink in은 '이해하다'라는 의미로 시사 잡지에서 자주 등장하는 2어 동사이다.

[어휘] implication 함축, 암시 stand in 대리하다
sink in 이해하다 sleep on 연기하다, 미루다
set on 공격하다

24 [유형] 2어 동사

A: Do you like your would-be daughter-in-law?

B: As a matter of fact, she didn't ___________ up to my expectations, but I will accept my son's decision.

   (a) get
   (b) come
   (c) take
   (d) answer

[해석] A: 장래의 며느릿감이 마음에 드세요?
B: 사실 그 아이는 내 기대에 미치지 못했지만 아들의 결정을 받아들일 겁니다.

[해설] '도달하다'가 된다면 가장 무난한 표현이 reach가 되겠지만, 선택지로 제시되지 않았으므로, (b)가 정답이 된다.

[어휘] come up to ~에 미치다, 다다르다

25 [유형] 이디엄

A: I guess you really need to take a day off before you ___________ under the strain.

B: Tell me about it.

   (a) strike
   (b) break
   (c) crack
   (d) bust

[해석] A: 너 정말 스트레스로 몸이 상하기 전에 하루 쉬어야 할 것 같아.
B: 그러게 말이야.

[해설] '~하기 전에 휴식을 취하라'는 조언으로 볼 때, 빈칸에는 스트레스를 받아 몸이 상하게 된다는 표현을 완성하는 단어가 적절하다. crack under the strain은 '지나친 긴장으로 인해 몸이 상하게 되다'라는 의미.

[어휘] strain 중압감, 정신적 긴장
Tell me about it. 그러게 말이야.

Part Ⅱ Questions 26-50

26 유형 이디엄

Every time Ann hopes to buy something, she asks me for some money. I guess she thinks that I have money to ___________ .

(a) buy
(b) grant
(c) burn
(d) mock

해석 Ann은 뭔가 사고 싶을 때마다 내게 돈을 요청한다. 그녀는 내가 돈이 많다고 생각하는 모양이다.

해설 '돈이 많다'는 의미의 표현으로 have money to burn이 있다. 한 단어처럼 알아두자.

어휘 **have money to burn** 돈이 많다 **grant** 주다
mock 흉내내다

---

27 유형 고난도 어휘

Surprisingly, the plants that listen to classical music frequently are likely to be better able to ___________ infection and disease.

(a) faze
(b) withdraw
(c) withstand
(d) fumble

해석 놀랍게도, 클래식 음악을 자주 듣는 식물이 감염이나 질병에 더 잘 견뎌내는 경향이 있다.

해설 withstand를 단순히 '견디다'로 해석하면 쉽지 않은 문제지만, '저항해서 견디다'의 의미로 본다면 답을 찾을 수 있다.

어휘 **infection** 감염 **faze** 당황하게 하다
withdraw 인출하다, 후퇴시키다
withstand 저항하다, 견디다 **fumble** 손으로 더듬다

---

28 유형 구어

I have been concerned that my favorite friends, Tom and Mary, don't have ___________ with each other in the least.

(a) heart
(b) history
(c) mind
(d) chemistry

해석 내가 제일 좋아하는 친구인 Tom과 Mary가 서로 궁합이 전혀 맞지 않아서 걱정스럽다.

해설 주로 두 사람이 헤어진다는 표현을 말할 때 history를 사용해서 답으로 내는 TEPS 문제가 많아서, 급하게 읽으면 (b)를 답으로 생각하기 쉽다. 그러나 분명히 빈칸 앞에 don't have라는 표현이 나오기에 문맥은 '서로 잘 맞는다'라는 긍정의 말이 나와야 한다.

어휘 *cf.* They are history. 그들은 오래 전에 헤어졌다.
They are chemistry. 그들은 서로 끌린다./ 서로 궁합이 잘 맞는다.

---

29 유형 연어

The moment the prodigal son got back home, his mother ___________ her arms around him and gave him a hearty and big hug.

(a) infuriated
(b) wrapped
(c) razed
(d) hugged

해석 방탕한 아들이 집에 돌아오자, 어머니는 두 팔로 안아 진심으로 꼭 껴안아 주었다.

해설 '감싸 안다'라는 의미에서는 wrap one's arm의 표현이 적절하다. 그냥 사람을 안을 때는 hug를 쓰는 것이 나을 것이다.

어휘 **prodigal** 방탕한, 낭비하는 **hearty** 진심어린
give a big hug 꼭 껴안다 **wrap** 감싸다
infuriate 화나게 하다 **raze** 파괴하다 **hug** 안다

30 고난도 어휘

On the grounds that the rain really ___________ it
was no use even though I had an umbrella.

   (a) hoisted

   (b) sprinkled

   (c) pelted

   (d) hurled

해석 비가 억수같이 내렸기 때문에 나는 우산이 있어도 소용없었다.

해설 문맥상 비가 심하게 온다는 것이므로 pelt가 적절하다.

어휘 hoist 높이 들어 올리다 sprinkle (물을) 뿌리다
pelt (비가) 심하게 내리다 hurl 던지다

---

31 고난도 어휘

Although David and Susan didn't know that the film
would be so ___________, they wound up laughing
for the whole time.

   (a) sober

   (b) scrupulous

   (c) diurnal

   (d) hilarious

해석 David와 Susan은 그 영화가 그렇게 즐거울 거라고는 생각하지 못했지만, 결국 그들은 영화 내내 웃었다.

해설 문맥상 '재미있는, 즐거운'의 의미가 자연스러우므로 (d)가 정답이다.

어휘 sober 맑은 정신인 scrupulous 양심적인
diurnal 주행성의 hilarious 즐거운

---

32 고난도 어휘

Even though the oral presentation was ___________,
it was quite well-organized.

   (a) complimentary

   (b) convulsant

   (c) ambiguous

   (d) boisterous

해석 구두 발표 내용은 애매하기는 했지만, 잘 구성되어 있었다.

해설 문제 자체는 크게 어렵지는 않지만, 양보 접속사 even though를 고려하여 뒤의 well-organized와 어울리는 답을 찾기가 다소 힘든 문제이다.

어휘 complimentary 공짜의 convulsant 경련을 일으키는
ambiguous 애매한 boisterous 시끄러운

---

33 고난도 어휘

To her disappointment, she got abruptly
___________ without any prior notification.

   (a) crammed

   (b) crushed

   (c) sanctioned

   (d) sacked

해석 실망스럽게도, 그녀는 아무런 사전통지도 없이 갑자기 해고되었어요.

해설 문맥상 필요한 단어는 해고되는 것이므로 (d)가 정답이다.

어휘 abruptly 갑자기 notification 통지, 통보
cram 벼락치기하다 crush 밀어 넣다
sanction 허가하다 get sacked 해고당하다

34 유형 연어

Smith had ___________ himself to the issue for the primary purpose of redistribution of wealth.

    (a) concealed

    (b) addressed

    (c) beckoned

    (d) demised

[해석] Smith는 부의 재분배라는 주 목적을 위해서 그 문제에 전념했다.

[해설] address는 상당히 다양한 뜻을 가지고 있는 단어이다. 그래서 TEPS에서 가장 자주 출제되는 단어 중의 하나이다. 여기에서는 oneself와 어울려 '전념하다'의 의미로 쓰였다.

[어휘] redistribution 재분배 conceal 감추다
address 말을 걸다, 연설하다, 다루다, 전념하다
beckon 신호하다, 손짓하다 demise 서거하다

35 유형 고난도 어휘

In autocratic times, the authors ___________ the secret society to dodge crack by the government.

    (a) censored

    (b) chided

    (c) treasured

    (d) undermined

[해석] 독재시대에 작가들은 정부의 단속을 피하기 위해 비밀 결사를 소중하게 여겼다.

[해설] 문맥상 보물처럼 '소중히 여기다'라는 뜻은 treasure이다.

[어휘] autocratic 독재의 dodge 피하다 censor 검열하다
chide 혼내다 treasure 소중하게 생각하다
undermine (명성 등을) 훼손시키다

36 유형 고난도 어휘

The presidential election results were ___________ on the ground of voter fraud.

    (a) negotiated

    (b) nullified

    (c) championed

    (d) ameliorated

[해석] 대통령선거 결과는 부정투표 때문에 무효가 되었다.

[해설] 답 자체가 어렵다기보다는 voter fraud가 '부정투표'를 의미한다는 사실이 더 어렵게 느껴질 수 있는 문제이다.

[어휘] on the ground of ~의 이유로 negotiate 협상하다
nullify 무효화하다 champion 지지하다
ameliorate 개선하다

37 유형 형태상 혼동 어휘

After an exhaustive and thorough examination of the patient's mental condition, the ___________ prescribed some drugs.

    (a) psychopath

    (b) pharmacist

    (c) psychiatrist

    (d) psychologist

[해석] 환자의 정신 상태를 철저하고 꼼꼼하게 검사한 후에 그 정신과 의사는 몇 가지 약을 처방했다.

[해설] 문맥상 약을 처방하는 사람이면서, 그 분야는 정신과여야 한다. 따라서 정답은 (c)이다.

[어휘] psychopath 사이코패스(반사회적 성격 장애자)
pharmacist 약사 psychiatrist 정신과 의사
psychologist 심리학자

38 유형 고난도 어휘

When Jane learned that she was expecting, she wanted to meet with a proficient ___________.

    (a) plastic surgeon

    (b) orthopedist

    (c) dermatologist

    (d) obstetrician

해석 | Jane은 자신이 임신 중이라는 것을 알았을 때 능숙한 산부인과 의사를 만나기를 원했다.

해설 | 미국은 산과의사, 부인과 의사를 구별하기도 한다.

어휘 | plastic surgeon 성형외과 의사
orthopedist 정형외과 의사
dermatologist 피부과 의사
obstetrician 산과의사
cf. gynecologist 부인과 의사

39 유형 고난도 어휘

On the basis of the incidents with drinking problems which occurred two weeks ago, the school resolved to ___________ the rules that allow serving alcohol on the campus.

    (a) emaciate

    (b) cow

    (c) rescind

    (d) falter

해석 | 2주 전 발생했던 음주로 인한 사고 때문에 그 학교는 캠퍼스 내에서 주류판매를 허용하는 규칙을 폐지하기로 결정했다.

해설 | 공(公)적인 것을 '없애다, 폐기하다'는 의미로 rescind를 알아두자.

어휘 | emaciate 쇠약하게 하다 cow 위협하다
rescind 폐지하다, 철폐하다
falter 비틀거리다, 말을 더듬거리다

40 유형 고난도 어휘

A longer war would harm the U.S. at home, ___________ racial tensions on the grounds of the disproportionate number of blacks on the front lines.

    (a) extinguishing

    (b) consummating

    (c) exacerbating

    (d) transacting

해석 | 조금만 더 전쟁이 길어지면 전방에 불균형하게 배치된 흑인들의 수로 인해 인종간의 갈등을 악화시켜 미국 내에 해를 입히게 될 것이다.

해설 | 문맥상 인종간의 긴장을 '악화시킨다'는 의미의 단어는 (c)가 적절하다.

어휘 | at home 국내에 disproportionate 불균형의
consummate 완성하다 exacerbate 악화시키다
transact 거래하다

41 유형 형태상 혼동 어휘

According to the report, the aircraft set off to ___________ away from the runway due to the inclement visibility.

    (a) sway

    (b) swing

    (c) swerve

    (d) swamp

해석 | 보고서에 따르면, 항공기는 출발 후 악천후로 인한 시계 불량 때문에 활주로에서 벗어났다고 했다.

해설 | 활주로 위에 있었으므로 (a), (b)는 정답이 아니고 (d)는 전혀 무관한 표현이며 (c) swerve가 가장 적절한 답이다.

어휘 | set off 출발하다 inclement 날씨가 험한
sway 흔들리다 swing 흔들다 swerve 벗어나다
swamp 쇄도하다

42 유형 고난도 어휘

It has been so __________ for us to lose a year's harvest on account of the huge typhoon.

    (a) mesmerizing

    (b) unnerving

    (c) fuzzy

    (d) cumbersome

해석 우리가 대형 태풍으로 인해 한 해 수확을 잃은 것은 너무나 맥 빠지는 일이었다.

해설 가끔 익숙치 않은 단어에 자신이 아는 뜻을 대입시켰다가 문맥에 맞지 않아서 정답인데도 답이 아니라고 생각하는 경우가 많다. 여기에서 unnerving도 그러한 차원의 단어 이다. 이 단어에는 '맥 빠지는'이라는 의미가 있다.

어휘 mesmerizing 매혹하는
unnerving 맥 빠지게 하는, 낙담시키는 fuzzy 애매한
cumbersome 성가시게 하는

43 유형 연어

Every step forward will meet with more impediments if we are bent on maintaining the __________.

    (a) pro-choicer

    (b) pros and cons

    (c) status quo

    (d) archetype

해석 우리가 현상 유지에 급급해한다면 앞으로의 모든 단계에서 더 많은 방해물을 만나게 될 것이다.

해설 여러 가지 합성어들의 뜻을 구별할 수 있는지를 물어보는 문제이다. 문맥상 '현 상태'라는 의미를 가지는 status quo 가 타당하다.

어휘 pro-choicer 낙태에 찬성하는 사람
pros and cons 찬반 양론
status quo 현 상태 archetype 전형, 원형

44 유형 의미상 혼동 어휘

When a hostage situation takes place, the police have a tight security __________ around the building.

    (a) lane

    (b) line

    (c) hurdle

    (d) cordon

해석 인질극이 발생하면, 경찰은 건물 주위에 삼엄한 비상 경계 선을 친다.

해설 여기서는 단순한 선의 의미가 아니라 안전이나 수사를 위 한 선의 의미이므로 cordon을 사용한다.

어휘 hostage 인질 lane 육상 트랙의 코스, 좁은 길
hurdle 장애물 cordon (경찰의) 비상 경계선

45 유형 연어

According to the research by the sociologist, there are __________ differences between the East and the West in their support for the death penalty.

    (a) ample

    (b) stark

    (c) profuse

    (d) fecund

해석 사회학자들의 연구에 따르면 사형제를 지지함에 있어서 동 서양 간에 극명한 차이가 있다.

해설 연어(collocation) 문제이다. '극명한[뚜렷한] 차이'는 stark difference이다.

어휘 death penalty 사형 제도 ample 풍부한
stark 현저한, 뚜렷한, 극명한
profuse 많은 양을 생산하는 fecund 땅이 기름진

46 유형 고난도 어휘

Some researchers announced that when children make some mistakes, for example, breaking a vase or spilling water, if they are chided for them, it contributes to ___________ children's creativity.

(a) circumscribing
(b) digressing
(c) dislodging
(d) infuriating

[해석] 아이들이 실수를 할 때, 예를 들어 꽃병을 깨거나 물을 엎질렀을 때 그로 인해 혼난다면 그것이 아이들의 창의성을 제한하는 원인이 된다고 몇몇 연구자들이 발표했다.

[해설] 문맥상 creativity와 어울리게 나올 표현은 '제한하다'는 의미를 가지는 circumscribe이다.

[어휘] circumscribe 제한하다 digress 옆길로 새다
dislodge 쫓아내다 infuriate 극도로 화나게 하다

47 유형 이디엄

I surmise that without a ___________ of doubt, Mr. Choo will be a member of the all star team.

(a) fracture
(b) room
(c) trace
(d) cream

[해석] 나는 추호의 의심도 없이 추 선수가 올스타 중 한 명이 될 거라고 생각한다.

[해설] trace of doubt은 '의심의 흔적[기미]'이라는 의미로 반드시 without과 붙여서 숙어로 쓰인다.

[어휘] surmise 추측하다 fracture 골절, 금이 감, 부서짐
room 공간, 여지 trace 흔적
cf. the cream of the crop 수확한 것 중 최고로 좋은 것

48 유형 연어

This is a fantastic machine that is designed to fix a ___________ which has taken place in the course of making things.

(a) swatch
(b) paralysis
(c) glitch
(d) laud

[해석] 이것은 물건을 만드는 과정에서 발생한 결함을 고치기 위해 고안된 대단한 기계이다.

[해설] fix가 여기서는 '고정하다'의 의미가 아니라, '고치다'의 뜻으로 쓰였다. 그래서 '결함을 고치다' 라는 의미가 된다.

[어휘] swatch 직물의 견본 paralysis 마비
glitch 사소한 결함[고장] laud 칭찬, 찬사

49 유형 고난도 어휘

Edward's father admonished him that if he didn't brush his teeth three times a day after meals, his teeth would get infirm and easily broken, contributing to ___________.

(a) dentures
(b) diarrhea
(c) hepatitis
(d) wisdom teeth

[해석] Edward의 아버지는 식사 후에 하루 세 번 이를 닦지 않으면 이가 약해져서 쉽게 부러질 것이고 그 결과 의치를 하게 될 것이라고 Edward를 훈계했다.

[해설] dentures, 즉 '의치'라는 말이 어려워서가 아니라 contribute to 부분이 문맥의 해석과 관련해 어렵게 느껴져서 고난도 문제가 될 수 있다.

[어휘] dentures 의치 diarrhea 설사 hepatitis 간염
wisdom teeth 사랑니

50 유형 의미상 혼동 어휘

Forgetting what he had done in the past, Matt resolved to be __________ to remember it.

   (a) enchanted

   (b) hypnotized

   (c) bewitched

   (d) intrigued

해석   Matt는 과거에 자기가 무엇을 했는지를 잊어버려서 그것을 기억해내려고 최면을 걸기로 결심했다.

해설   '최면을 걸다'라는 답을 이끌어내기까지 문장 전체의 논리 구조를 유추하기가 쉽지 않은 문제이다.

어휘   enchant 매혹시키다 hypnotize 최면을 걸다
bewitch 마법을 걸다 intrigue 호기심을 돋우다

1. (c)	2. (d)	3. (a)	4. (a)	5. (c)	6. (c)	7. (c)	8. (b)	9. (c)	10. (a)
11. (c)	12. (d)	13. (b)	14. (b)	15. (d)	16. (d)	17. (a)	18. (c)	19. (c)	20. (b)
21. (c)	22. (a)	23. (c)	24. (d)	25. (d)	26. (c)	27. (c)	28. (c)	29. (c)	30. (b)
31. (a)	32. (c)	33. (d)	34. (a)	35. (c)	36. (c)	37. (a)	38. (a)	39. (b)	40. (b)
41. (d)	42. (c)	43. (a)	44. (c)	45. (a)	46. (a)	47. (c)	48. (b)	49. (a)	50. (c)

Part I Questions 1-25

1 유형 이디엄

A: The manager says that Tom will ___________.

B: I can understand the manager. Tom is always rude to the customers.

  (a) get cold feet

  (b) get to the bottom of something

  (c) get the boot

  (d) get down to brass tacks

해석 A: 지배인이 Tom을 해고할 거래.

B: 난 지배인을 이해할 수 있어. Tom은 항상 고객들에게 무례하게 굴잖아.

해설 B의 말에서 Tom이 고객들에게 무례하게 굴고 있기 때문에 그가 '해고될' 것이라고 추측할 수 있다.

어휘 get cold feet 겁을 먹다
get to the bottom of something 진실을 알아내다
get the boot 해고당하다
get down to brass tacks 본론으로 들어가다

2 유형 형태상 혼동 어휘

A: Shanna, what is your religion?

B: My whole family is Catholic but I am still an ___________.

  (a) ardent

  (b) antipodal

  (c) ambience

  (d) agnostic

해석 A: Shanna, 넌 종교가 뭐야?

B: 우리 가족은 다 천주교 신자인데 난 아직은 불가지론자야.

해설 '가족은 전부 천주교 신자이지만 ~'이라고 했으므로 뒤에는 상반되는 내용이 나와야 한다. 그러므로 불가지론자의 뜻을 가진 agnostic이 답이다. 불가지론의 정확한 의미를 몰라 틀릴 수 있는 문제이다.

어휘 ardent 열정적인 antipodal 지구상의 정반대의
ambience 분위기 agnostic 불가지론자

3 유형 형태상 혼동 어휘

A: I've never seen that couple raises their voice at each other before. Have you?

B: Oh, I'm sure they do have an __________ once in a while.

(a) altercation

(b) alternation

(c) alternant

(d) alignment

해석 A: 난 저 커플이 한 번도 서로한테 언성을 높이는 것을 본 적이 없어. 넌 본 적 있니?

B: 에이, 그래도 어쩌다 한 번씩 말싸움은 할 거야.

해설 커플의 의견 충돌, 언쟁에 대해 이야기하고 있다. 한 번도 싸우는 것을 보지 못했다고 하는 A와는 달리 그래도 한 번쯤은 그랬을 거라 이야기하고 있는 B이므로 답은 (a) altercation이다.

어휘 altercation 논쟁, 언쟁 alternation 교대, 교체
alternant 교대 함수 alignment 가지런함

4 유형 이디엄

A: Dad! What are we having for your birthday dinner tonight?

B: I'm sorry Howard, but I'm afraid we will just have to make __________ with something at home.

(a) do

(b) to

(c) out

(d) believe

해석 A: 아빠! 우리 오늘 아빠 생신 기념 저녁으로 뭐 먹어요?

B: 미안하지만, Howard, 오늘은 그냥 집에서 대충 때워야 할 것 같구나.

해설 아들이 생일 저녁에 대한 기대를 나타내고 있지만 아빠는 그냥 집에서 먹어야 될 것 같다고 말하고 있으므로 답은 (a) make do(그런대로 때우다)가 되어야 한다.

어휘 make do with ~으로 임시 변통하다, 때우다
make out 지내다 make believe ~인 척하다

5 유형 고난도 어휘

A: You have a huge issue when you date someone.

B: I know, I try not to __________ myself too much but it's hard not to.

(a) spurt

(b) dodge

(c) pamper

(d) disentangle

해석 A: 넌 연애할 때 정말 큰 문제가 있어.

B: 알아, 너무 멋대로 굴지 않으려 노력하지만 그러지 않기가 힘들어.

해설 누군가와 사귈 때 큰 문제가 있다고 말했으므로 그것이 부정적인 것이라고 예측할 수 있다. 따라서 제멋대로 행동하지 않으려고 하지만 힘들다는 것이 자연스럽다. pamper oneself는 '제멋대로 처신하다'라는 뜻.

어휘 spurt 뿜어내다 dodge 기피하다
pamper 애지중지하다
disentangle oneself (from) ~와 인연을 끊다

6 유형 고난도 어휘

A: Part-time jobs are a waste of time, don't you think?

B: No. It may seem __________, but it can be a great experience in life.

(a) precious

(b) flaunting

(c) ephemeral

(d) external

해석 A: 아르바이트는 시간낭비야, 그렇지 않니?

B: 아니, 덧없어 보일 수도 있지만 인생에 있어 소중한 경험이 될 수도 있어.

해설 A는 아르바이트가 시간낭비라고 하지만 B는 덧없어 보일 수는 있지만 인생에 있어 소중한 경험이 될 수도 있다고 말하고 있다. 따라서 답은 ephemeral(덧없는)이다. 특히 (b)는 flau-의 스펠링 때문에 제대로 뜻을 외우지 않은 사람은 그 의미를 혼동할 수 있는 단어이다.

어휘 flaunting 과시하는 ephemeral 덧없는
external 외부의

7 유형 고난도 어휘

A: How is Shayna these days? Is she still depressed?

B: Yeah, I feel so bad. She used to be so joyful and
___________.

(a) abstruse

(b) frigid

(c) vivacious

(d) vigilant

해석 A: Shayna는 요즘 어때? 아직도 우울해 해?
B: 응, 참 안됐어. 예전엔 무척 즐거워 보이고 활기찼었는데.

해설 used to be가 과거의 성격이 현재 그녀의 우울한 상태와는 다르다는 것을 말해준다. 따라서 그녀는 '항상 즐겁고 활기 있었다'가 답이 되어야 한다.

어휘 abstruse 난해한 frigid 불감증의 vivacious 활기 있는 vigilant 바짝 경계하는

8 유형 이디엄

A: How is your plan for a trip to China going?

B: Ha ha, I finally decided to take the ___________!

(a) decision

(b) plunge

(c) itinerary

(d) eaves

해석 A: 중국 여행 계획은 어떻게 되어가?
B: 하하, 드디어 모험을 하기로 결정했어!

해설 드디어 결정했다고 했기 때문에 뒤에는 take the plunge라는 '오랜 궁리 끝에 결정을 내렸다'는 뜻이 와야 한다.

어휘 take the plunge (오랜 궁리 끝에) ~을 단행하기로 하다
itinerary 여행 일정표 eaves (지붕의) 처마

9 유형 연어

A: How did that theory go?

B: Fortunately the market behaved precisely as assumed, so it finally hit the ___________!

(a) booze

(b) brake

(c) mark

(d) roof

해석 A: 그 이론 어떻게 됐어?
B: 다행히도 예측한 대로 시장이 반응해 주어서 드디어 성과를 거뒀어!

해설 B의 말에서 긍정적인 결과를 가져왔다는 것을 알 수 있다. 따라서 답은 성과를 거두었다는 (c)가 되어야 한다.

어휘 hit the booze 술을 마시다
hit the brake 급브레이크를 걸다
hit the mark 성과를 거두다
hit the roof (몹시 화가 나서) 길길이 뛰다

10 유형 이디엄

A: I think that Maria has a talent for the piano. She won every musical contest that she attended.

B: Didn't you know that Maria's father is a pianist? She is a ___________.

(a) chip off the old block

(b) drop in the ocean

(c) run-of-the-mill

(d) all thumbs

해석 A: 내 생각에 Maria는 피아노에 재능이 있는 거 같아. 참가한 모든 음악 콘테스트에서 우승을 했어.
B: Maria의 아버지도 피아니스트인 거 몰랐어? 그녀는 아빠를 그대로 닮은 거야.

해설 a chip off the old block은 '부모를 닮은 것'을 의미

어휘 a chip off the old block 부모의 행동이나 성격을 꼭 닮은 사람
a drop in the ocean 새발의 피
run-of-the-mill 평범한
all thumbs 손재주가 없음

11 [유형] 형태상 혼동 어휘

A: Jenna, how do you want me to pay you back?

B: Oh! I almost forgot. You can just ___________ the money.

(a) revere

(b) retrieve

(c) remit

(d) restore

[해석] A: Jenna야, 돈 어떻게 갚아줄까?
B: 아! 깜박할 뻔했다. 그냥 송금해주면 돼.

[해설] 돈을 어떠한 수단으로 갚길 바라냐고 물어 보았다. 따라서 돈을 전달하는 수단 중 하나가 나와야 하므로 답은 송금의 뜻을 가진 (c)이다. 혹시 되돌린다는 의미로 (b)를 답으로 선택했다가 낭패를 볼 수도 있는 문제이다.

[어휘] revere 존경하다 retrieve 회수하다 remit 송금하다 restore 회복하다

12 [유형] 형태상 혼동 어휘

A: What is the primary requirement you want from a potential employee?

B: From many aspects, we first want them to be ___________ in making decisions.

(a) rebuked

(b) retentive

(c) repellent

(d) resolute

[해석] A: 입사 지원자에게 가장 우선적으로 원하는 능력은 무엇입니까?
B: 여러 가지 점 중에서, 우리는 우선 결정을 내릴 때 단호하길 바랍니다.

[해설] '어떠한 능력을 바라느냐'고 물어 보았으므로 사람의 능력에 대한 답이 와야 한다.

[어휘] potential employee 입사 지원자
rebuked 꾸중을 들은 retentive 기억력이 좋은
repellent 혐오감을 주는 resolute 단호한, 확실한

13 [유형] 2어 동사

A: Is there a problem with the light? It doesn't work.

B: The electricity was ___________ for hours to change an old cable.

(a) cut down

(b) cut off

(c) cut out

(d) cut up

[해석] A: 전등에 무슨 이상이 있나요? 켜지지 않네요.
B: 오래된 전선을 교체하느라 몇 시간 동안 전기가 끊겼습니다.

[해설] 전선 교체를 위해 잠시 전기를 차단했을 것이기에 전기, 가스 등의 공급을 중단한다는 의미의 cut off가 맞다.

[어휘] cut down 감소시키다
cut off 공급을 멈추다, 단절시키다
cut out 삭제하다 cut up 조각조각 오리다

14 [유형] 형태상 혼동 어휘

A: Who have you met recently among our ___________?

B: Remember Jack who was in our math class? I ran into him the other day!

(a) altar

(b) alumni

(c) alumnus

(d) alchemy

[해석] A: 우리 동창들 중 최근에 누구 만났어?
B: 우리와 수학 수업을 같이 들었던 Jack 기억나? 저번에 우연히 마주쳤어!

[해설] 같은 수업을 들었던 사람이므로 두 사람 다 아는 사람일 가능성이 크다. 따라서 '동창'이라는 (b)와 (c)가 답이 되어야 하는데, among에서 여러 동창을 지칭함을 알 수 있으므로 복수형인 alumni가 답이 된다.

[어휘] altar 제단 alumni 동창들 alumnus 동창
alchemy 연금술

15 유형 이디엄

A: Jenny admitted she came close to losing her business.

B: But, she __________. She doesn't cry at all.

(a) gets cracking
(b) twists her arm
(c) spills the beans
(d) keeps a stiff upper lip

해석 A: Jenny는 자기 사업이 거의 망하게 된 걸 인정했어.
B: 하지만 그녀는 꿋꿋이 잘 버티고 있어. 전혀 울지 않아.

해설 Jenny가 사업을 잃게 된 위기에도 불구하고 전혀 울지 않고 있기 때문에 '꿋꿋이 버티고 있다'는 표현을 고르면 된다.

어휘 get cracking 서두르다
twist one's arm 억지로 잡아끌다
spill the beans 비밀을 털어놓다
keep a stiff upper lip 의연하다, 꿋꿋이 버티다

16 유형 이디엄

A: I'm very worried about my son. He doesn't do anything without watching TV.

B: That's too bad. He is just __________.

(a) the pick of the bunch
(b) turning the table
(c) pulling his socks up
(d) marking time

해석 A: 나는 내 아들이 걱정이에요. TV 보는 것 외에는 아무것도 하지 않아요.
B: 참 안됐네요. 그 아이는 그냥 허송세월을 하고 있네요.

해설 A의 문장에서 아무것도 하지 않는다는 힌트가 있으므로 허송세월이라는 의미를 찾으면 된다.

어휘 the pick of the bunch 가장 좋은 것
turn the table 형세를 역전시키다
pull one's socks up 분발하다
mark time 허송세월하다

17 유형 고난도 어휘

A: Did you know you had a sickly __________ last night?

B: Really? I really didn't feel good yesterday.

(a) pallor
(b) pittance
(c) magnitude
(d) iota

해석 A: 너 어젯밤에 아픈 사람처럼 창백했던 거 알아?
B: 정말? 나 어제는 정말 몸이 안 좋았어.

해설 건강하지 못함, 아픈 것에 대해 이야기하고 있으므로 빈칸에는 건강을 나타내는 단어가 와야 적당하다. 따라서 '창백함'의 뜻을 가진 pallor가 답이다. 특히 (b)와 (d)가 까다로운 뜻의 단어여서 답을 찾기가 수월치 않을 수도 있는 문제이다.

어휘 sickly 병약한, 허약해 보이는 pallor 창백함
pittance 아주 적은 돈[보수] magnitude 규모, 중요도
iota 아주 조금

18 유형 고난도 어휘

A: Did you get your results back from the hospital?

B: Yeah, and I have bad news. Doctors found a __________ tumor in my breast.

(a) colossal
(b) infinite
(c) malignant
(d) penurious

해석 A: 너 병원에서 결과 받았어?
B: 응, 근데 안 좋은 소식이 있어. 의사들이 내 가슴에서 악성 종양을 발견했어.

해설 병원에서 나온 결과에 대해 이야기하고 있으므로 건강에 대한 내용이 나와야 한다. 안 좋은 소식이라는 말을 했으므로 빈칸에는 부정적 상태를 뜻하는 '악성의(malignant)'라는 단어가 와야 한다. 예를 들어서 (a)처럼 단지 크다는 의미만으로는 (c)보다 설득력이 떨어진다.

어휘 colossal 거대한 infinite 무한한 malignant 악성의
penurious 인색한

19 유형 고난도 어휘

A: If you put the trash there, a ___________ odor comes into our house.

B: I'm really sorry, but this is where it's supposed to be.

  (a) cogent

  (b) impregnable

  (c) rancid

  (d) colossal

[해석] A: 그곳에 쓰레기를 두시면 역겨운 냄새가 저희 집으로 들어와요.

B: 정말 죄송하지만 원래 여기다가 두는 겁니다.

[해설] 쓰레기와 관련된 내용에서 odor(냄새)를 꾸며주는 단어가 와야 하므로 rancid(역겨운)가 알맞다.

[어휘] cogent 사람을 납득시키는 impregnable 난공불락의 rancid 역겨운 colossal 거대한

20 유형 연어

A: How did Kristen get to be in charge of that project?

B: I don't know, I guess the boss gave her a ___________ for the last time.

  (a) remiss

  (b) crack

  (c) scrutiny

  (d) leave

[해석] A: 어떻게 Kristen이 그 프로젝트를 맡게 된거야?

B: 몰라, 상사가 마지막으로 기회를 줬나 봐.

[해설] crack은 '갈라진 틈'이라는 의미가 있지만 '~에 대한 기회'의 의미도 있다.

[어휘] remiss 태만한 give a crack 기회를 주다
scrutiny (면밀한) 조사

21 유형 이디엄

A: Honey, look at this report card. Our son Jake got 5 F's this semester.

B: He ___________ himself. He just hung around with his friends studying nothing during the whole semester.

  (a) served right

  (b) came to

  (c) brought that upon

  (d) went wrong with

[해석] A: 여보, 이 성적표 좀 봐요. 우리 아들 Jake가 이번 학기에 F를 다섯 개나 받았어요.

B: 자업자득이에요. Jake는 지난 학기 내내 공부도 하지 않고 친구들과 어울렸잖아요.

[해설] 대화 내용으로 미루어 보아 Jake가 공부를 하지 않고 놀러 다녔기 때문에 좋지 않은 성적을 받았다고 하므로 '인과응보, 자업자득'이라는 뜻을 가진 표현을 찾아야 한다. bring something upon himself = serve someone right = have it coming 등의 표현이 있다. (a)는 It serves someone right과 같은 형태로 쓰이므로 문제에서 적절한 답이 될 수 없다.

[어휘] report card 성적표
hang around with someone 누구와 어울려 놀다

A: Did you hear there is a shot that can cure swine flu?

B: Yeah, I heard the drug will ___________ the virus.

   (a) attenuate

   (b) endear

   (c) reimburse

   (d) discard

[해석] A: 돼지 인플루엔자를 치료할 수 있는 주사가 나왔다는 말 들었어?

     B: 응, 그 약이 바이러스를 약화시킨다며?

[해설] 독감에 대한 약이 나왔다고 말했으므로 병을 약화시키는 내용의 긍정적인 의미를 가진 단어가 와야 한다. (d)는 '버린다'는 의미이나, virus에 쓰기에는 적합하지 않다.

[어휘] attenuate 약화시키다, 희석시키다
endear 사랑받게 하다 reimburse 보상하다
discard 버리다

A: Do you want me to explain every single detail of the case or get to the point?

B: You'd better ___________ as we have no time at the moment.

   (a) beat around the bush

   (b) bark up the wrong tree

   (c) cut to the chase

   (d) wander from the subject

[해석] A: 사건의 모든 전말을 설명해주기를 바랍니까, 아니면 본론을 말해주기를 바랍니까?

     B: 지금은 시간이 얼마 없으니 바로 본론으로 들어가는 게 낫겠어요.

[해설] 사건의 상세한 부분까지 설명해 줄지, 아니면 본론으로 들어갈지를 묻는 A의 물음에 시간이 없으므로 본론으로 바로 들어가는 게 낫겠다고 하는 것이 가장 적절하다.

[어휘] get to the point 본론으로 들어가다
beat around the bush 말을 빙빙 돌리다
bark up the wrong tree 잘못 짚다
cut to the chase 바로 본론으로 들어가다
wander from the subject 본론에서 벗어나다

A: Do you think ___________ people are irresponsible or wise?

B: I'm not sure, but I don't see what's bad about enjoying their own lives.

   (a) esthetic

   (b) olfactory

   (c) burly

   (d) hedonistic

[해석] A: 넌 쾌락을 추구하는 사람들이 무책임하다고 생각하니, 현명하다고 생각하니?

     B: 그건 잘 모르겠지만, 자기 인생을 즐기는 것이 뭐가 잘못된 건지는 모르겠어.

[해설] 문맥상 특정 부류의 인생 방식(enjoying their own lives)에 대해 이야기한다는 것을 알 수 있다. 그러므로 '쾌락주의의'라는 의미의 단어 hedonistic이 와야 알맞다.

[어휘] irresponsible 무책임한 esthetic 미적인
olfactory 후각의 burly 건장한
hedonistic 쾌락주의의

25 유형 고난도 어휘

A: How do you know so many great tasting restaurants?

B: Ha ha, I have such ___________ taste. I find eating one of my great pleasures in life.

(a) quirky

(b) tangible

(c) culinary

(d) epicurean

해석 A: 어떻게 이렇게 맛있는 음식점을 많이 알아요?
B: 하하, 제가 미식가라서요. 먹는 게 제 인생에서 가장 큰 즐거움을 주는 것들 중 하나 같아요.

해설 epicurean은 '쾌락주의'라는 원래의 뜻 외에 '미식가'라는 의미도 가지고 있다. 맛과 음식에 대해 말하고 있으므로 문맥상 epicurean(미식의)라는 의미가 와야 알맞다.

어휘 quirky 변덕스러운 tangible 만질 수 있는
culinary 요리의 epicurean 미식의

Part Ⅱ Questions 26-50

26 유형 이디엄

In spite of the low attendance, the party went on without a ___________.

(a) bean

(b) blink

(c) hitch

(d) hatch

해석 참석률이 저조했지만 파티는 지체 없이 잘 진행되었다.

해설 in spite of(~에도 불구하고)로 보아 파티는 그럼에도 불구하고 잘 진행되었다는 의미가 와야 한다.

어휘 without a bean 한 푼 없이 without a blink 태연히
without a hitch 지체 없이 hatch 부화

27 유형 구어

An environmentalist having radical ideas about making the world green is called ___________.

(a) a green hand

(b) all nature

(c) a tree-hugger

(d) a sanguine nature

해석 세상을 푸르게 만든다는 급진적인 생각을 가진 사람들인 환경 운동가들은 '나무를 끌어안는 사람(환경운동가)'이라고 불린다.

해설 환경운동가, 즉 environmentalist를 부르는 다른 말, 흔히들 말하는 애칭에 대해서 묻고 있는 문제이다.

어휘 environmentalist 환경운동가 radical 급진적인
a green hand 미숙한 사람 all nature 만물
tree-hugger 급진적인 환경보호운동가
a sanguine nature 낙천가

28 고난도 어휘

The musical 'Rent' has enchanted everyone who watched it and it acquired some __________ fame.

  (a) notorious

  (b) flagrant

  (c) illustrious

  (d) dubious

해석 뮤지컬 '렌트'는 관람한 모든 이들을 사로잡았고 눈부신 명성을 얻었다.

해설 뮤지컬 '렌트'가 모든 이들을 매혹시켰다는 표현으로 미루어 보아 빈칸의 표현도 긍정적인 의미의 명성이 알맞다. 따라서 '빛나는, 눈부신'의 뜻을 지니고 있는 illustrious가 가장 적절하다.

어휘 enchant 매혹시키다 acquire 얻다
notorious 악명 높은 flagrant 악명 높은
illustrious 빛나는 dubious 미심쩍어하는

29 연어

Lawschool, which is an institution specializing in legal education, was successful in the U.S. while it was a(n) __________ in Japan.

  (a) fatal blunder

  (b) minor setback

  (c) utter failure

  (d) fast track

해석 법 교육을 전문적으로 가르치는 기관인 로스쿨은 미국에서는 성공적이었지만 일본에서는 완전한 실패작이었다.

해설 '~하는 반면'이라는 뜻을 지닌 while로 이어지는 빈칸에 successful과 반대되는 표현이 와야 한다. 가장 적절한 것은 '완전한 실패' 라는 뜻의 utter failure이다.

어휘 institution 기관 specialize in ~을 전문으로 하다
minor setback 사소한 실패
fatal blunder 치명적인 실수 utter failure 완전한 실패
fast track 성공 가도

30 2어 동사

If one of our customers __________ the contract, he should compensate us for loss.

  (a) abides by

  (b) reneges on

  (c) enters into

  (d) falls out

해석 만약 고객 중 한 명이 계약을 위반한다면, 그 고객은 우리에게 손실을 보상해야 합니다.

해설 고객이 어떠한 행위를 했을 경우 손실을 보상해야 하는지를 생각하면 답을 쉽게 고를 수 있다.

어휘 abide by 지키다 renege on (계약 등을) 위반하다
enter into (계약 등을) 체결하다 fall out 다투다

31 형태상 혼동 어휘

Be careful, that pottery was rated as " __________ " by experts because of its origin and age.

  (a) valuable

  (b) variable

  (c) vaticinal

  (d) vagarious

해석 조심해, 그 자기는 기원과 시기 때문에 전문가들에게 "가치 있는" 것으로 평가 받은 것이야.

해설 가치 있는 것으로 '평가되었다'는 문장이다. 따라서 빈칸에는 알맞은 의미를 가진 valuable(가치가 있는)이 들어가야 한다.

어휘 variable 가변성의 vaticinal 예언의
vagarious 상식을 벗어난

32 유형 형태상 혼동 어휘

The President announced that he would focus on solving the ___________ poverty.

(a) abstract
(b) abridged
(c) abject
(d) absurd

해석 대통령은 극빈을 해결하는 데에 집중하겠다고 발표하였다.

해설 abject poverty라고 하면 가난 중에서도 매우 심각한 '극빈'을 말한다.

어휘 abstract 추상적인 abridged 요약된
abject 극도로 비참한 absurd 우스꽝스러운

33 유형 연어

The U.S. government on Monday ___________ sanctions on four people and eight organizations accused of aiding North Korea's government through illicit trade, the Treasury Department said.

(a) slashed
(b) smacked
(c) skimmed
(d) slapped

해석 재무부 발표에 따르면, 미국 정부는 월요일에 불법적인 거래를 통해서 북한 정부를 도운 혐의를 받고 있는 네 명과 8개 기구에 대한 제재를 가했다.

해설 sanction이라는 단어는 주로 복수 형태로 slap과 결합해서 과격하게 처분을 내릴 때 쓰는 연어이다. slap sanctions는 '제재를 가하다'라는 의미.

어휘 accuse 혐의를 씌우다 illicit 불법적인
Treasury Department 재무부
slash (날카로운 것으로) 긋다, 베다 smack 때리다
skim 스쳐지나가다 slap 치다

34 유형 이디엄

I am warning you for the last time, do not try to hand me a ___________.

(a) lemon
(b) bowl
(c) pepper
(d) fiddle

해석 내가 마지막으로 경고하겠는데, 나를 속이려고 들지 마.

해설 hand a person a lemon은 거래상에서 '속이는 것'을 뜻한다. lemon에 '불량품'의 의미가 있다는 점은 TEPS 수험자들에게 익히 알려져 있지만, '속인다'는 뜻이 있다는 것은 잘 모르는 경우가 있다.

어휘 fiddle 바이올린

35 유형 고난도 어휘

Just like any other typical politician, she also gave us a(n) ___________ answer.

(a) retorted
(b) nostalgic
(c) equivocal
(d) equivalent

해석 다른 전형적인 정치인들과 마찬가지로 그녀 또한 우리에게 애매모호한 대답을 해주었다.

해설 어떠한 대답을 해주었다는 내용으로 보아 문맥상 equivocal(애매모호한)이 와야 한다. 특히 (a)로 착각하지 않도록 조심해야 한다. 정치인들의 습성이 왜곡된 발언을 하는 것이라는 의미에서 선택지가 distorted였다면 정답의 여지가 있을 것이다.

어휘 retort 말대꾸하다 nostalgic 그리워하는
equivocal 애매한, 모호한 equivalent 동등한

36 유형 고난도 어휘

I prefer simple designs over flaring and ___________ interior designs.

    (a) mere
    (b) dull
    (c) gaudy
    (d) infantile

해석 저는 요란하고 화려한 인테리어 디자인보다는 심플한 디자인을 더 좋아해요.

해설 '요란한'이라는 의미의 flaring과 어울릴 수 있는 단어가 와야 한다. 따라서 gaudy(화려한)가 답이다.

어휘 flaring (외관이) 요란한 mere 단순한 dull 지루한 gaudy 화려한 infantile 유치한

37 유형 형태상 혼동 어휘

The ___________ seem to dislike me, for they misapprehend that I overwhelmed them with knowledge.

    (a) pundits
    (b) bandits
    (c) transits
    (d) misfits

해석 지식인들은 나를 싫어하는 것 같다, 내가 지식면에 그들을 압도한다고 오해하니까.

해설 지식에서 남을 압도한다면 빈칸의 인물들 역시 지식인이 되어야 한다. 그래서 정답은 (a)가 된다.

어휘 pundit 지식인 bandit 강도 transit 수송 misfit 부적응자

38 유형 고난도 어휘

The greatest concern of Obama was that many of the hard-core supporters would rather lose the election than ___________ the vote.

    (a) court
    (b) entangle
    (c) face
    (d) pry

해석 Obama의 가장 큰 걱정은 그들의 많은 핵심 지지자들이 표를 모으기는커녕 선거에서 패할 것이라는 것이다.

해설 court는 다양한 의미가 있는 단어인데, 여기서는 '끌어오다'의 의미로 쓰였다.

어휘 court 얻으려고 하다 entangle 얽어매다 face 직면하다 pry 꼬치꼬치 캐다

39 유형 형태상 혼동 어휘

I will give you another copy of our contract for you to ___________ after the meeting.

    (a) procrastinate
    (b) peruse
    (c) perceive
    (d) procreate

해석 회의가 끝난 후 정독하실 수 있도록 계약서 한 부를 드릴게요.

해설 계약서를 한 부 더 주겠다고 하고 있으므로 문맥상 peruse(정독하다)가 알맞다.

어휘 procrastinate 미루다, 질질 끌다 peruse 정독하다 perceive 감지하다 procreate 아이[새끼]를 낳다

40 유형 이디엄

Are you still waiting for the judge to drop the other
____________?

(a) boot

(b) shoe

(c) sandal

(d) slipper

해석 아직도 판사의 마지막 판결을 기다리고 있나요?

해설 안 좋은 일의 끝마무리를 한다는 것을 drop the other shoe 라고 한다. 따라서 재판의 결과를 기다리고 있다는 뜻이 되어야 한다.

어휘 drop the other shoe (주로 좋지 않은 일의) 끝마무리를 하다

41 유형 형태상 혼동 어휘

North Korean spies ____________ into South Korea
in order to watch troop movements.

(a) instigated

(b) intimated

(c) intermediated

(d) infiltrated

해석 북한 간첩들은 군의 움직임을 감시하기 위해 남한에 침투했다.

해설 스파이들이 관찰하기 위해서는 몰래 침투를 해야 한다. 따라서 의미상 infiltrate(침투하다)가 알맞다.

어휘 instigate 실시하다, 착수하다 intimate 넌지시 알리다
intermediate 중재하다
infiltrate 잠입하다, 침투하다

42 유형 형태상 혼동 어휘

The man next door was accused of ____________ a
convicted felon.

(a) hankering

(b) hooting

(c) harboring

(d) harrowing

해석 옆집 남자가 중범죄인을 숨겨준 죄로 기소되었다.

해설 harbor에는 '항구'라는 뜻 외에 '피난처, 은신처' 또는 '숨겨주다, 은닉하다'라는 뜻이 있다.

어휘 be accused of -ing ~의 혐의로 기소[고발/고소]당하다
hanker 갈망하다 hoot 야유하다
harrow 괴롭히다

43 유형 고난도 어휘

The craving for excitement is deeply ____________ in
humankind of all periods.

(a) rooted

(b) drooled

(c) convicted

(d) awry

해석 자극적인 것에 대한 열망은 모든 시대에 걸쳐 인간에게 깊이 뿌리 박혀 있다.

해설 문맥상 알맞은 단어는 rooted(뿌리 박혀 있는)이다.

어휘 craving 열망 drool 침을 흘리다
convicted 유죄를 선고받은 awry 비뚤어진

44 유형 고난도 어휘

History is not just a list of events arranged in a careless manner like a ___________ of things.

(a) dictate
(b) measure
(c) heap
(d) bore

해석 역사는 물건 더미처럼 아무렇게나 배열한 사건 더미가 아니다.

해설 문맥상 알맞은 단어는 heap(더미)이다.

어휘 dictate 명령, 요구 measure 단위, 표시 heap 더미
bore 따분한 일

45 유형 형태상 혼동 어휘

One must understand that suffering and failure are not only ___________ but also beneficial.

(a) inevitable
(b) inedible
(c) inert
(d) inexorable

해석 시련과 실패가 불가피한 것일 뿐 아니라 도움이 된다는 것을 이해해야 한다.

해설 문맥상 의미가 알맞은 것은 '피할 수 없는'의 뜻을 가진 inevitable이다.

어휘 inevitable 불가피한 inedible 먹을 수 없는
inert 기력이 없는 inexorable 멈출 수 없는, 냉혹한

46 유형 형태상 혼동 어휘

When the company restructured its employment policies, Harper and more than 6,000 fellows found most of their benefits had ___________ through their fingers.

(a) slipped
(b) smashed
(c) spruced
(d) sizzled

해석 회사가 고용정책을 개편했을 때, Harper와 6,000명이 넘는 동료들은 자신들의 수당이 순식간에 날아간 것을 알게 되었다.

해설 slip through라고 하면 감쪽같이 없어진 것을 의미한다.

어휘 restructure 개편하다, 재정비하다
benefits (회사에서 받는) 복리후생 급부, 수당
smash 강타하다 spruce 장식하다
sizzle 지글지글거리다

47 유형 2어 동사

Experts announced that bad habits often ___________ up on us while we are not conscious of them.

(a) curse
(b) thrust
(c) creep
(d) strike

해석 전문가들은 나쁜 버릇은 흔히 무의식중에 몸에 밴다고 발표했다.

해설 creep up은 '소리없이 다가오다'라는 뜻으로 무의식중과 가장 어울리는 표현이다.

어휘 curse 욕[악담]을 퍼붓다 thrust 밀치다
creep up 소리없이 다가오다
strike up (대화 또는 관계를) 시작하다

48 유형 고난도 어휘

Although I have a handicap, I am __________ with a fierce resolution to succeed in the world.

    (a) empowered

    (b) possessed

    (c) convinced

    (d) controlled

해석 나는 불리한 조건을 갖고 있지만 세상에서 성공하겠다는 굳은 다짐에 사로잡혀 있다.

해설 문맥상 '사로잡힌'의 뜻을 가진 possessed가 답이 되어야 한다.

어휘 empower 권한을 주다
be possessed with ~에 홀리다, 사로잡히다
convince 설득하다 control 조종하다

49 유형 형태상 혼동 어휘

How can we __________ those natural resources that can be used to produce nutritious foods for thousands who are starving?

    (a) squander

    (b) scavenge

    (c) scrounge

    (d) swamp

해석 굶고 있는 수많은 사람들을 위해서 영양가 높은 음식을 만들어내는 데 쓸 수도 있을 그 천연자원을 어떻게 허비할 수가 있죠?

해설 '천연자원을 허비해서는 안 된다'라는 뜻을 전달하는 목적이 있다. 따라서 정답은 낭비의 뜻을 가진 squander가 되어야 한다.

어휘 squander 낭비하다 scavenge (찾으려고) 뒤적이다
scrounge 구걸하다 swamp 쇄도하다

50 유형 연어

In order to stop the virus from spreading, we must keep suspicious patients in __________ from others.

    (a) reconciliation

    (b) usefulness

    (c) quarantine

    (d) nomination

해석 바이러스의 확산을 막기 위해 우리는 의심 가는 환자들을 다른 사람들로부터 격리시켜야 한다.

해설 keep ~ in quarantine은 '~를 격리시키다'라는 뜻을 가지고 있다. 따라서 답은 문맥상 (c)가 가장 적합하다.

어휘 reconciliation 화해, 조정 usefulness 유용성
quarantine 격리 nomination 임명, 지명

1. (b)	2. (c)	3. (a)	4. (a)	5. (d)	6. (a)	7. (a)	8. (c)	9. (d)	10. (b)
11. (b)	12. (b)	13. (c)	14. (b)	15. (a)	16. (b)	17. (b)	18. (d)	19. (d)	20. (c)
21. (d)	22. (c)	23. (a)	24. (b)	25. (d)	26. (a)	27. (b)	28. (d)	29. (a)	30. (b)
31. (c)	32. (a)	33. (c)	34. (d)	35. (b)	36. (a)	37. (c)	38. (b)	39. (a)	40. (b)
41. (c)	42. (d)	43. (c)	44. (a)	45. (d)	46. (b)	47. (c)	48. (d)	49. (a)	50. (b)

Part I Questions 1-25

1 유형 이디엄

A: I really love professor Kim's lectures on physical anthropology. He always helps us understand difficult matters so easily in his lectures.

B: I couldn't agree with you more. Today's lecture was also ___________ and no one needed to ask any questions.

(a) as good as his words

(b) as plain as day

(c) a word out of season

(d) around the corner

해석 A: 난 김 교수님의 자연인류학 강의가 정말 좋아. 교수님은 항상 강의 시간에 어려운 주제들을 쉽게 이해할 수 있도록 도와주셔.

B: 전적으로 동감이야. 오늘 강의도 일목요연해서 그 누구도 질문을 할 필요가 없었지.

해설 A와 B의 대화 내용으로 미루어 보아 교수의 강의가 이해하기 쉽고 명료함을 알 수 있다. 따라서 이와 같은 내용에 알맞은 표현은 '명명백백한, 일목요연한'이라는 뜻을 지닌 as plain as day가 적절하다.

어휘 physical anthropology 자연인류학
as good as one's word 약속을 지키는
a word out of season 때에 맞지 않은 말
around the corner 코앞에 있는

2 유형 이디엄

A: I hate Lisa singing out so loud at midnight. I can't possibly go to sleep and it drives me crazy.

B: You know what? Lisa loves singing alone at midnight but never sings in front of the others and always tries to ___________ even when she has to sing.

(a) sink a shoot

(b) have the last word

(c) get out of that

(d) go out of date

해석 A: 자정에 Lisa가 큰소리로 노래하는 게 정말 싫어. 거의 잠을 잘 수가 없고 나를 미치게 만들어.

B: 그거 알아? Lisa는 한밤중에 혼자 노래 부르는 걸 좋아하지만 다른 사람들 앞에서는 절대 노래하는 법이 없고 노래를 불러야 할 때조차 빼려고 해.

해설 노래 부르는 것을 좋아하는 Lisa가 정작 다른 사람들 앞에서는 노래를 부르지 않고 빼려고 한다는 내용에 알맞은 표현을 찾아야 한다. get out of something이 가장 적절하다.

어휘 sing out 크게 노래하다 sink a shoot 슛을 성공시키다
have the last word (토론 등에서) 끝까지 양보하지 않다
get out of ~을 회피하다, 발뺌하다
go out of date 시대에 뒤지다

3 유형 연어

A: Is there any difference between these apples?

B: Yes, these apples are tree- ___________, so the price is 30% higher.

(a) ripened
(b) fledged
(c) seasoned
(d) harvested

해석 A: 이 사과는 다른가요?
B: 예, 이 사과는 갓 수확한 것이라서 30퍼센트 비쌉니다.

해설 tree-ripened는 '갓 수확한'이라는 뜻이다.

어휘 ripened 익은, 숙성된
fledged (새끼 새가) 날 수 있게 된 seasoned 양념이 된
harvested 수확한

4 유형 2어 동사

A: I guess the monsoon season is finally over.

B: To my sadness, it's not over yet. The National Weather Service said it's just ___________ for a moment.

(a) holding off
(b) holding in
(c) holding at
(d) holding up

해석 A: 장마철이 드디어 끝난 것 같아.
B: 애석하게도 아직 끝난 게 아니야. 기상청에서 그러는데 잠시 소강상태일 뿐이래.

해설 장마철이 마침내 끝났다는 A의 말에 B는 기상청의 발표를 인용하며 동의하지 않고 있다. 따라서 '소강상태'를 의미하는 hold off가 가장 적절하다.

어휘 monsoon season 장마철, 우기 hold in 자제하다
hold up 견디다

5 유형 고난도 어휘

A: It seems you're living quite a busy life!

B: You think so? I am volunteering for a host of ___________ traveling around the country.

(a) pavement
(b) sparks
(c) proceeds
(d) causes

해석 A: 아주 바쁘게 사시는 것 같아요!
B: 그래요? 전국을 돌아다니며 수많은 운동에 자원하고 있어요.

해설 자원봉사를 의미할 수 있는 것은 사회적인 운동을 뜻하는 cause이다.

어휘 a host of 수많은 pavement 포장도로 spark 불꽃
proceeds 수익금 cause 사회적인 운동, 대의

6 유형 이디엄

A: I'm so sorry, I couldn't make it to the meeting.

B: Never mind, but promise me you will never ___________ your word again.

(a) go back on
(b) flare up at
(c) get hold of
(d) make up for

해석 A: 정말 죄송해요, 미팅에 참석하지 못했어요.
B: 됐어요. 그런데 다시는 약속을 깨지 않겠다고 약속하세요.

해설 A가 미팅에 참석하지 못한 데 대해 사과를 한다. B는 괜찮지만 다시는 약속을 깨지 않겠다고 약속해달라고 하므로 '(약속을) 깨다'를 의미하는 go back on이 알맞다.

어휘 go back on 배반하다, 약속을 깨다
flare up at 화를 내다 get hold of 연락을 취하다
make up for 보충하다

7 유형 이디엄

A: Did you hear that the company is going to downsize our production crew?

B: No, I didn't. That news really ____________.

(a) brings me down

(b) trips me up

(c) runs me down

(d) holds me down

해석 A: 우리 회사가 생산 인력을 줄일 것이라는 소식 들었어요?
B: 아니요, 듣지 못했어요. 그 소식을 들으니 정말 맥이 빠지네요.

해설 회사가 인력을 감축하는 구조조정을 할 예정이라는 소식을 듣고 B의 반응으로 적절한 것은 '맥이 빠지게 하다'라는 뜻의 bring someone down이다.

어휘 trip up 넘어뜨리다, 실수를 하게 만들다
run someone down ~를 치다
hold someone down ~를 제압하다

8 유형 이디엄

A: My dentist pulled out an intact tooth even though I had paid a high hospital fee.

B: You must feel ____________ advantage of.

(a) clipped

(b) given

(c) taken

(d) ripped off

해석 A: 내가 병원비를 많이 지불했는데도 치과의사가 멀쩡한 이를 뽑아버렸어요.
B: 이용당한 느낌이겠네요.

해설 take advantage of 는 '기회를 틈타다, 역이용하다'라는 표현이다. ripped off는 '바가지를 쓴'이라는 뜻이다. 문맥상 맞으려면 advantage가 없었어야 한다. 병원비를 많이 내었는데 멀쩡한 이를 뽑았다는 건 병원비를 지불한 입장에서는 '이용당했다'라는 생각이 들 것이다.

어휘 intact tooth 멀쩡한 이 clip 자르다, 깎다
rip off 바가지를 씌우다

9 유형 의미상 혼동 어휘

A: How would you like to be ____________?

B: You can call me Parker.

(a) anointed

(b) designated

(c) named

(d) addressed

해석 A: 어떻게 불러드릴까요?
B: Parker라고 부르세요.

해설 이름이나 칭호를 '~라고 부르다'고 할 때는 address라는 단어를 쓴다. designate는 '(직책 따위에) 임명하다', name은 '명명하다'라는 의미이다.

어휘 anoint 성유[성수]를 바르다

10 유형 이디엄

A: You will be more economical if you make a list of things to buy before shopping.

B: Don't worry. I make mental ____________ of what I buy whenever I shop.

(a) willies

(b) tallies

(c) rallies

(d) fillies

해석 A: 쇼핑을 하기 전에 구매 목록을 만들면 더 경제적일 텐데요.
B: 걱정 마세요. 쇼핑할 때마다 제가 사는 것을 마음속으로 계산해요.

해설 make mental tallies는 '~의 숫자를 마음속으로 일일이 세다(기록하다)'라는 뜻이다.

어휘 rally 대집회 willies 불편함, 소름 filly 말괄량이

11 [유형] 의미상 혼동 어휘

A: Do I get my money back if I'm not satisfied with this product?

B: Of course, our refund guarantee is ___________.

(a) sturdy

(b) solid

(c) genial

(d) potent

[해석] A: 이 제품에 대해 만족하지 못하면 제 돈을 돌려받나요?
B: 당연하죠. 환불 보장은 확실합니다.

[해설] 환불 정책이 믿을 만한가에 관해 얘기하고 있다. 분명하다는 의미가 포함된 solid가 가장 적절한 단어이다. 유사한 의미의 단어인 (a)나 (d)를 쓰지 않도록 조심한다.

[어휘] sturdy 완강한 solid 고체의, 틀림없는
genial 친절한, 온화한
potent 유력한, (약이나 술이) 강한

12 [유형] 의미상 혼동 어휘

A: Could I send these glasses to Korea by express mail?

B: It is possible but you need to write down "___________" on the box because they break easily.

(a) vulnerable

(b) fragile

(c) feeble

(d) tender

[해석] A: 이 유리잔들을 속달로 한국으로 보낼 수 있을까요?
B: 가능하겠지만, 깨지기 쉽기 때문에 상자에 "파손 주의"라고 써야 될 거예요.

[해설] 유리잔들이 깨지기 쉽다는 의미로 fragile을 쓴다. vulnerable은 신체적이나 정신적으로 취약하다는 뜻이고, feeble 또한 효과나 의지가 취약하다는 뜻이다.

[어휘] vulnerable 취약한 fragile 약한, 깨지기 쉬운
feeble 아주 약한, (효과나 의지가) 약한 tender 연한

13 [유형] 의미상 혼동 어휘

A: I'm moving out next week, how can I get my mail ___________?

B: Please fill out the form and submit it to me.

(a) received

(b) remitted

(c) forwarded

(d) transmitted

[해석] A: 다음 주에 이사 가는데 제 우편물은 어떻게 받아야 하나요?
B: 신청서를 작성해서 제출하세요.

[해설] 이사를 가게 되어 새 집으로 우편물을 보내달라고 부탁하는 상황인데, received를 쓰면 안 된다. 이것은 특정 우편물을 받을 때 쓰는 단어이고 여기서는 '계속 우편물이 새 주소로 보내지도록 하는 것'이므로 forward가 답이다.

[어휘] receive 수령하다 remit 송금하다
forward 새 주소로 전송하다 transmit 전송하다

14 [유형] 의미상 혼동 어휘

A: My check ___________. What's going on?

B: Let's see. It's because you're overdrawn.

(a) withdrawn

(b) bounced

(c) broke

(d) bankrupted

[해석] A: 제 수표가 부도가 되어 되돌아 왔어요. 무슨 일이죠?
B: 어디 볼까요. 예금을 너무 많이 찾으셨네요.

[해설] 예금을 너무 많이 찾아서 통장에 잔고가 없으므로 발행한 수표가 부도가 나게 되었다는 문맥이므로 bounce가 적절하다. broke는 돈이 없어서 '파산했다'는 뜻이다.

[어휘] withdraw 철수하다, 인출하다, 중단하다
broke 파산한 bankrupted 파산한

15 유형 의미상 혼동 어휘

A: I'm earning a great deal of money. It's the
___________ of my career.

B: That's great!

   (a) pinnacle

   (b) crest

   (c) vertex

   (d) plateau

해석 A: 난 엄청나게 돈을 많이 벌어. 지금이 내 경력의 전성기
야.
B: 멋지다!

해설 돈을 많이 번다고 하면서 자기 경력에서 최고의 시점이라
고 말하고 있으므로, 인생이나 경력에서 가장 성공적인 시
점이나 직위 등을 의미하는 pinnacle이 가장 알맞다.

어휘 pinnacle 절정, 정점 crest 볏, 꼭대기, 물마루
vertex 삼각형의 꼭짓점 plateau 정체기

---

16 유형 의미상 혼동 어휘

A: I'd like to have this white T-shirt ___________
because I spilt some black ink on it.

B: Sure. Is there anything else?

   (a) altered

   (b) bleached

   (c) dry-cleaned

   (d) starched

해석 A: 이 하얀 티셔츠에 잉크를 쏟아서 그런데 표백해 주세요.
B: 예. 다른 거 뭐 또 있나요?

해설 하얀 티셔츠에 검정색 잉크를 쏟았으니 표백을 해야 할 것
이므로 bleach라는 단어가 가장 잘 어울린다.

어휘 alter 수선하다 bleach 표백하다 starch 풀 먹이다

---

17 유형 고난도 어휘

A: The clouds look so ___________.

B: You're right. I suspect that a heavy rainstorm is
coming.

   (a) ambivalent

   (b) ominous

   (c) biped

   (d) affluent

해석 A: 구름이 아주 불길해 보여.
B: 맞아. 심한 폭풍우가 올 것 같아.

해설 구름을 보고 폭풍우가 올 것이라는 예측을 하는 것은
구름이 불길해 보여서이므로 ominous라는 단어가 적
절하다.

어휘 ambivalent 상반된 감정이 있는, 양면적인
ominous 불길한, 험악한 biped 발이 두 개 있는
affluent 부유한

---

18 유형 이디엄

A: I feel tired. Can you ___________?

B: Sure, but I suggest you take a shower before you
go to bed. You smell bad.

   (a) hit the spot

   (b) let me up

   (c) play sick

   (d) tuck me in

해석 A: 나 피곤해. 이불 좀 덮어줄래?
B: 그래, 근데 자기 전에 샤워 좀 하고 와. 냄새가 나.

해설 잠자기 전에 샤워를 하라고 하는 상황에서는 '이불을 덮어
달라'는 숙어인 tuck me in이라는 표현이 적절하다.

어휘 hit the spot 딱 그것이다, 만족스럽다
let up (비나 눈 등이) 그치다, 완화되다
play sick 꾀병 부리다
tuck someone in[up] ~에게 이불을 덮어주다

19 유형 2어 동사

A: Let's ___________ for a present on Sue's birthday.

B: Good idea. I will contact everyone who adores her.

   (a) keep the chin up

   (b) buy off

   (c) cash in

   (d) chip in

해석 A: 돈을 조금씩 내서 Sue 생일선물을 사자.
B: 좋은 생각이야. Sue를 좋아하는 모든 사람한테 전화할게.

해설 대화의 흐름상 선물을 위해 '돈을 모으자'는 뜻이므로 chip in이 적당하다.

어휘 keep the chin up 의연한 자세를 유지하다, 용기를 잃지 않다 buy off 매수하다 cash in 입금하다
chip in (돈을) 조금씩 내다

20 유형 고난도 어휘

A: Why did you spank Marty?

B: He ___________ despite my warning even when the traffic was very heavy.

   (a) overworked

   (b) retarded

   (c) jaywalked

   (d) underwrote

해석 A: Marty를 왜 때렸어?
B: 하지 말라는데도 교통이 몹시 혼잡할 때조차 무단횡단을 하잖아.

해설 경고를 했는데도 차가 많이 다니는 곳에서 무단횡단했다는 뜻이므로 jaywalked가 적절하다.

어휘 spank 엉덩이를 때리다 overwork 과로하다
retard 지연시키다 jaywalk 무단횡단하다
underwrite 서명으로 승낙하다

21 유형 고난도 어휘

A: Would you stop ___________ me, please?

B: It's too cramped here so I can't help it.

   (a) gushing

   (b) wiping

   (c) hissing

   (d) poking

해석 A: 나 좀 그만 찔러댈래?
B: 여기가 너무 비좁아서 나도 어떻게 할 수가 없어.

해설 비좁은 곳에서 일어나는 대화이다. 서로 몸이 부딪히는 상황에서 어떤 대화가 오갈지 생각해 봐야 한다.

어휘 cramped 비좁은
gush (말, 액체 등이) 세차게 흘러나오다
hiss 쉬 소리를 내다 poke 찌르다

22 유형 의미상 혼동 어휘

A: How was the food at the new Chinese restaurant?

B: Fantastic! The food was delicious, not to ___________ cheap.

   (a) speak

   (b) state

   (c) mention

   (d) talk

해석 A: 새로운 중국집 음식이 어땠어?
B: 최고야! 음식이 참 맛있더라, 싸기도 하고.

해설 speak, state, mention, talk는 전부 '말하다'라는 뜻의 유의어이지만 not to와 같이 쓰이는 단어는 mention뿐이다. (a)를 쓰기 위해서는 speak 뒤에 of 를 붙인 형태를 사용한다.

어휘 state 진술하다 not to mention ~은 물론이고

23 유형 의미상 혼동 어휘

A: I've heard that you recently started to play golf. Are you enjoying it?

B: Of course. It's a(n) ___________ from my daily life.

   (a) diversion
   (b) divergence
   (c) evasion
   (d) conversion

해석 A: 최근에 골프를 시작했다고 들었어요. 재미있으세요?
B: 당연하죠. 일상을 벗어나 기분 전환이 돼요.

해설 빈칸에는 골프를 즐긴다는 의미와 어울려야 한다. evasion은 '회피, 기피'라는 뜻인데 일상을 회피하면서 골프를 즐길 수는 없다. divergence는 '분기'라는 의미이므로 어울리지 않는다. 그리고 conversion은 '전환'이라는 뜻으로 쓰인다. 따라서 '기분 전환'이라는 뜻인 diversion이 답이다.

어휘 diversion 방향 전환, 분위기 전환
divergence 분기, 차이 evasion 회피, 기피
conversion 전환, 개종

24 유형 고난도 어휘

A: Do you think he is good-looking?

B: Yes, he's tall and has ___________ features.

   (a) engraved
   (b) chiseled
   (c) exempted
   (d) hassled

해석 A: 그가 잘생겼다고 생각하니?
B: 응. 키도 크고 조각 같은 얼굴을 하고 있어.

해설 한국말로 잘생겼다는 표현으로 '조각 같은 얼굴'이라고 하는데 영어도 비슷하다. chisel이라는, '조각칼로 깎다'라는 표현을 쓴다. 특히 (a)를 답으로 선택하지 않도록 조심한다.

어휘 feature 얼굴, 용모 engrave (나무나 돌에) 새기다
exempt 면제시키다 hassle 재촉하다, 들볶다

25 유형 형태상 혼동 어휘

A: Tell me the time and the ___________ of the meeting?

B: It's Lecturer's Common Room, 2 pm next Tuesday.

   (a) vendition
   (b) vendor
   (c) venison
   (d) venue

해석 A: 회의 시간과 장소 좀 알려줄래?
B: 다음 주 화요일 오후 2시, 공동연구실이야.

해설 B의 말을 참고하면 빈칸 안에는 '장소'라는 단어가 들어가야 한다.

어휘 vendition 환매, 매각 vendor 잡상인
venison 사슴고기 venue 장소

26 유형 형태상 혼동 어휘

Desperate to hide the test result, Jack ____________ his parents signature and submitted the sheet back.

(a) **forged**

(b) forwent

(c) forfeited

(d) forsaw

해석 시험 결과를 숨기고 싶은 절박함에 Jack은 부모님의 서명을 위조하여 성적표를 다시 제출했다.

해설 시험 결과를 숨기려는 절박함이 나왔으므로 뭔가 바람직하지 않은 일이 나와야 한다. 따라서 '위조하다'의 뜻을 가진 forge가 답이 된다.

어휘 desperate 필사적인 forge 위조하다 forgo 삼가다 forfeit 박탈하다 foresee 예견하다

27 유형 형태상 혼동 어휘

Actress Angelina ____________ a suit against her manager for revealing her private life to the public.

(a) inspected

(b) **instituted**

(c) inscribed

(d) inverted

해석 배우 Angelina는 자신의 사생활을 대중에 공개한 매니저에 대해 소송을 제기하였다.

해설 institute a suit은 '소송을 제기하다'라는 뜻이 된다.

어휘 inspect 검사하다 institute a suit 소송을 제기하다 inscribe 쓰다, 새기다 invert 뒤집다

28 유형 형태상 혼동 어휘

We must hold our president ____________ for the continuous economic recession.

(a) applicable

(b) accusable

(c) appliable

(d) **accountable**

해석 우리는 계속되는 경제 불황에 대해 대통령이 책임을 지게 해야 한다.

해설 '~에게 책임을 지우다'라는 표현은 hold ~ accountable for 이다. 따라서 답은 accountable이 되어야 한다.

어휘 recession 불황 applicable 적당한
accusable 고소해야 할, 비난받을 만한

29 유형 형태상 혼동 어휘

We have reached a conclusion that any kind of plagiarism will not go ____________, and will be punished.

(a) **uncensured**

(b) uncensored

(c) uncanny

(d) uncaring

해석 우리는 어떠한 종류의 표절도 비난을 면치 못할 것이며, 처벌받을 것이라는 결론에 도달했다.

해설 uncensured는 'un(아닌)+censure(책망하다)+ed(~당한)'으로 분석된다. censure(책망하다)와 censor(검열하다)를 혼동하지 않아야 한다.

어휘 plagiarism 표절
go uncensured 비난받지 않다
uncensored 검열 받지 않은 uncanny 이상한, 묘한
uncaring 냉담한

30 유형 고난도 어휘

Some celebrities earn their talents through intense training, but most of them are born with ___________ talents.

    (a) excessive

    (b) congenital

    (c) accused

    (d) conceded

해석 몇몇 연예인들은 강도 높은 훈련을 통해 재능을 얻는 사람도 있지만 대부분은 끼를 타고났다.

해설 '~ 재능을 가지고 태어나다'와 가장 어울리는 단어는 '선천적'이라는 단어이다. 또한 앞에선 '(후천적으로) 얻는 반면'이라고 했으므로 뒤에는 그에 반대되는 '선천적'이 와야 한다.

어휘 excessive 과도한 congenital 타고난
accused 고발당한 conceded 양보된

31 유형 고난도 어휘

In order to resolve the ___________ over North Korea's nuclear weapons program, diplomats from six nations gathered at the table.

    (a) digression

    (b) nomination

    (c) impasse

    (d) implication

해석 북한의 핵개발 프로그램을 둘러싼 교착 상태를 해결하기 위해 여섯 개 나라의 외교관들이 한 곳에 모였다.

해설 첫 부분에서 '해결한다'는 내용이 나왔으므로 다 같이 모여 '교착 상태'를 해결하기 위해서라고 볼 수 있다. 따라서 문맥상 impasse(교착 상태)가 알맞다.

어휘 digression (본래의 주제로부터의) 일탈
nomination 지명, 추천, 임명 impasse 교착 상태
implication 암시

32 유형 형태상 혼동 어휘

Geographers claim that major cities nearby the ocean basin will be ___________ due to natural hazards such as tsunami.

    (a) obliterated

    (b) obedient

    (c) obliged

    (d) obeisant

해석 지리학자들은 대양 분지에 접한 주요 도시들이 쓰나미 같은 자연 재해로 인해 완전히 파멸될 것이라고 주장한다.

해설 자연 재해와 쓰나미 같은 말로 미루어 보아 파괴적인 것이라는 것을 예측할 수 있다. 따라서 '흔적을 없애다, 제거하다'의 뜻을 가진 obliterated가 와야 한다.

어휘 basin 분지 obliterate 없애다, 완전히 제거하다
obedient 순종하는 oblige 강요하다, 의무를 지우다
obeisant 공손한

33 유형 고난도 어휘

A growing number of teenagers these days tend to think that keeping their ___________ is not that important if they use the protection.

    (a) polygamy

    (b) asceticism

    (c) celibacy

    (d) percept

해석 요즘은 피임을 한다면 순결을 지키는 것은 그다지 중요하지 않다고 생각하는 청소년들의 수가 늘고 있다.

해설 protection은 '피임'의 뜻도 있다. 따라서 문맥상 '육체적 순결'을 뜻하는 celibacy가 답이 된다.

어휘 polygamy 일부다처제 asceticism 금욕주의
celibacy (육체적) 순결, 독신 상태[생활]
percept 인식의 대상

34 유형 형태상 혼동 어휘

Eight ___________ doctors who used licenses from real doctors were taken into custody.

- (a) quota
- (b) quorum
- (c) quirk
- **(d) quack**

해석 진짜 의사로부터 구한 자격증을 사용한 여덟 명의 돌팔이 의사가 구속되었다.

해설 의사 자격증을 빌렸다고 했으므로 '의사 흉내를 낸' 사람을 뜻하는 단어가 와야 한다.

어휘 quota 할당량 quorum (의결) 정족수
quirk (우연히 생긴) 기이한 일
quack 돌팔이 의사

35 유형 형태상 혼동 어휘

It is your responsibility to ___________ if you feel any physical pain. We are not in charge of your accident.

- (a) abominate
- **(b) abort**
- (c) alleviate
- (d) advert

해석 어떠한 신체적 고통을 느낄시 도중하차하는 것은 여러분의 책임입니다. 저희는 여러분의 사고에 책임지지 않습니다.

해설 사고에 책임지지 않으므로 도중하차하는 것은 자신이 판단할 일이라고 전달하고 있다.

어휘 abominate 증오하다, 혐오하다
abort 도중하차하다 alleviate 경감하다, 완화하다
advert 주의를 돌리다

36 유형 고난도 어휘

According to the statistical view economists have come up with, it alone ___________ the possibility of economic recession.

- **(a) negates**
- (b) legitimates
- (c) integrates
- (d) justifies

해석 경제학자들이 내놓은 통계에 의한 견해에 따르면 경기 침체의 가능성은 없다.

해설 가능성에 대해 말하고 있으므로 문맥상 negate(무효화하다, 부인하다)가 알맞다.

어휘 negate 무효로 만들다, (존재 · 정당성을) 부정하다
legitimate 합법화하다 integrate 통합시키다
justify 정당화하다

37 유형 형태상 혼동 어휘

We not only look at the essay's content, logicality, and grammar, but we also consider the ___________.

- (a) bribery
- (b) braid
- **(c) brevity**
- (d) brevet

해석 우리는 에세이의 내용, 논리성, 문법 등을 볼 뿐 아니라 간결성도 고려한다.

해설 에세이를 평가하는 것들에 대해 이야기하고 있다. 따라서 문맥상 의미가 맞는 것은 brevity(간결성)이다.

어휘 logicality 논리성 bribery 뇌물 수수
braid 장식용 수술 brevity 간결성 brevet 명예 진급

38 유형 고난도 어휘

Politicians who are ___________ between what they say and what they actually do usually raise people's frustration.

    (a) spilt

    (b) dichotomous

    (c) sporadic

    (d) convergent

해석 말과 실제 행동이 양분되는 정치인들은 대개 사람들의 짜증을 불러일으킨다.

해설 dichotomous는 뒤에 흔히 between A and B의 형태를 수반하며 '양분한, 이분의'라는 뜻을 가진다. 정치인의 양면을 말하고 있으므로 정답은 dichotomous가 된다.

어휘 spilt 엎질러진 dichotomous 양분된
sporadic 산발적인, 이따금 발생하는
convergent 한 점에 모이는

---

39 유형 형태상 혼동 어휘

When you are at a workplace, you need to be more serious at your work than giving ___________ opinions during the meeting.

    (a) frivolous

    (b) ferocious

    (c) fervent

    (d) felicitous

해석 직장에 있을 때는 회의 중에 경솔한 의견을 내뱉지 않고 일에 더 진지할 필요가 있다.

해설 '~한 것보다 ~해야 한다'라고 말하고 있으므로 문맥상 경솔함보다는 진지함이 필요하다고 말해야 한다.

어휘 frivolous 경솔한 ferocious 격렬한, 맹렬한
fervent 열렬한 felicitous 적절한

---

40 유형 형태상 혼동 어휘

As technology developed, many means of communication became ___________.

    (a) oblivious

    (b) obsolete

    (c) oblique

    (d) obliterate

해석 과학 기술이 발달함에 따라 많은 통신 수단이 쓸모없어졌다.

해설 과학 기술이 발달하면서 나타난 결과를 의미하는 단어가 와야 한다.

어휘 means 수단 oblivious 의식하지 못하는
obsolete 쓸모가 없는, 구식의 oblique 완곡한
obliterate 없애다, 지우다

---

41 유형 고난도 어휘

Without any survey or research done, it is___________ to think that the plan could succeed.

    (a) averse

    (b) elliptical

    (c) ludicrous

    (d) immense

해석 아무런 사전조사나 설문조사 없이 그 계획이 성공할 수 있을 거라 생각하는 것은 터무니없다.

해설 조사 없이 실시된 그 계획은 실패하는 것이 당연했다고 말하고 있다.

어휘 averse 싫어하는 elliptical 타원형의
ludicrous 터무니없는 immense 거대한

42 유형 고난도 어휘

During the presentation today, could you clearly point out the ___________ feature of your idea to the investors?

- (a) shallow
- (b) amiable
- (c) introverted
- **(d) salient**

해석 오늘 발표 도중에 투자자들에게 당신 아이디어의 핵심을 분명히 짚어줄 수 있겠어요?

해설 투자자들은 중요 인물이라는 것을 예측할 수 있다. 아이디어의 '~를' 명확하게 알려달라고 했으므로 문맥상 빈칸에 들어갈 단어의 뜻은 '핵심'이 되어야 한다.

어휘 shallow 얕은 amiable 상냥한
introverted 내성적인 salient 가장 두드러진, 핵심적인

43 유형 고난도 어휘

Because mistakes are not intentionally made, I do not want to ___________ Bryan for the accident that he caused.

- (a) vent
- (b) creep
- **(c) castigate**
- (d) diffuse

해석 실수는 일부러 저지르는 것이 아니기 때문에 이번 사고를 일으킨 Bryan을 크게 책망하고 싶진 않다.

해설 실수 또는 사고는 일부러 저질러지는 것이 아니라고 말하고 있으므로 '크게 책망하고 싶지 않다'는 의미가 되어야 한다.

어휘 vent 내보내다 creep 살금살금 몰래 걷다
castigate 크게 책망하다 diffuse 발산하다

44 유형 이디엄

An educator's job is not only to provide knowledge but also to ___________ their students into life.

- **(a) galvanize**
- (b) vent
- (c) ladle
- (d) cram

해석 교육자의 임무는 지식을 전달하는 것뿐만이 아니라 학생들에게 활력을 불어넣어줄 수 있어야 한다.

해설 galvanize a person into life는 '~에게 활력을 넣어주다'라는 뜻이 있다. 교육자의 임무에 대해 말하는 것이므로 문맥상 가장 알맞은 것은 (a)이다.

어휘 vent 내보내다 ladle 국자로 뜨다
cram 벼락치기 공부하다

45 유형 고난도 어휘

Many immigrant workers were ___________ against the company's owner because of the excessive workload and delay in paying wages.

- (a) moribund
- (b) plagued
- (c) relieved
- **(d) incensed**

해석 많은 이주 노동자들은 과도한 업무량과 임금 체불 때문에 회사 소유주에게 분개했다.

해설 against는 주로 무언가에 반하는 때에 많이 쓰인다. 여러 가지 부당한 대우에 대해 노동자들이 분개하고 있다는 뜻이 되어야 한다. 따라서 incensed against ~(~에 대해 분개하다)가 답이 된다.

어휘 moribund 죽어가는 plague 괴롭히다 relieved 안심한

46 유형 고난도 어휘

The judge should not have been so ___________ with that sex offender at the court last week.

    (a) utter

    (b) lenient

    (c) slothful

    (d) overbearing

해석 지난주 법정에서 판사는 그 성 범죄자에 대해 그렇게 관대하지 말았어야 했다.

해설 판사가 범죄자에 대해 너무 '~했다'라는 의미가 되어야 하므로 lenient(관대한)이 적절하다.

어휘 utter 철저한　slothful 굼뜬　overbearing 고압적인

47 유형 고난도 어휘

The process in which ___________ cancer cells multiply has not been fully understood by the experts yet.

    (a) extinct

    (b) vigorous

    (c) malignant

    (d) vehement

해석 악성 암세포가 증식하는 과정은 전문가들에 의해 아직 완전히 밝혀지지 않았다.

해설 '~한 암세포'라는 의미가 되어야 한다. 따라서 문맥상 malignant(악성의)가 알맞다.

어휘 extinct 사멸한　vigorous 힘 있는　vehement 격렬한

48 유형 연어

If you let them walk, they will sooner or later develop a nasty ___________ for committing a crime again.

    (a) coarseness

    (b) destituteness

    (c) insolvency

    (d) penchant

해석 지금 그들을 풀어준다면 머지않아 또 범죄를 저지르는 추악한 성향이 나타날 것입니다.

해설 앞에 나온 단어 nasty와 어울리는 단어는 penchant(성향)이다. 범죄를 저지르는 행위는 nasty penchant(추악한 성향)이므로 문맥상 의미가 알맞다.

어휘 coarseness 조잡함　destituteness 빈곤　insolvency 파산

49 유형 형태상 혼동 어휘

Most of the newly released cars these days are ___________ with the latest technology.

    (a) replete

    (b) replicative

    (c) replenished

    (d) repopulated

해석 요즘 새로이 출시되는 대부분의 차들은 최신 기술을 완비하고 있다.

해설 '충분히 가지고 있다'라는 의미가 되어야 하므로 replete(가득한, 충만한)이 와야 알맞은 의미가 된다.

어휘 replenish 보충하다
repopulate ~에 사람을 다시 살게 하다
replicative 증식하는

50 유형 고난도 어휘

The unstable economic and political situation were
__________ to the cause of the conflict between the
two countries.

    (a) trifled

    (b) ancillary

    (c) secluded

    (d) resilient

해석 불안한 경제 및 정치적 상황은 양국 갈등의 부차적인 원인이었다.

해설 be ancillary to는 '~에 대해 부차적인 일이다'를 의미한다. 문맥상 ancillary(부차적인)가 와야 알맞다.

어휘 trifle 희롱하다, 무시하다 secluded 외딴
resilient 쾌활한, 발랄한

1. (c)	2. (a)	3. (b)	4. (b)	5. (d)	6. (b)	7. (c)	8. (b)	9. (d)	10. (a)
11. (a)	12. (b)	13. (d)	14. (c)	15. (b)	16. (a)	17. (b)	18. (d)	19. (a)	20. (c)
21. (b)	22. (a)	23. (a)	24. (c)	25. (d)	26. (b)	27. (c)	28. (b)	29. (b)	30. (d)
31. (c)	32. (d)	33. (b)	34. (a)	35. (a)	36. (d)	37. (a)	38. (b)	39. (c)	40. (b)
41. (d)	42. (a)	43. (a)	44. (d)	45. (b)	46. (c)	47. (a)	48. (b)	49. (d)	50. (b)

Part I Questions 1-25

1 유형 고난도 어휘

A: It is no use for you to be ___________ after you have committed such a cruel crime.

B: I know, but could you please reconsider?

(a) rumpled
(b) dilapidated
(c) contrite
(d) deplorable

해석 A: 그렇게 잔인한 범행을 저질러 놓은 후에 뉘우쳐도 소용없어요.
B: 알아요, 하지만 제발 한번만 다시 생각해 주시겠어요?

해설 흉악한 범죄를 저지른 후 '~ 해도 소용없다'라고 하였으므로 문맥상 '후회하는, 뉘우치는'의 의미가 어울린다. 따라서 contrite(참회하는)가 답이 된다.

어휘 rumpled 쭈글쭈글한 dilapidate 황폐한
contrite 크게 뉘우치는 deplorable 개탄스러운

2 유형 고난도 어휘

A: An example of ___________ is "You told me that story a thousand times!"

B: Oh, and another one is "She nodded her head a million times."

(a) hyperbole
(b) hibernation
(c) decrepit
(d) induction

해석 A: 과장법의 한 가지 예는 "너 그 얘기 나한테 천 번 했어!"야.
B: 아, 그리고 또 다른 예로는 "그녀는 고개를 백만 번 끄덕였다."가 있지.

해설 대화에서 예시로 들고 있는 것들은 모두 과장법에 해당한다. 따라서 답은 hyperbole(과장법)이 된다.

어휘 hibernation 동면 decrepitude 노쇠
induction 귀납법

3 유형 고난도 어휘

A: Government's ___________ plan will threaten the country's social security system.

B: They must plan so that the country develops as time goes by.

(a) deriding

(b) myopic

(c) sporadic

(d) tenacious

해석 A: 정부의 근시안적인 계획은 나라의 사회보장제도를 위협할 거야.

B: 시간이 갈수록 나라가 발전할 수 있도록 계획을 세워야 해.

해설 대화의 전반적인 내용을 이해해야 한다. 뒤에서 미래에, 시간이 갈수록 나라가 발전할 수 있도록 계획해야 한다고 했으므로 근시안적인 계획은 바꾸어야 한다는 내용이 되어야 한다.

어휘 deriding 비웃는 myopic 근시안적인
sporadic 산발적인 tenacious 고집스런

4 유형 고난도 어휘

A: What is the reason for the troops still remaining there?

B: I think the ___________ reason for their presence is to keep the peace, but you never know.

(a) prerogative

(b) ostensible

(c) grudging

(d) grimacing

해석 A: 그 부대가 아직도 거기 머무르는 이유가 뭐야?

B: 표면상 이유는 평화를 지키기 위해서인 것 같은데, 다른 이유가 있을지 누가 알아.

해설 부대가 아직도 그곳에 머무르는 이유를 말해야 한다, 하지만 뒤에 but you never know(진짜 이유는 아무도 모른다)라는 말이 왔으므로 문맥상 빈칸에는 ostensible(명목상, 표면상의)이 들어가야 한다.

어휘 prerogative 특권의 ostensible 명목상의
grudging 마지못해 하는 grimacing (얼굴을) 찡그리는

5 유형 고난도 어휘

A: How did the ___________ meeting for the concert go?

B: It went well, all the members were present and they all had great ideas.

(a) enunciate

(b) perilous

(c) prenuptial

(d) preliminary

해석 A: 콘서트에 대비한 예비 회의는 어땠어?

B: 좋았어, 멤버들이 모두 참석했는데 다들 좋은 아이디어가 있었어.

해설 preliminary란 중요한 행동이나 행사에 대해 '예비의~'라는 뜻을 가지고 있다. 콘서트 전 미팅이 어떻게 됐냐는 것이므로 답은 preliminary가 된다.

어휘 enunciate 선언하다 perilous 아주 위험한
prenuptial 혼전의
preliminary (중요한 행동, 행사에 대한) 예비의

6 유형 고난도 어휘

A: Once you start a conversation with her, you will know that she is very ___________.

B: I realized! She was socializing very well at the party.

(a) acquitted

(b) gregarious

(c) perverse

(d) sedulous

해석 A: 그녀와 한번 대화를 나누기 시작하면 굉장히 붙임성이 좋다는 것을 알게 될 거야.

B: 그렇더라! 파티에서 굉장히 잘 어울리고 있었어.

해설 그녀의 사회성, 붙임성에 대해 이야기하고 있으므로 문맥상 의미는 gregarious(사교적인, 붙임성 좋은)이 되어야 한다.

어휘 socialize 사람들과 어울리다 acquit 석방하다
perverse 비뚤어진, 괴팍한
sedulous 정성을 다하는

7 `유형` 이디엄

A: The brand 'Dior Homme' succeeded in its undertaking thanks to Hedi Slimane.

B: After he left 'Dior Homme', the brand tried to ___________ by recruiting innovative and creative designers.

   (a) make dry bones alive

   (b) come back alive

   (c) keep it alive

   (d) keep the matter alive

`해석` A: 브랜드 '디올 옴므'는 Hedi Slimane 덕분에 사업에 성공했어.

B: 그가 '디올 옴므'를 떠난 이후에, 이 브랜드는 혁신적이고 창조적인 디자이너들을 영입함으로써 활력을 유지하려고 노력했지.

`해설` Hedi Slimane이 '디올 옴므'를 성공으로 이끈 장본인인데, 그가 디올 옴므를 떠난 이후에도 혁신적인 디자이너들의 영입을 통해 활력을 유지하려고 노력한다는 내용을 유추할 수 있으므로 keep something alive가 가장 적절하다. keep the matter alive는 '아직도 토론을 계속하다'라는 표현이다.

`어휘` **make dry bones alive** 못쓰게 된 것을 되살리다
come back alive 살아 돌아오다, 생환하다
keep alive 명맥[활기]을 유지하다
keep the matter alive 토론을 계속하다

---

8 `유형` 고난도 어휘

A: I wish you and Jack would stop fighting.

B: We can't help it. I guess we are just ___________ enemies.

   (a) unsolicited

   (b) implacable

   (c) premature

   (d) uncharted

`해석` A: 너랑 Jack이 그만 좀 싸웠으면 좋겠어.

B: 우리도 어쩔 수가 없어. 그냥 우린 화해할 수 없는 적인가 봐.

`해설` 두 명은 계속 싸운다는 것을 알 수 있다. an implacable enemy라고 하면 '화해할 수 없는 적, 철천지 원수'라는 뜻으로 문맥상 가장 알맞다.

`어휘` **unsolicited** 요구받지 않은 **premature** 너무 이른 **uncharted** 미지의

---

9 `유형` 고난도 어휘

A: What is your essential point in your job?

B: I always try to be ___________ in keeping the records up-to-date.

   (a) dealing

   (b) adjunct

   (c) abstract

   (d) meticulous

`해석` A: 당신이 일을 할 때 주안점은 무엇입니까?

B: 저는 항상 꼼꼼하게 기록을 가장 최근 내용까지 정리해 두려고 노력합니다.

`해설` 기록을 최신으로 갱신하는 것이 자신의 담당이라고 말하고 있으므로 기록 관리를 어떻게 하는가가 빈칸에 와야 한다. 따라서 meticulous(꼼꼼한, 세심한)가 가장 적절한 표현이다.

`어휘` **up-to-date** 최신의 **adjunct** 부속품 **abstract** 추상적인

10 유형 고난도 어휘

A: Why do so many politicians lie about what they
have done?

B: I guess they are just lying on the ___________ of
protecting the country.

   (a) pretext

   (b) launching

   (c) retainment

   (d) meddling

해석 A: 왜 이렇게 많은 정치인들이 자신이 한 행동에 대해 거짓말을 하지?

B: 나라를 보호한다는 구실도 그냥 거짓말하는 것이겠지.

해설 거짓말하는 이유가 나와야 하므로 문맥상 '~라는 구실로, ~을 빙자하여'가 답이 되어야 한다. 따라서 pretext가 답이다.

어휘 launching 출시, 내보냄 retainment 보유
meddling 참견

---

11 유형 고난도 어휘

A: What do you think of my poem?

B: Wow… it's very concise but the words
___________ with such complex and deep
expressions.

   (a) resonate

   (b) infringed

   (c) stifled

   (d) pre-empted

해석 A: 내가 쓴 시에 대해 어떻게 생각해?

B: 우와… 정말 간결하지만 어휘가 참 복잡하고 심오한 표현들로 가득 차있어.

해설 시에 대한 평가를 기대하고 있으므로 빈칸에는 시가 '~로 되어 있다, 어떠하다'는 의미가 와야 한다. 따라서 '(어떤 기운·느낌으로) 가득한'이라는 뜻의 표현 resonate (with)가 와야 한다.

어휘 infringe (권리 등을) 침해하다
stifle 숨막히게 하다, 억제하다 pre-empt 선취하다

---

12 유형 연어

A: What is the worst thing about your boyfriend?

B: You need to see him at a restaurant… He's a real
___________ eater.

   (a) exacerbated

   (b) voracious

   (c) formidable

   (d) incumbent

해석 A: 네 남자친구의 가장 나쁜 점이 뭐야?

B: 음식점에서 그를 봐야 해… 완전 게걸스럽게 먹어.

해설 voracious eater는 게걸스럽게 먹는 사람을 뜻한다. 가장 안 좋은 점을 대라고 했는데 음식점에서 최악이라고 했으므로 문맥상 voracious가 와야 한다. 과격하고 극단적인 의미를 가졌다고 해서 (c)를 쓰지 않도록 주의해야 한다.

어휘 exacerbate 악화시키다 formidable 무서운
incumbent 현직에 의무가 있는

---

13 유형 이디엄

A: I heard that you had a fight with Ms. Kelly the
other day. Did you apologize to her?

B: No. Her sharp words ___________ so I don't want
to apologize.

   (a) took me off

   (b) gave a little

   (c) rained favors on me

   (d) cut me to the quick

해석 A: 너와 Kelly 양이 일전에 싸웠다고 하던데. 사과했니?

B: 아니. 그녀의 신랄한 말이 마음에 사무쳐서 사과하고 싶지 않아.

해설 B에게 Ms. Kelly가 싸운 적이 있는데 사과했냐는 A의 물음에 B가 그렇지 않다고 대답하고 있다. 따라서 빈칸에는 '마음에 사무치게 하다'라는 부정적인 표현이 알맞다.

어휘 take someone off ~를 (재미로) 흉내내다
cut someone to the quick 마음에 사무치게 하다
give a little 양보하다
rain favors on a person ~에게 은혜를 많이 베풀다

14 유형 고난도 어휘

A: The documentary last night dealt with the
___________ of modern society.

B: That must have been interesting. I've always
wanted to make a documentary myself.

  (a) introvert

  (b) extrovert

  (c) decadence

  (d) levity

해석 A: 어젯밤 다큐멘터리에서 현대 사회의 타락에 대해 다뤘어.

B: 정말 흥미로웠겠다. 난 늘 그런 걸 하나 만들고 싶었는데.

해설 현대 사회의 어떠한 성향을 다룬 다큐멘터리에 대해 이야기하고 있다. 따라서 문맥상 빈칸에는 현대 사회의 특징을 표현할 만한 명사가 와야 한다. decadence은 '타락, 퇴폐'를 뜻한다. 나머지 선택지들은 사람의 성격이나 행동에 대한 표현이므로 적절치 않다.

어휘 introvert 내성적인 사람 extrovert 외향적인 사람
levity 경솔, 경박

15 유형 고난도 어휘

A: That infamous construction company got accused
again.

B: Again? They are the most ___________ corporation
I've ever heard of.

  (a) uncanny

  (b) nefarious

  (c) predominant

  (d) preceding

해석 A: 그 악명 높은 건설 회사가 또 고소를 당했대.
B: 또? 그 회사는 내가 들어본 기업 중에서 가장 극악무도한 기업이야.

해설 infamous를 통해 두 사람이 말하는 기업이 악명 높은 곳이라는 것을 알 수 있다. 따라서 뒤의 내용도 그 기업이 들어본 것 중에서 가장 '극악무도한 기업'이라는 내용이 되어야 한다.

어휘 uncanny 이상한, 묘한 nefarious 극악무도한, 불법적인
predominant 우세한, 두드러진
preceding 앞선, 이전의

16 유형 고난도 어휘

A: Were there any complaints with the service?

B: There was one woman who felt one of the workers
was too ___________.

  (a) standoffish

  (b) gregarious

  (c) preamble

  (d) staunch

해석 A: 서비스에 대한 불만이 있었나요?
B: 어떤 여자 분이 직원 중 한 명이 너무 무뚝뚝하다고 느끼셨대요.

해설 불만이 들어온 게 있었냐고 물어보고 있으므로 직원에 대해 부정적인 면이 빈칸에 와야 의미가 알맞다.

어휘 standoffish 냉담한 gregarious 붙임성이 있는
preamble 서문 staunch 충성스러운, 지조가 있는

17 유형 이디엄

A: When Miranda appeared on the catwalk with a fashionable outfit, she ___________.

B: I was also invited to that fashion show and she was really awesome.

(a) scored in public

(b) brought down the house

(c) acted on her own volition

(d) covered up the stage

해석 A: Miranda가 멋진 의상을 입고 패션쇼에 나왔을 때 모든 사람의 박수 갈채를 받았어.

B: 나도 그 패션쇼에 초대받았었는데 그녀는 정말 멋졌어.

해설 A와 B의 대화 내용으로 미루어 보아 Miranda의 패션쇼 무대가 굉장히 멋졌다는 것을 알 수 있다. 따라서 이에 상응하는 긍정적 의미를 지닌 표현으로 '만장의 박수 갈채를 받다'라는 뜻의 bring down the house가 적절하다.

어휘 score in public 버젓이 비난하다
bring down the house 만장의 박수 갈채를 받다
act on ~에 따라서 행동하다 cover up 덮다, 은폐하다

18 유형 고난도 어휘

A: As an educator, what do you think is the most ___________ obstacle to a high quality education?

B: I think the current trend of private education is the biggest factor that deters the development of quality education at public school.

(a) heartening

(b) forlorn

(c) formative

(d) formidable

해석 A: 교육자로서 양질의 교육에 가장 큰 걸림돌이 무엇이라고 생각하십니까?

B: 제 생각엔 요즘의 사교육 추세가 공립 학교의 질 높은 교육의 발전을 가로막는 가장 큰 요인이라고 생각합니다.

해설 앞의 내용과 뒤에 내용은 동등하다고 볼 수 있다. 뒤의 문장의 뜻을 고려하자면 biggest와 비슷한 뜻을 가진 formidable(강력한)이 답이 되어야 한다.

어휘 deter 막다, 단념시키다 heartening 고무적인
forlorn (버림받아) 비참한 formative 형성의

19 유형 2어 동사

A: Don't get too close to him. There are rumors ___________ about him.

B: Really? But he seems totally innocuous to me.

(a) going around

(b) hanging around

(c) winding down

(d) chucking up

해석 A: 저 남자애랑 너무 가까워지지 마. 돌고 있는 소문이 있어.

B: 진짜? 전혀 악의가 없어 보이는데.

해설 한 사람에 대한 안 좋은 소문이 돌고 있다고 하는데 but이 나오면서 그 반대인 것처럼 보인다는 흐름의 대화이다. 소문이 돈다는 의미에서 go around가 타당하다.

어휘 innocuous 악의 없는
hang around (남과) 돌아다니며 놀다
wind down 느슨해지다 chuck up 그만두다

20 유형 고난도 어휘

A: Don't you think the new assignment is too much for us to do by ourselves?

B: I don't know, it's pretty ___________ but I am going to try my best.

    (a) opaque

    (b) lustrous

    (c) onerous

    (d) unhindered

해석 A: 새로운 과제가 우리가 스스로 하기에는 너무 버겁다는 생각이 들지 않아?

B: 모르겠어, 꽤 부담되지만 난 최선을 다할 거야.

해설 too much라는 것과 비슷한 의미를 가진 단어를 찾아야 한다. '꽤 ~ 하지만 최선을 다할 것'이라고 했으므로 문맥상 onerous(부담되는)가 가장 알맞다. 원래 onerous는 '의무적인'이라는 뜻이지만, 문맥상 '부담되는'으로 해석이 된다는 것도 알아야 한다.

어휘 opaque 애매한 lustrous 윤기 나는
unhindered 방해받지 않은

---

21 유형 고난도 어휘

A: In order to survive in a highly competitive society, you must try not to be ___________.

B: I know that I need to be more tactful, thanks for your advice.

    (a) hindered

    (b) unheeding

    (c) elucidated

    (d) eluded

해석 A: 경쟁이 심한 사회에서 살아남으려면 부주의하지 않도록 노력해야 해요.

B: 좀 더 요령이 있어야 한다는 거 압니다. 충고 감사합니다.

해설 뒤에서 더 요령 있어야 한다는 것을 안다고 말했으므로 충고한 내용 또한 그러한 내용이라는 것을 알 수 있다. 따라서 답은 unheeding(부주의한)이 된다.

어휘 tactful 재치[요령]있는 hinder 방해하다
unheeding 부주의한 elucidate 명확히 하다
elude 회피하다

---

22 유형 연어

A: Why do you look at him like that?

B: I don't know, I just don't like his ___________ grin.

    (a) impish

    (b) impious

    (c) imposing

    (d) impoverished

해석 A: 너 왜 그를 그렇게 쳐다봐?

B: 몰라, 난 그냥 저 장난꾸러기 같은 웃음이 싫어.

해설 impish grin은 '장난꾸러기 같은 웃음'을 뜻한다.

어휘 impious 불경스러운
imposing 눈길을 끄는
impoverished 가난해진, 허약해진

---

23 유형 2어 동사

A: Most politicians have used spies.

B: Right, they did to ___________ some useful information on the opponent.

    (a) ferret out

    (b) dig up

    (c) gussy up

    (d) map out

해석 A: 대부분의 정치가들은 스파이를 이용해왔어.

B: 맞아, 그들은 정적에 대한 유용한 정보를 캐기 위해서 그랬어.

해설 '정보를 캐다'라는 표현으로는 ferret out을 사용한다.

어휘 opponent 상대, 적수 dig up 우연히 발견하다
gussy up 멋을 내다 map out 계획하다

24 유형 고난도 어휘

A: What are you planning on doing after retirement?

B: I want to build a foundation that helps those who are ___________.

    (a) far-fetched

    (b) frivolous

    (c) indigent

    (d) opulent

해석 A: 은퇴 후에 무엇을 할 계획이세요?
B: 궁핍한 사람들을 돕는 재단을 만들고 싶어요.

해설 돕는다는 내용이 나왔으므로 빈칸에는 문맥상 '어려운 처지의' 사람들이 들어올 것을 예상할 수 있다.

어휘 far-fetched 억지스러운 frivolous 경박한, 사소한 indigent 궁핍한 opulent 부유한, 풍부한

---

25 유형 고난도 어휘

A: Police found some inappropriate actions between the two ___________ companies.

B: Wow, but too bad they don't exist anymore.

    (a) pecuniary

    (b) prissy

    (c) debunked

    (d) defunct

해석 A: 지금은 없어진 두 회사 사이에서 부적절한 행위를 경찰이 발견했대.
B: 우와, 근데 더 이상 존재하지 않으니 아깝다.

해설 더 이상 존재하지 않는, 문을 닫은 회사들에 대해 이야기하고 있다는 것을 알 수 있다.

어휘 inappropriate 부적절한 pecuniary 금전적인 prissy 깐깐한 debunked 거짓임이 밝혀진 defunct 현존하지 않는

Part Ⅱ   Questions 26-50

26 유형 연어

Due to current CEO's bad investment decisions, the company had to go through a ___________ loss.

    (a) refined

    (b) pecuniary

    (c) chagrin

    (d) eclectic

해석 현 CEO의 잘못된 투자 결정 때문에 회사가 재정적 곤란을 겪어야만 했다.

해설 pecuniary loss는 '재정 손실'을 뜻한다. 투자 실패로 손해를 봤다는 내용이므로 답은 (b)이다.

어휘 refined 정제된 pecuniary 금전상의 chagrin 원통함, 분함 eclectic 다방면에 걸친

---

27 유형 고난도 어휘

Although we overcame the critical situation, there is no room to be ___________.

    (a) myriad

    (b) furtive

    (c) complacent

    (d) perfunctory

해석 우리는 위기 상황은 넘겼지만 안주하고 있을 여유가 없다.

해설 There's no room to be는 '~할 여지가 없다, 여유가 없다'를 뜻하는 표현으로 위기를 모면했어도 안도해선 안 된다는 내용이 와야 한다.

어휘 myriad 무수히 많은, 막대한 furtive 은밀한, 엉큼한 complacent 현실에 안주하는, 자기만족적인 perfunctory 형식적인, 겉치레의

28 유형 고난도 어휘

The coach has still not made a decision of how he will ___________ me for my inexcusable behavior.

(a) serene

(b) reprimand

(c) convince

(d) acclimatize

해석 코치는 변명의 여지없는 나의 행동에 대해 어떻게 질책할지 아직 결정을 내리시지 못했다.

해설 reprimand는 '~를 질책하다'라는 의미가 있다. 변명의 여지없는, 즉 커다란 잘못에 대해 코치가 어떻게 자신을 벌할지 아직 결정을 내리지 않았다는 내용이다.

어휘 serene 평온하게 하다 convince 납득시키다 acclimatize 적응시키다

29 유형 이디엄

Now that you apologize for it, it's ok. But I was so upset when you ___________ and got angry without any understanding.

(a) accounted for that

(b) jumped the gun

(c) scooped in

(d) distressed yourself

해석 이제 사과하시니 괜찮습니다만, 당신이 어떠한 이해도 하려 하지 않고 다짜고짜 화를 냈을 때 저도 정말 속상했어요.

해설 글의 내용으로 미루어 보아 상대방이 화자의 말을 자세히 들어보지 않고 성급하게 화를 냈다는 것을 알 수 있다. 따라서 이와 같은 상황에 가장 잘 어울리는 표현은 '성급하게 행동하다'라는 뜻의 jump the gun이다.

어휘 account for ~을 해명하다 scoop in (사람을) 유인하다 distress oneself 고민하다

30 유형 이디엄

The world ___________ South Korea to the skies about organizing the ministerial talks with North Korea and Russia.

(a) solicit

(b) sojourn

(c) probed

(d) extolled

해석 한국이 북한과 러시아와의 장관급 회담을 준비하는 것에 대해 세계가 극찬하였다.

해설 '극구 칭찬하다'라는 뜻으로 extol to the skies가 쓰인다. 빈칸 뒤에 somebody to the skies가 나왔으므로 빈칸에는 extol(칭찬하다)라는 단어가 와야 한다.

어휘 solicit 간청하다 sojourn (일시) 체류하다 probe 면밀히 조사하다

31 유형 고난도 어휘

The journalist Cameron Stucky was criticized for being ___________ in his essay written about a politician.

(a) defiled

(b) irrevocable

(c) hard-hitting

(d) tentative

해석 저널리스트 Cameron Stucky는 한 정치가에 대해 쓴 에세이가 직설적이라는 이유로 비난 받았다.

해설 문장의 전체적인 의미를 파악해야 한다. 에세이가 어떤 특징 때문에 비난을 받았을지를 생각하면, 답은 '직설적인, 강력한'이라는 뜻의 hard-hitting이 되어야 한다.

어휘 defiled 더럽혀진 irrevocable 돌이킬 수 없는 tentative 잠정적인

32 유형 고난도 어휘

We had a special guest to give us a lecture but he kept on talking about topics ___________ to the issue at hand.

   (a) pseudonymous

   (b) parsimonious

   (c) intravenous

   (d) extraneous

해석 우리에게 강의를 해달라고 특별 게스트를 불러왔지만 그는 현 쟁점과는 거리가 먼 이야기만 계속했다.

해설 issue at hand는 '현재의 문제, 쟁점'이라는 뜻을 가지고 있다. 즉 쟁점과는 거리가 먼 이야기만 계속했다는 내용으로 답은 extraneous(관련 없는)가 되어야 한다.

어휘 pseudonymous 가명의 parsimonious (극히) 인색한 intravenous 정맥으로 주입하는

33 유형 형태상 혼동 어휘

I doubt he can predict the outcome; it's almost impossible with any degree of ___________.

   (a) chagrin

   (b) certitude

   (c) commotion

   (d) circumference

해석 그는 아마 결과를 예측하지 못할 것이다. 확실하게 예상하는 것은 거의 불가능하니까.

해설 맨 앞의 문장에서 결과를 예측하기 힘들다고 했으니, 그와 같은 뜻으로 확실함의 정도(degree of certitude)를 예측하기란 거의 불가능하다고 하면 문맥에 어긋나지 않는다.

어휘 chagrin 원통함 commotion 소란 circumference 원주, 둘레

34 유형 2어 동사

In his address, the spokesperson made a clever attempt to ___________ the many failures of his company.

   (a) gloss over

   (b) jump at

   (c) dote on

   (d) kick off

해석 대변인은 연설에서 회사의 많은 실패를 미화하려는 교활한 시도를 하였다.

해설 gloss over는 유약을 바른다는 말에서 유래한 '미화하다'라는 뜻의 표현이다.

어휘 jump at ~을 덥석 붙잡다, 받아들이다
dote on 홀딱 빠지다
kick off 경기를 시작하다, 버럭 화를 내다

35 유형 고난도 어휘

The communist leader lamented, "Why is the road to the West so ___________?"

   (a) bumpy

   (b) glum

   (c) heretical

   (d) medicinal

해석 그 공산당 지도자는 "어째서 서방으로 가는 길은 험난한가?"라고 탄식했다.

해설 탄식을 했다면, 그 내용은 부정적이면서도 road라는 말과 어울려야 한다. 그러기 위해서는 '험난한, 울퉁불퉁한'의 의미를 가지는 (a)가 가장 타당하다.

어휘 glum 우울한 heretical 이교의, 이단의
medicinal 약효가 있는

36 유형 고난도 어휘

Many reporters were striving to find more information about the president's assassination in order to write the ___________ for their newspaper.

    (a) olfactory
    (b) vicinity
    (c) lethargy
    (d) obituary

해석 많은 기자들이 자신들의 신문에 그 부고기사를 쓰기 위해서 대통령 암살에 관한 더 많은 정보를 얻으려고 애쓰고 있었다.

해설 대통령의 죽음을 알릴 기사를 신문에 쓰기 위해 정보를 찾고 있다는 내용이므로 '사망 기사'라는 뜻의 obituary가 답이 되어야 한다.

어휘 olfactory 후각기관 vicinity 부근 lethargy 무기력

37 유형 고난도 어휘

Widespread ___________ towards public order and morality among teenagers today is becoming a serious issue.

    (a) apathy
    (b) minor
    (c) conclave
    (d) caucus

해석 요즘 청소년들 사이에 팽배해 있는 공중도덕과 도덕성에 대한 무관심은 심각한 문제가 되고 있다.

해설 청소년들의 문제에 대해 이야기하고 있다. 따라서 후자에 대한 무관심이 심각한 문제가 되고 있다라는 문맥이 자연스러우므로 답은 apathy(무관심)이다. (c)는 어떤 불순한 목적이 언급되었다면 답이 되겠지만 공중도덕과 도덕성과는 어울리지 않으므로 오답이다.

어휘 public order 공중도덕 morality 도덕성
minor 미성년자 conclave 비밀회의 caucus 의원 총회

38 유형 이디엄

Everyone at the conference was very impressed by the information provided and thought the content really hit the ___________.

    (a) air
    (b) spot
    (c) buffers
    (d) bull's-eye

해석 회의에 참석한 모든 사람들은 제공된 정보에 대해 매우 감명을 받았으며 내용이 아주 만족스러웠다고 생각했다.

해설 대단히 감명을 받고 '만족스러웠다' 등의 긍정적인 반응이 나올 것을 예상할 수 있으므로 답은 hit the spot(만족스럽다)가 되어야 한다.

어휘 hit the air 방송하다 hit the spot 만족스럽다
hit the buffers (계획 등이) 갑자기 잘못되다, 실패로 돌아가다 hit the bull's-eye 적중하다

39 유형 이디엄

Politicians really need to hold their ___________ and discuss the matters thoughtfully rather than make a violent scene.

    (a) corner up
    (b) course
    (c) horses
    (d) ground

해석 정치가들은 폭력적인 상황을 만드는 대신 진정하고, 현안들을 진지하게 토론해야 한다.

해설 hold one's horses는 '진정하다'라는 뜻으로 정치가들이 폭력적이기보다는 차분하게 의논해야 한다는 내용이 나와야 한다.

어휘 hold one's corner up 자기 역할[책무]을 다하다
hold one's course 방향을 지속하다
hold one's ground 자기의 입장을 고수하다

40 유형 형태상 혼동 어휘

Carter's plan to re-start exports of U.S. beef angers
Korean ___________.

(a) rangers

(b) ranchers

(c) rapports

(d) respecters

해석 미국 쇠고기를 다시 수출하려는 Carter 계획은 한국의 축산업자들을 분노케 했다.

해설 축산업자(rancher)가 미국의 쇠고기 수출에 대해서 가장 분노를 느끼게 될 것이다.

어휘 ranger 관리인 rancher 축산업자 rapport 친밀한 관계 respecter 차별 대우하는 사람

41 유형 이디엄

Our company has a strict dress code. It is out of
___________ to wear any inappropriate clothes to
work.

(a) a hat

(b) upright

(c) the gate

(d) bounds

해석 우리 회사는 엄격한 복장 규정이 있습니다. 어떤 부적절한 옷이라도 입고 출근하는 것은 금지되어 있습니다.

해설 엄격한 복장 규정이라는 말을 통해 뒤에 그러한 옷들이 '금지되어 있다'는 내용이 오리라는 것을 추측할 수 있다.

어휘 out of a hat 무작위로 out of upright 기울어져
out of the gate 시작하자마자, 즉시, 당장에
out of bounds 금지되어, 도가 지나쳐

42 유형 고난도 어휘

They will praise the student even if he is not
___________.

(a) unassuming

(b) abusive

(c) bleak

(d) agonizing

해석 그 학생이 겸손하지 않더라도 그들은 그를 칭찬할 것이다.

해설 문맥상 빈칸에는 not과 결합되어서 부정적인 내용이 나와야 '설사 ~하더라도' 칭찬을 할 것이라는 내용이 완성될 것이다. 따라서 정답은 '겸손한'의 의미를 가지는 (a)가 정답이다.

어휘 abusive 남용하는, 학대하는 bleak 황량한, 음침한
agonizing 고통스러운

43 유형 형태상 혼동 어휘

After the company went out of business, everyone
started to doubt the former owner's ___________
because of his strange behavior caught by the
paparazzi.

(a) sanity

(b) sanitary

(c) sanctuary

(d) saturation

해석 회사가 부도난 후 파파라치에게 포착된 전 사주의 이상한 행동 때문에 모든 사람들은 그의 정신이 온전한지 의심하기 시작했다.

해설 이상한 행동을 하는 것을 포착했다고 했으므로 제정신인가를 의심해 본다는 내용이 와야 한다. 그래서 답은 '제정신'의 의미의 sanity이다.

어휘 sanitary 위생 sanctuary 보호지역
saturation 포화(상태)

44 유형 이디엄

Four people were arrested at the scene while trying to sell illegal drugs under the ___________.

    (a) corporal

    (b) affidavit

    (c) backlash

    (d) counter

해석   네 명이 불법 마약을 비밀리에 판매하려는 도중에 현장에서 체포되었다.

해설   under the counter는 원래 '처방전 없이' 약을 줄 때에 쓰는 말이지만, '비밀리에, 암거래로'라는 뜻이 있다. 불법마약을 어떻게 거래하려 했을지 추측하면 답을 찾을 수 있다.

어휘   corporal 상병, 하사   affidavit 진술서
backlash 강력한 반발

45 유형 이디엄

It was impressive to see how Cindy coped in her new job considering she was up to her ___________ in work.

    (a) lark

    (b) eyes

    (c) tricks

    (d) ears

해석   Cindy가 일에 몰두하는 걸 생각하면 새로운 직장에서 얼마나 잘 해내는지 알 수 있어서 인상적이었어.

해설   up to one's eyes는 '몰두하다'의 뜻이 있다. 그 외에도 up to one's elbows, up to one's neck 등도 같은 뜻을 가지고 있다.

어휘   up to one's lark 장난에 팔려
up to one's tricks 장난을 치고(치려고)
up to one's ears (궁지에 빠져) 꼼짝 못하게 되어

46 유형 이디엄

My irresponsible brother-in-law seems to always stay ___________ financially.

    (a) in the works

    (b) in there pitching

    (c) in the soup

    (d) in the bag

해석   나의 무책임한 매형은 늘 금전적으로 곤란한 지경에 있는 것으로 보인다.

해설   '곤경에 처하여'라고 할 때 in the soup이라는 표현을 쓴다.

어휘   in the works 진행중인
in there pitching 열심히 노력하는
in the bag 확실하여

47 유형 2어 동사

You should not have ___________ up at the reporter even though you were offended.

    (a) flared

    (b) fired

    (c) skewed

    (d) antiquated

해석   너는 기분이 상했더라도 그렇게 기자에게 버럭 화를 내지 말았어야 했어.

해설   be offended는 '기분이 불쾌하다[상하다]'라는 뜻으로 그것에 대한 반응을 안 좋게 보였다고 예측할 수 있다. flare up은 '벌컥[버럭/불끈] 화를 내다'라는 의미의 표현.

어휘   fire up 작동시키다, 흥미를 불어넣다   skew 왜곡하다
antiquate 한물가게 하다

48 유형 이디엄

There is no good in making a mountain out of a molehill, because this case is something we don't want to make a big ___________ about.

(a) pose

(b) fuss

(c) dirt

(d) pinch

해석 우리는 이 일로 소란을 피우고 싶지 않기 때문에 사소한 문제를 크게 만들 필요가 없다.

해설 make a big fuss는 make a mountain out of a molehill과 같은 뜻이다. 문맥상 앞뒤가 상응하는 의미를 만들어 줘야 하기 때문에 (b)가 답이 된다.

어휘 molehill 두더지가 파놓은 흙더미 pose 자세
pinch 꼬집기, 난관

49 유형 이디엄

Whenever there is an argument or a disagreement, I always try to sit on the ___________ and try to settle things down.

(a) rock

(b) tree

(c) swing

(d) fence

해석 언쟁이나 의견 충돌이 있을 때마다 난 항상 중립을 지키면서 상황을 진정시키기 위해 노력한다.

해설 sit on the fence란 '중립을 지키다, 형세를 관망하다'라는 뜻이다.

어휘 disagreement 의견 차이
settle down 진정시키다, 편안히 앉다

50 유형 이디엄

Thanks to the taxi driver, I was saved by the ___________.

(a) air

(b) bell

(c) hand

(d) sound

해석 택시 운전사 덕분에 난 간신히 곤경을 면했다.

해설 be saved by the bell은 원래 '(권투 선수가) 종이 울려 KO를 면하다'라는 뜻을 가지고 있다. 동시에 '곤경을 피해가다'라는 의미가 될 수 있다.

고난도 Actual Training 08

1. (b)	2. (a)	3. (b)	4. (d)	5. (b)	6. (b)	7. (d)	8. (a)	9. (d)	10. (a)
11. (c)	12. (b)	13. (d)	14. (d)	15. (a)	16. (a)	17. (a)	18. (d)	19. (c)	20. (c)
21. (b)	22. (a)	23. (d)	24. (b)	25. (b)	26. (a)	27. (c)	28. (d)	29. (c)	30. (c)
31. (a)	32. (a)	33. (a)	34. (d)	35. (d)	36. (a)	37. (b)	38. (a)	39. (d)	40. (b)
41. (b)	42. (c)	43. (a)	44. (b)	45. (d)	46. (b)	47. (c)	48. (b)	49. (b)	50. (d)

Part I Questions 1-25

1 유형 이디엄

A: Have you ever had a(n) ____________ that someone is hiding something from you?

B: No, never in my life. I'm really slow at catching things.

(a) wink

(b) inkling

(c) eye

(d) itch

해석 A: 누가 너한테 뭘 숨기고 있다는 걸 눈치챈 적 있어?
B: 아니, 여태까지 한 번도 없어. 난 뭘 알아차리는 데 정말 둔해.

해설 B가 부정하는 동시에 눈치채는 것, 알아차리는 것이 굉장히 둔하다고 했으므로 앞에서는 그러한 적이 있냐고 물어보는 내용이 와야 한다. get an inkling of...는 '~를 눈치채다, 어렴풋이 알다'라는 뜻이다.

어휘 get an eye to ~을 주목하다
get an itch 가렵다, 흥분하다

2 유형 이디엄

A: You look so fat. What about doing a little ___________ on your beer belly?

B: I know I've grown fleshy but I don't want to undergo any operations.

(a) nip and tuck

(b) back and belly

(c) Botox injections

(d) breast augmentation

해석 A: 당신 너무 뚱뚱해 보여요. 술배에 지방제거 수술을 받는 거 어때요?
B: 내가 뚱뚱해졌다는 건 알지만 어떤 수술도 받고 싶지 않아요.

해설 beer belly (술배)에 지방제거 수술을 받는 것이 어떠냐는 제안으로, 이에 적절한 표현은 nip and tuck이다. '보톡스 시술을 받다'라는 표현을 쓸 때는 동사 get이 쓰임에 유의한다.

어휘 beer belly 술배 grow fleshy 비만이 되다
undergo an operation 수술을 받다
nip and tuck 피부성형 수술; 막상막하
back and belly 완전히
breast augmentation 가슴확대 수술

3 유형 연어

A: The government's aim is to make all the companies compete on a ___________.

B: I doubt it since it doesn't have any policies to guarantee the equality of opportunity for reaching new markets.

  (a) ground plan

  (b) level playing field

  (c) high ground

  (d) gray area

해석 A: 정부의 목표는 모든 회사들이 공평한 경쟁의 장에서 경쟁하도록 만드는 것입니다.

B: 새로운 시장에 진출하기 위한 기회의 균등을 보장하는 어떠한 정책도 마련되지 않았으니 믿기 어려운데요.

해설 B의 말에서 기업에 균등한 기회를 보장하는 것이 정부 목표의 주된 내용임을 알 수 있다. 따라서 이와 비슷한 표현으로 level playing field(공평한 경쟁의 장)이 적절하다.

어휘 ground plan 건물의 1층 평면도
level playing field 공평한 경쟁의 장
the equality of opportunity 기회의 균등
high ground (논쟁 등에서의) 우위
gray area 애매한 부분[상황]

4 유형 이디엄

A: Hello Mr.Clark, nice to meet you. I am just going to cut to the ___________ since we don't have much time.

B: Yes sure, let's get down to business right away.

  (a) quick

  (b) a point

  (c) bone

  (d) chase

해석 A: 안녕하세요, Clark씨, 만나서 반갑습니다. 시간이 별로 없는 관계로 바로 본론으로 들어가겠습니다.

B: 네, 바로 시작합시다.

해설 cut to the chase는 '본론으로 들어가다'라는 뜻을 가지고 있다. 뒤에서 Let's get down to business라고 비슷한 의미의 문장을 말해주었으므로 앞 문장도 비슷한 뜻을 가지도록 만들어 주면 된다.

어휘 cut someone to the quick ~에게 깊은 상처를 주다
cut to a point 끝을 뾰족하게 하다
cut to the bone 지출을 최대한 줄이다

5 유형 이디엄

A: This new product ready for next month's launch will decide the future of our company.

B: I know, I'll really make a ___________ for its success.

  (a) bad break

  (b) pitch

  (c) tally

  (d) big splash

해석 A: 다음 달 출시를 앞두고 있는 이 신제품에 우리 회사의 미래가 걸려 있어요.

B: 알고 있습니다, 제품의 성공을 위해 열과 성을 다하겠습니다.

해설 make a pitch for ~ 는 '~을 손에 넣으려고[설득하려고] 열을 올리다'라는 뜻을 가지고 있다. B의 문장은 그것의 성공을 위해 열과 성을 다하겠다는 뜻이 된다.

어휘 make a bad break 실수를 저지르다
make a tally (경기에서) 득점하다
make a big splash 화제를 불러일으키다

6 유형 이디엄

A: Why are you mad at me?

B: I'd prefer not to see you ___________ over my share.

   (a) fluttering

   (b) drooling

   (c) squabbling

   (d) snuggling

해석 A: 나한테 왜 화났어?
B: 내 몫에 네가 침을 흘리지 말았으면 좋겠어.

해설 빈칸 뒤의 my share(내 몫)에서 힌트를 얻는다. 내 몫을 건드리거나, 탐내거나 하는 등의 행동으로 화가 났을 것이다. 선택지에서 그와 같은 표현은 (b) drooling(침을 흘리는)이다.

어휘 flutter 펄럭거리다 drooling 침을 흘리는
squabble 싸움하다 snuggle 달라붙다

---

7 유형 고난도 어휘

A: Let's set up a modern hospital in a third world country, perhaps one in Africa.

B: Sounds like a good plan but do you think it's realistically and financially ___________?

   (a) supercilious

   (b) innate

   (c) autonomous

   (d) feasible

해석 A: 아프리카 같은 개발 도상국가에 현대식 병원을 세우자.
B: 좋은 계획 같은데 현실적으로나 재정적으로 실현 가능할까?

해설 좋은 계획 같지만 현실적이냐라는 내용이 나와야 한다.

어휘 supercilious 안하무인인 innate 천부적인
autonomous 자치의

---

8 유형 형태상 혼동 어휘

A: What ability do you look for the most in hiring a worker?

B: Our company lacks people who are ________ in computer usage, therefore we need those who are highly proficient in dealing with computers.

   (a) literate

   (b) literary

   (c) literal

   (d) illiterate

해석 A: 직원을 고용할 때 어떠한 능력을 가장 많이 기대합니까?
B: 우리 회사는 컴퓨터 사용 기술을 가진 사람들이 부족해서, 컴퓨터를 다루는 데 통달한 사람이 필요해요.

해설 뒷부분에 컴퓨터 다루는 기술이 좋았으면 한다는 내용을 바탕으로 앞의 내용도 같아야 한다는 것을 알 수 있다. literate in computer usage는 '컴퓨터 사용 기술을 가진'이라는 뜻이므로 가장 알맞다.

어휘 proficient 능숙한 literary 문학의
literal 글자 그대로의 illiterate 문맹의

---

9 유형 고난도 어휘

A: Why did you turn down her offer like that?

B: The idea seemed pretty ingenious, but it was hardly ___________ to what I am looking for.

   (a) blistering

   (b) potent

   (c) dire

   (d) germane

해석 A: 왜 그녀의 제안을 그렇게 거절하셨어요?
B: 아이디어는 꽤 창의적인 것처럼 보였지만 내가 찾는 것과는 관련성의 거의 없었어.

해설 but이 나왔으므로 부정적인 내용이 이어질 것을 예측할 수 있다. 따라서 '관련성이 희박한'의 뜻이 예상되므로 (hardly) germane이 가장 적합하다.

어휘 blistering (속도 등이) 맹렬한
potent 강력한 dire (결과 등이) 심각한
germane 밀접히 연관된

10 유형 고난도 어휘

A: Although that church stood ___________ for decades, some features still remained.

B: You're right. We can still observe the very detailed decorations on the church wall.

   (a) derelict

   (b) implacable

   (c) snug

   (d) lush

해석 A: 저 교회는 몇 십 년간 방치되었지만 몇몇 특징들이 남아 있어.
B: 맞아. 아직도 교회 벽에 새겨진 아주 섬세한 장식을 관찰할 수 있어.

해석 전체적인 내용상 교회가 오랜 기간 동안 방치되었지만 아직도 정교한 장식을 볼 수 있다고 말하고 있으므로 답은 '방치된'이라는 뜻의 derelict가 적당하다.

어휘 preserve 보존하다 implacable 무자비한 snug 아늑한 lush 울창한

11 유형 형태상 혼동 어휘

A: Everything is closely related to cash these days.

B: I think that's why it is believed that poverty is ___________ to the next generation.

   (a) consecrated

   (b) perspired

   (c) perpetuated

   (d) procured

해석 A: 요즘 모든 것들이 돈에 밀접하게 관련되어 있어.
B: 그래서 빈곤은 다음 세대로 영속된다고 여겨지는 것 같아.

해석 다음 세대라는 대상으로 빈곤이 계속 이어진다는 의미를 예측할 수 있다. '영속시키다'의 뜻을 가진 perpetuate의 수동태 perpetuated가 답이 된다.

어휘 consecrate 신성하게 하다 perspire 땀을 흘리다 procure 조달하다

12 유형 고난도 어휘

A: I was really shocked that James beat Chad up.

B: Me too, he was so obsequious that no one expected him to be ___________.

   (a) riotous

   (b) pugnacious

   (c) gluttonous

   (d) stupendous

해석 A: James가 Chad를 때렸다니 굉장히 놀랐어.
B: 나도. 그는 너무 고분고분해서 아무도 그가 호전적으로 나올 거라고 예상하지 못했어.

해석 그가 호전적으로 나올 것이라고는 예상하지 못했다는 내용이 와야 알맞으므로 '싸움을 좋아하는(pugnacious)' 사람일 거라곤 사람들이 예상하지 못했다고 해야 문맥에 맞다.

어휘 riotous 아주 재미있는 gluttonous 탐욕스러운 stupendous 굉장한

13 유형 연어

A: We should respect the other people regardless of gender, creed and nation.

B: To do that, we must get rid of any ___________ first.

   (a) relative concept

   (b) compulsive idea

   (c) popular opinion

   (d) preconceived notion

해석 A: 우리는 성별, 신념 그리고 국적에 관계없이 타인을 존중해야만 해요.
B: 그러기 위해서는, 먼저 선입견을 없애야 하겠지요.

해석 성별, 신념, 국적 등 외부조건에 관계없이 사람들을 존중해야 한다는 A의 말과 가장 잘 어울리는 표현으로 B의 빈칸에 들어갈 말은 편견 또는 선입견(preconceived notion)이다.

어휘 regardless of ~와 관계없이 creed 신조, 신념
relative concept 상대개념
compulsive idea 강박관념 popular opinion 여론
preconceived notion 선입견

14 유형 연어

A: Why do you always force me to study but not tell my younger sister to do so?

B: I believe that she will follow __________ if you first demonstrate it to her.

  (a) boots

  (b) footprints

  (c) behind

  (d) suit

해석 A: 왜 항상 저한테만 공부하라고 강요하고 여동생한테는 안 그러세요?

B: 네가 먼저 모범을 보이면 동생이 따라 할 거라고 믿기 때문이야.

해설 먼저 모범을 보이라고 했으므로 문맥상 follow suit가 가장 적당하다. follow suit은 '따라 하다'라는 뜻을 가지고 있다.

어휘 force 강요하다 demonstrate 시범을 보이다
footprint 발자국

15 유형 연어

A: Honey, you should discuss the problem with me before taking any measures.

B: Stop __________. Our discussion always ends up in a bitter quarrel.

  (a) fussing around

  (b) pampering yourself

  (c) spoiling the game

  (d) blowing it wide open

해석 A: 여보, 당신은 어떤 조치를 취하기 전에 나와 문제에 대해 의논해야 해요.

B: 내게 잔소리 좀 그만해요. 우리의 의논은 항상 지독한 말다툼으로 끝나잖아요.

해설 앞 사람의 말에 대해서 간섭을 싫어한다는 다음 사람의 이야기를 핵심적으로 나타낸 표현을 찾는다. fuss around는 '잔소리를 하다'라는 의미로 쓰인다.

어휘 take measures 조치를 취하다
pamper oneself 제멋대로 처신하다
spoil the game 실수하다
blow... (wide) open ~을 못쓰게 만들다, 망치다

16 유형 이디엄

A: It costs too much money to ship these by truck.

B: There's more than one way to __________ a cat. Let's check with the railroad.

  (a) skin

  (b) grab

  (c) kill

  (d) catch

해석 A: 트럭으로 이것들을 배송하려면 비용이 너무 많이 들어.

B: 문제를 해결하는 데는 여러 가지 방법이 있어. 기차로 하는 것을 알아보자.

해설 There's more than one way to skin a cat 문제를 해결하는 데는 여러 가지 방법이 있다

어휘 ship 운송하다 skin 껍질을 벗기다

17 유형 2어 동사

A: Were you able to see the face of the person who broke into your house last night?

B: No, I was just able to ___________ a figure in the dark.

(a) make out
(b) make in
(c) make through
(d) make up

해석 A: 어제밤 집에 침입했던 사람의 얼굴을 볼 수 있었습니까?
B: 아니요, 그냥 어둠 속에 어떤 형체가 있다는 것만 알 수 있었어요.

해설 make out은 '지내다, 알아보다, 작성하다, 이해하다' 등의 여러 뜻이 있다. 이 문장에서는 '알아보다'라는 뜻으로 쓰여야 알맞다. make out이 '이해하다'의 의미로는 많이 알고 있지만, 이런 식의 의미로는 모르는 경우도 있어 어려운 문제이다.

어휘 make in ~에 들어가다 make through 해내다
make up 화해하다, 이루다, 형성하다

18 유형 2어 동사

A: I hear that Mr. Kim has a good command of English.

B: Indeed. His British accent is excellent! He'd ___________ an Englishman anytime.

(a) pass over
(b) pass off
(c) pass out
(d) pass for

해석 A: 나는 김 선생님이 영어를 잘한다고 들었어.
B: 그래, 그의 영국식 발음은 훌륭하지. 언제든 그는 영국인으로 통할 거야.

해설 영어를 잘하고 발음이 훌륭하다면 영국 사람으로 통할 (pass for) 수도 있을 것이다.

어휘 pass over 피하다, 무시하다
pass off 점차적으로 사라지다 pass out 기절하다
pass for ~라고 생각되다, ~로 통하다

19 유형 연어

A: When filing your complaint, you must follow the chain of command.

B: I already attended the orientation and was educated about the company ___________.

(a) precedent
(b) contrivance
(c) protocol
(d) brunt

해석 A: 불만사항을 제출할 때에는 반드시 지휘 계통을 따라야만 합니다.
B: 이미 예비교육에 참가해서 회사 규정에 대해 교육을 받았습니다.

해설 chain of command란 지휘 계통을 말한다. 따라서 회사 규정에 대한 이야기를 하고 있다는 것을 알 수 있다.

어휘 precedent 선례 contrivance 장치
protocol 의례, 규정 brunt (공격, 타격의) 주력

20 유형 이디엄

A: What did the consultant say about your mental state?

B: She told me I need to correct my habit of spitting ___________.

  (a) joust

  (b) crash

  (c) tacks

  (d) stifle

해석 A: 상담원이 너의 정신 상태에 대해 뭐라고 했어?
B: 화내는 버릇을 고쳐야 된다고 말했어.

해설 spit tacks는 '화내다, 격노하다'의 뜻이 있다. 화를 내는 버릇을 고쳐야 한다는 내용이 가장 알맞다.

어휘 joust 마상 창 시합 stifle 무릎 관절; 질식시키다

21 유형 이디엄

A: Do you think there is a possibility of Alex getting the job?

B: No need to worry. According to his talent and ability, it's a(n) ___________ conclusion.

  (a) muddled

  (b) foregone

  (c) outmoded

  (d) absolute

해석 A: Alex가 취직이 될 가능성이 있다고 생각해?
B: 전혀 걱정할 필요 없어. 그의 재능과 능력을 고려하면 이미 따 놓은 당상이야.

해설 foregone은 '전의, 이전의, 과거의'라는 뜻으로 foregone conclusion은 이미 결정된 것이나 마찬가지인 '빤한 일'을 뜻한다. 걱정 없다고 말했으므로 B는 Alex의 취업을 확신하고 있다.

어휘 muddled 뒤섞인, 낭비된 outmoded 유행에 뒤떨어진 absolute 절대적인

22 유형 형태상 혼동 어휘

A: I learned from the lecture, in order to be successful one has to be ___________ about the flow of money.

B: I agree, I think the richer someone is, the more uptight they are about dealing with money.

  (a) savvy

  (b) suave

  (c) sagging

  (d) salubrious

해석 A: 그 강좌에서 배웠는데, 성공하기 위해서는 돈의 흐름에 대해 굉장히 밝아야 한대.
B: 나도 그렇게 생각해. 내 생각엔 부자일수록 돈 문제에는 더 깐깐한 것 같아.

해설 B가 A의 의견에 동의한다고 했으므로 앞뒤 내용이 일치해야 한다. 따라서 뒤에 나온 uptight란 단어와 비슷한 맥락이 되어야 하므로 savvy(정통한, 약은, 꾀 많은)가 가장 알맞다.

어휘 suave 온화한, 세련된, 점잖은 sagging 축 처진 salubrious 건강에 좋은

23 유형 고난도 어휘

A: What happened to Major John Watson of the Marine Corps who was involved in the murder case?

B: It's pretty obvious. He got ___________ of his position as a result of his misconduct.

(a) struck
(b) entitled
(c) served
(d) stripped

해석 A: 살인 사건에 관련되었던 해병대 소령 John Watson은 어떻게 됐어?
B: 뻔하지 뭐. 범죄를 저지른 대가로 계급장을 떼게 됐어.

해설 뒤에 position(지위, 신분)이 나온 것을 고려해보면 문맥의 의미상 계급장을 빼앗겼다는 뜻이 되어야 한다. be stripped of는 '~을 빼앗기다'라는 뜻이다.

어휘 be[get] struck 타격을 입다 entitled ~할 권리가 있는
serve 쓸모 있다, 목적에 들어맞다

24 유형 이디엄

A: What happened to the people who lost their houses due to the flood damage?

B: Nothing ___________, they all started working on restoring their residential district.

(a) inquired
(b) daunted
(c) compelled
(d) inducted

해석 A: 홍수 피해 때문에 집을 잃은 사람들은 어떻게 됐어?
B: 그들 모두 조금도 굴하지 않고 거주 지역에 대한 복구 작업을 시작했어.

해설 nothing daunted는 '조금도 굴하지[기죽지] 않고'라는 뜻의 표현이다. 따라서 복구 작업을 시작한 사람들의 태도를 나타낼 수 있는 표현으로는 nothing daunted가 가장 알맞다.

어휘 inquire 묻다, 문의하다 compel 강요하다
induct 인도하다;임명하다

25 유형 형태상 혼동 어휘

A: Look how ___________ they look after the news on Maria's successful pregnancy.

B: They must be pretty rapturous after a long, depressing 5 years of infertility.

(a) erratic
(b) ecstatic
(c) enigmatic
(d) eclectic

해석 A: Maria가 임신에 성공했다는 얘기를 들은 뒤에 두 사람이 얼마나 기뻐하는지 좀 봐.
B: 5년 동안 임신이 안 돼서 길고 우울하게 보낸 뒤라 아주 기쁠 거야.

해설 B는 임신에 성공한 부부의 심정을 rapturous(황홀해하는)로 표현하고 있다. 따라서 동의어인 단어를 찾으면 된다.

어휘 infertility 불임 erratic (언행이) 별난, 괴상한
ecstatic 기쁨에 벅찬, 황홀한
enigmatic 불가사의한 eclectic (취미 등이) 폭넓은

26 유형 이디엄

We voted on how to handle it before we spoke
____________ word.

 (a) another
 (b) rather
 (c) such
 (d) enough

해석　우리는 그 문제를 어떻게 처리할지에 대해 즉석에서 투표했다.

해설　before we speak another word는 '즉석에서'의 의미를 가진다. 상황에 대한 파악과 함께 숙어 표현을 알아야 하는 좋은 문제이다.

어휘　rather 차라리, 정말로

27 유형 이디엄

The lawyer ____________ his brains to find decisive evidence that the opponent was bought off through bribery.

 (a) pushed
 (b) squeezed
 (c) beat
 (d) tied

해석　변호사는 상대편이 뇌물에 매수되었다는 결정적인 증거를 찾기 위해 머리를 짜냈다.

해설　beat one's brains는 '머리를 짜내다'라는 뜻의 숙어로, 문맥상 가장 알맞은 표현이다. 짜낸다는 의미라고 해서 squeeze를 쓰지 않는다는 것을 알고 있어야 한다.

어휘　decisive 결정적인 squeeze 짜다

28 유형 연어

Regarding the vitality of this matter, please make sure you ____________ up all the consequences before reporting the final draft to the boss.

 (a) depose
 (b) repose
 (c) draw
 (d) weigh

해석　이 문제의 중요성을 고려하여 사장님께 최종안을 보고하기 전에 모든 결과를 신중히 고려해 주십시오.

해설　weigh up은 '깊이 생각하다, 가늠하다'의 뜻을 가진다. 문맥상 중요한 사안이니 보고하기 전에 충분히 고려하라는 내용이 와야 한다.

어휘　vitality 중요성 depose 면직하다
repose 쉬다, 휴식하다

29 유형 이디엄

After Jake got dismissed, he immediately went to government offices in search of a job but he always got ____________.

 (a) the sack
 (b) the`show on the road
 (c) the run-around
 (d) the picture

해석　Jake는 해고당한 후 즉시 관공서에 가서 일자리를 찾아보았으나 항상 변명만 들었다.

해설　관공서에 일자리를 요청했는데, 뒤에 역접의 접속사 but이 있기에 요청에 대한 답변이 좋지 못했다는 내용이 와야 한다. 즉 get the run-around(변명을 듣다)가 적합하다.

어휘　get the sack 해고되다
get the show on the road 시작하다
get the run-around 변명을 듣다, 바람 맞다
get the picture 이해하다

30 유형 고난도 어휘

The whole world is worried sick about the little kids who are living in ___________ conditions, which leave them exposed to all sorts of diseases.

    (a) binary
    (b) respective
    (c) sordid
    (d) gratifying

해석   지저분한 환경에서 살고 있어 온갖 질병에 노출되어 있는 아이들에 대해 온 세계가 몹시 걱정하고 있다.

해설   sordid는 '더러운, 지저분한'이라는 뜻이 있다. 병의 전염을 걱정하고 있다고 말했으므로 굉장히 더럽고 지저분한 환경에서 살고 있는 아이들이란 것을 알 수 있다.

어휘   **worry sick** 대단히 걱정하다
binary 두 부분으로 이루어진, 2진법의
respective 각각의   **gratifying** 기쁜

31 유형 형태상 혼동 어휘

What you are saying is perfectly ___________, but I have a somewhat doubtful feeling.

    (a) viable
    (b) vivid
    (c) vital
    (d) vial

해석   당신의 말은 일리가 있지만, 저는 왠지 석연치 않은 느낌입니다.

해설   석연치 않다는 느낌을 가지게 한다는 말이 but의 뒤로 이어지므로, 그 전에 일리가 있다는 언급이 있어야 한다. 실행 가능하거나 일리가 있음을 말할 때 viable이라는 단어를 쓴다.

어휘   **viable** 일리가 있는   **vivid** 선명한   **vial** 유리병의

32 유형 이디엄

After a week I neglected boss's unresonable demand, I was given the ___________.

    (a) boot
    (b) slip
    (c) layoff
    (d) fire

해석   상사의 부당한 부탁을 거절하고 일주일 뒤, 난 해고 통지서를 받았다.

해설   문맥상 해고와 관련된 표현이 정답이다. pink slip이란 해고 통지서를 뜻하지만, 여기에서는 pink의 표현이 없으므로 (b)는 오답이다. layoff는 '해고'의 뜻이 있지만 give와 함께 쓰이지는 않으며, fire는 '해고하다'의 의미의 동사로는 쓰이지만 명사로는 적절하지 않다.

어휘   **neglect** 무시하다
give someone the boot 해고하다; 연인을 차버리다

33 유형 형태상 혼동 어휘

The steel house is so ___________ that only a few people lived without inconvenience.

    (a) cramped
    (b) curbed
    (c) cozy
    (d) curfewed

해석   그 철로 된 집은 너무 비좁아서 단지 몇 사람만이 불편하지 않게 살았다.

해설   불편을 느끼지 않은 이가 소수였다는 것은 그만큼 공간이 넓지 않았다는 뜻일 것이다. 그래서 정답은 (a)가 된다. curbed는 '제약을 받는'의 의미로 문맥과는 거리가 있다.

어휘   **inconvenience** 불편   **cramped** 비좁은   **curb** 억제하다
cozy 아늑한   **curfew** 통행을 금지시키다

34 형태상 혼동 어휘

The journal reported the unprecedented number of
____________ deaths at age one or younger.

    (a) griping
    (b) crippling
    (c) grasping
    (d) crib

해석   그 잡지는 한 살 이하 아이들의, 전례 없는 영아 사망자 수에 대해서 보도했다.

해설   crib death라고 하면 '유아, 영아 상태에서의 사망'을 말한다.

어휘   unprecedented 전례 없는   grip 꽉 쥐다, 이해하다   cripple 절름거리다   grasp 이해하다

35 연어

Many new words that are used these days were
____________ from what teenagers started using as slang.

    (a) supplied
    (b) related
    (c) ditched
    (d) coined

해석   요즘 쓰이고 있는 많은 신조어들은 청소년들이 유행어로 쓰기 시작했던 단어들로부터 만들어진 것이다.

해설   a new word를 목적어로 취하기에 가장 적절한 단어는 '만들어내다'라는 뜻의 coin이다. coin a word는 '단어를 새로 만들어내다'라는 뜻이다.

어휘   relate 관련짓다   ditch 도랑을 파다   coin 만들어내다

36 고난도 어휘

To gain more support, you must get rid of your
____________ attitude and try to be more modest.

    (a) haughty
    (b) cordial
    (c) residual
    (d) transitory

해석   지지를 더 받으려면 건방진 태도를 없애고 더 겸손해지도록 노력해야 한다.

해설   더 겸손해지도록 노력하라고 했으므로 그것과 반대되는 성향을 가지고 있다는 것을 짐작할 수 있다. 따라서 의미상 '오만한, 건방진'이라는 뜻의 haughty가 와야 알맞다.

어휘   get rid of ~을 없애다   haughty 오만한, 건방진
cordial 마음에서 우러나온
residual 나머지의, 찌꺼기의
transitory 일시적인, 덧없는

37 2어 동사

He seemed to seek a compromise, so he suggested to
____________ in for gas.

    (a) give
    (b) chip
    (c) rake
    (d) take

해석   그는 타협안을 찾는 것 같아 보였다. 그래서 그는 기름 값을 십시일반하자고 제안했다.

해설   chip in은 '(돈 따위를) 나누어내다'의 의미이다.

어휘   compromise 타협(안)   rake in 긁어모으다
take in 흡수하다

38 유형 연어

A: I am afraid you ___________ the wrong person.

B: Sorry. My mistake.

(a) **have**

(b) get

(c) lose

(d) put

해석 A: 사람을 잘못 보신 것 같습니다.
B: 죄송합니다. 실수했네요.

해설 여기서의 afraid는 '두려워하다, 무서워하다'가 아니라 약간 염려스럽다는 의미로 보면 된다. A의 말 자체가 '사람 잘못 보셨습니다'의 표현이 됨을 유념해야 한다.

39 유형 고난도 어휘

I am not aiming for a ___________ of awards and honors from people, in other words, I do not expect anything in return.

(a) demoted

(b) exhumed

(c) morose

(d) **myriad**

해석 많은 상과 존경을 받는 것이 내 목적이 아니다. 다시 말하자면 난 그 어떠한 대가도 바라지 않는다.

해설 awards and honors 둘 다 복수형이므로 '많은'이 가장 적당하다.

어휘 demoted 강등된 exhumed 발굴된, 침식하여 노출된 morose 까다로운, 언짢은 a myriad of 무수히 많은

40 유형 고난도 어휘

When I heard the news about a sex offender's continuous crime, I was filled with _________ and was sick to my stomach.

(a) aberration

(b) **revulsion**

(c) volition

(d) extenuation

해석 성 범죄자의 계속되는 범행에 대해 들었을 때 난 극도의 불쾌감이 차 올라 몹시 화가 났다.

해설 sick to my stomach는 '화가 많이 나다, 몹시 걱정하다'라는 뜻의 표현이다. 좋지 않은 기분을 나타내고 있으므로 '불쾌함, 격변'의 뜻의 revulsion이 와야 한다.

어휘 aberration 일탈, 탈선
revulsion 극도의 불쾌감, (감정 따위의) 격변
volition 의지, 의욕 extenuation 정상 참작

41 유형 형태상 혼동 어휘

In case the participants of the conference are absent, the ___________ for every session will be provided for them.

(a) processes

(b) **proceedings**

(c) proceeds

(d) procedures

해석 회의 참가자들이 자리를 비울 경우 그들에게 매 회의에 대한 의사록이 제공될 것이다.

해설 every session에 대한 어떠한 것이 불참한 사람들에게 제공될 것이라고 말했으므로 빈칸에는 회의와 관련된 용어인 proceedings(의사록)가 가장 알맞다.

어휘 process 과정, 추이 proceeds 수입, 수익금
procedure 절차, 순서

42 유형 고난도 어휘

The reason why drugs are especially ___________ to teenagers is because they are not old enough to make rational decisions.

   (a) fastidious

   (b) repressive

   (c) pernicious

   (d) irksome

해석 마약이 청소년들에게 특히 더 치명적인 이유는 그들은 이성적인 판단을 내릴 수 있을 만큼의 나이가 되지 않았기 때문이다.

해설 마약과 가장 관련이 있는 단어를 골라야 하므로 '해로운, 치명적인'이라는 뜻의 pernicious가 답이다.

어휘 rational 이성적인 fastidious 까다로운 repressive 억압하는 irksome 지루한, 귀찮은

43 유형 고난도 어휘

Devastated by war and natural disasters, the city was ___________ and in desperate need of assistance.

   (a) destitute

   (b) affluent

   (c) exquisite

   (d) indulgent

해석 전쟁과 자연재해로 인해 황폐화되어, 그 도시는 매우 궁핍했으며 도움이 절실했다.

해설 도시의 상황이 매우 좋지 않음을 알 수 있다. 그에 맞는 단어를 택해야 한다.

어휘 devastate 완전히 파괴하다, 망연자실하게 하다 destitute 궁핍한 affluent 풍족한 exquisite 절묘한 indulgent 관대한

44 유형 형태상 혼동 어휘

Food aid to impoverished regions will be guaranteed if you promise the ___________ of developing nuclear weapons.

   (a) circulation

   (b) cessation

   (c) continuation

   (d) convergence

해석 핵무기 개발의 중단을 약속한다면 가난한 지역에 식량 지원을 보장할 것이다.

해설 협상을 하려는 내용이므로 식량지원에 대한 조건으로 핵무기 개발 중단을 제시하는 것이 적절하다. '중단, 중지'의 의미인 cessation이 답이다.

어휘 circulation 순환, 유통 cessation 중단 continuation 지속 convergence 전환, 변환

45 유형 고난도 어휘

By the time the pull-out was decided, the United Nation's premises were already ___________, destroyed, and burnt.

   (a) dispersed

   (b) feigned

   (c) probed

   (d) looted

해석 철수가 결정되었을 때에는 이미 국제연합의 공관들이 약탈당하고 파괴되고 불에 탄 상황이었다.

해설 재산이 '~되었다'라고 말해야 하므로 빈칸에는 부정적 의미의 looted(약탈)이 가장 알맞다.

어휘 premises (건물이 딸린) 부지 disperse 분산시키다 feign 가장하다, 꾸며내다 probe 조사하다 loot 약탈[강탈]하다

46 유형 고난도 어휘

In Yosep's furniture shop, you will see the cozy
__________.

(a) device

(b) sectional

(c) tool

(d) typo

해석 Yosep의 가구점에서 여러분은 아늑한 조립식 가구를 보시게 될 것입니다.

해설 여기서 sectional은 여기서 '조립식 가구'의 의미로 쓰인다. tool은 논리적으로 다소 동떨어진 감이 있다.

어휘 typo 오식, 오자

47 유형 고난도 어휘

I just got done with the __________ classes in business and now I am planning on taking more intense courses.

(a) selective

(b) formative

(c) rudimentary

(d) perpendicular

해석 나는 기초적인 비즈니스 수업들을 다 마쳤고 앞으론 더 심화된 강의를 들을 예정이다.

해설 앞으로의 계획을 말하면서 '더 심화된 수업을 듣겠다'라고 했으므로 그 전 수업들은 더 쉬웠다는 것을 예측할 수 있다.

어휘 selective 선택의, 엄선된 formative 조형의, 형성의 rudimentary 기초의, 기본의 perpendicular 수직의

48 유형 이디엄

This year I want to run a marathon come __________ or high water.

(a) sun

(b) hell

(c) flood

(d) snow

해석 올해는 어떠한 고난이 있어도 마라톤을 뛰고 싶다.

해설 보통 숙어에 water가 나오면 고난이나 역경을 상징하게 된다. 그래서 come hell or high water는 '어떠한 고난이 있어도'의 뜻이 된다.

49 유형 연어

I was __________ when I got the phone call that a close friend of mine ended his life by hanging himself.

(a) dissuaded

(b) frantic

(c) meditative

(d) gratified

해석 내 친한 친구가 목을 매달아 생을 마감했다는 전화를 받았을 때 난 제정신이 아니었다.

해설 end one's life는 '생을 마감하다'라는 뜻이므로 친구의 사망소식을 들었을 때의 심정으로 가장 알맞은 것을 골라야 한다.

어휘 dissuade 단념시키다 frantic 미친 듯한, 제정신이 아닌 meditative 숙고하는 gratified 만족해하는

50 유형 고난도 어휘

We are planning on renovating this run-down cultural property to make sure it can __________ the storm that is coming soon.

(a) maintain

(b) stop

(c) persist

(d) weather

해석 우린 이 낡은 문화재가 다가오는 폭풍을 꼭 이겨낼 수 있도록 수리를 계획하고 있다.

어휘 maintain 지속하다, 유지하다 stop 멈추게 하다 persist 지속되다 weather (폭풍우·곤란을) 이겨내다, 견디다

1. (c)	2. (a)	3. (d)	4. (b)	5. (b)	6. (d)	7. (a)	8. (c)	9. (d)	10. (c)
11. (b)	12. (a)	13. (d)	14. (c)	15. (a)	16. (b)	17. (d)	18. (a)	19. (c)	20. (b)
21. (c)	22. (a)	23. (c)	24. (d)	25. (a)	26. (b)	27. (a)	28. (a)	29. (c)	30. (b)
31. (a)	32. (a)	33. (d)	34. (b)	35. (c)	36. (a)	37. (d)	38. (b)	39. (c)	40. (a)
41. (d)	42. (b)	43. (b)	44. (c)	45. (a)	46. (a)	47. (b)	48. (b)	49. (c)	50. (a)

Part I Questions 1-25

1 유형 고난도 어휘

A: I am not ___________ about what's going on. I just trust their actions.

B: No. You think it's none of your business.

(a) alloted

(b) abated

(c) nonchalant

(d) augmented

해석 A: 어떻게 되어가는지에 대해 내가 무관심한 게 아니야. 그냥 그들의 조치를 믿을 뿐이야.

B: 그렇지 않아요. 당신은 그냥 당신이 알 바 아니라고 생각하고 있어요.

해설 B가 주장하는 것에 대해 A는 부인하고 있다. 따라서 여자의 생각과 부인하는 내용이 같아야 하므로 none of your business와 빈칸에 들어올 단어는 같은 뜻을 지녀야 한다.

어휘 allot 할당하다, 분배하다 abate 약해지다, 약화시키다
nonchalant 아랑곳하지 않는, 무관심한
augment 늘리다, 증가시키다

2 유형 2어 동사

A: What do you think of homosexual couples' adoption?

B: Sorry. I didn't ___________ over that matter.

(a) ponder

(b) brood

(c) maul

(d) unravel

해석 A: 동성 커플들의 입양에 대해 어떻게 생각해?

B: 미안해. 그 문제에 대해서는 깊이 생각해본 적이 없어.

해설 ponder over는 '깊이 생각하다'의 의미이다.

어휘 adoption 입양 brood over (불쾌한 일)을 곱씹다
maul 혹평하다 unravel (수수께끼 등을) 풀다

3 유형 고난도 어휘

A: How do the students evaluate her course?

B: Most of them think she gives quite a ___________ explanation and therefore are able to understand easily and precisely.

(a) docile

(b) ferocious

(c) frugal

(d) lucid

해석 A: 학생들이 그녀의 수업을 어떻게 평가하나요?
B: 대부분의 학생들은 그녀가 명쾌한 설명을 해주어서 더 쉽고 정확하게 이해할 수 있다고 생각해요.

해설 정확하고 쉽게 이해할 수 있다고 했으므로 그녀의 설명이 긍정적인 평가를 받는다는 것을 알 수 있다.

어휘 evaluate 평가하다 docile 유순한, 고분고분한
ferocious 격렬한 frugal 절약하는, 소박한
lucid 명쾌한, 명료한

4 유형 의미상 혼동 어휘

A: I don't agree with our company's staffing freeze because we are short of skilled people while there is too much work to deal with.

B: Yeah, I know the company is in financial difficulty but ___________ in staffing is going to aggravate the situation.

(a) gulf

(b) gaps

(c) lack

(d) shortage

해석 A: 처리해야 할 업무는 너무 많은데 숙련된 인력이 부족한 상황에서 우리 회사가 직원 채용을 동결하는 건 난 동의할 수가 없어요.
B: 맞아요, 우리 회사가 재정난에 처해 있다는 것은 알지만 직원의 결원은 상황을 더 악화시킬 거예요.

해설 '차이' 또는 '부족', '결핍'을 나타내는 단어들 중 문맥에 가장 적절한 표현은 gaps이다. 참고로 lack이 명사로 쓰일 때는 lack of something의 식으로 전치사 of와 함께 쓰인다. shortage도 of와 함께 쓰인다.

어휘 staffing freeze 직원 채용 동결
in financial difficulties 재정난에 처해 있는
aggravate 악화시키다
gulf (사고나 생활방식 등의) 큰 격차
gaps in staffing 직원의 결원

5 유형 이디엄

A: Nothing can ever seem to beat this product's practicality.

B: I don't think so. There are so many different features that come in ___________ out in the market that we missed.

(a) favor

(b) handy

(c) flocks

(d) sight

해석 A: 이 제품의 실용성을 이길 수 있는 건 전혀 없어 보여.
B: 내 생각은 달라. 지금 시장에 나와 있는 것 중 우리가 모르고 지나쳤지만 쓸모 있는 특징들이 정말 많아.

해설 come in handy는 '쓸모가 있다, 편리하다'라는 뜻을 가지고 있다. 실용성에 대해 이야기하고 있으므로 문맥상 의미는 come in handy가 되어야 한다.

어휘 come in favor of ~에 대한 지지를 표명하다
come in flocks 떼지어 오다, 몰려오다
come in sight 보이기 시작하다

6 유형 이디엄

A: How is everything going for you?

B: Nothing has changed, I am still up a ___________ without a paddle.

  (a) storm

  (b) island

  (c) cloud

  (d) creek

해석 A: 넌 요즘 어떻게 지내고 있니?
    B: 달라진 게 없어. 난 아직도 곤경에 빠져서 헤어 나오질 못하고 있어.

해설 be up a creek은 '궁지에 몰리다'라는 뜻으로 without a paddle과 같이 자주 쓰인다. 꼼짝없이 곤경에 빠졌을 때를 말한다.

어휘 up a storm 잔뜩, 극도로

---

7 유형 고난도 어휘

A: I heard on the news that a container coming from China was filled with ___________ goods such as imitations of high brands.

B: Why do people struggle so much to earn money by smuggling products that are prohibited?

  (a) contraband

  (b) cornerstone

  (c) deference

  (d) infidelity

해석 A: 뉴스를 들으니까 중국에서 들어오는 컨테이너에 명품 모조품 같은 밀수품들이 가득 들어 있었대.
    B: 왜 사람들은 금지된 것들을 밀수하려고 그렇게 노력을 하지?

해설 contraband goods는 '수출입 금지품'을 뜻한다. smuggle은 '밀수입[밀수출]'이라는 뜻으로 contraband goods와 가장 상응하는 단어이다.

어휘 contraband 수출입이 금지된 cornerstone 기초, 초석 deference 복종 infidelity 불신, 부정

---

8 유형 고난도 어휘

A: I was with Jack the whole time to console him upon his sudden ___________.

B: I'm so sorry to hear that. I did know that his mom was struggling with cancer for quite a while.

  (a) trespass

  (b) loiter

  (c) bereavement

  (d) imposture

해석 A: Jack이 어머니와 갑자기 사별하게 되어서 내가 위로하려고 내내 같이 있었어.
    B: 정말 안됐어. 한동안 그의 어머니가 암 투병을 하고 있다는 건 알고 있었는데.

해설 console(위로하다)와 암 투병으로 미루어 볼 때 좋지 않은 소식이라는 것을 알 수 있다. '유감스럽다'라고 표현하였으므로 bereavement(사별)이 가장 적당하다.

어휘 trespass 침입하다 loiter 빈둥거리다 bereavement 사별 imposture 사기, 협잡

---

9 유형 연어

A: He lacks sportsmanship when we play golf with him.

B: What he really needs is the ability to enjoy the game and accept the result even if it is a(n) ___________ defeat.

  (a) turbulent

  (b) derivative

  (c) sleuth

  (d) ignominious

해석 A: 그는 우리와 골프를 칠 때 스포츠맨 정신이 부족해.
    B: 그가 정말 필요한 건 경기를 즐기고 아무리 수치스러운 패배라 해도 결과를 받아들이는 능력이야.

해설 스포츠맨 정신이 부족한 사람에게 필요한 것들을 이야기하고 있다. ignominious defeat(수치스러운 패배)이라 해도 결과를 받아들이는 능력이 중요하다는 의미가 되어야 한다.

어휘 turbulent 격동의, 격변의 derivative 파생적인 sleuth 형사, 탐정 ignominious 수치스러운, 창피한

10 유형 고난도 어휘

A: What did the famous comedian get accused of?

B: He made a remark that accidently ___________ one company's name on last week's show.

(a) forestalled

(b) corroborated

(c) **slandered**

(d) reared

해석 A: 그 유명한 코미디언이 무엇 때문에 기소되었대?
B: 저번 주 쇼에서 한 발언이 뜻하지 않게 어떤 회사의 명예를 훼손했대.

해설 잘못 발언을 하여 한 회사의 이름을 더럽혔다는 의미가 되어야 하므로 문맥상 slander(명예를 훼손하다)가 가장 알맞다.

어휘 forestall 앞서다 corroborate 확증하다
slander 명예를 훼손하다 rear 사육하다, 양육하다

11 유형 숙어

A: What do you think of our company's policy of salary being ___________ with one's experience in the field?

B: I think it is fair since more experience means they are more precise in what they do.

(a) in a quandary

(b) **commensurate**

(c) flaunting

(d) exuded

해석 A: 그 분야의 경력에 상응하는 월급을 주는 우리 회사의 정책에 대해서 어떻게 생각합니까?
B: 경험이 더 많다는 것은 그들이 할 것에 대해서 더 정확하다는 것을 말하기에 정당하다고 생각합니다.

해설 be commensurate with는 '~에 어울리다, 상응하다'의 뜻으로 월급과 관련 분야 경험이 상응해야 하는가를 논하고 있는 대화이다.

어휘 in a quandary 당황하여
commensurate (크기, 중요도, 자질 등에) 어울리는, 상응하는 flaunting 과시하는 exude 스며나오다

12 유형 고난도 어휘

A: It makes me really mad that so many girls have to be sacrificed because of some people who are not wise and sane enough.

B: Yeah, I heard the news. I really ___________ with the victims who were wounded both mentally and physically.

(a) **commiserate**

(b) stricken

(c) disclaim

(d) back out

해석 A: 지각 없고 제정신이 아닌 사람들 때문에 너무 많은 여자 아이들이 희생될 수밖에 없다는 것이 정말 화가 나.
B: 맞아, 뉴스 들었어. 정신적으로나 육체적으로나 상처받은 피해자들이 정말 가여워.

해설 희생된 피해자들에 대한 심정을 나타내는 대화로 문맥상 알맞은 의미가 되려면 commiserate(동정하다, 가엽게 여기다)가 답이 되어야 한다.

어휘 stricken (병에) 걸린, 고통 받는
disclaim 권리를 포기하다 back out 철회하다

13 유형 고난도 어휘

A: Statistical data are ___________ for people who wish to see the constant rate of change at a glance.

B: You're right. Statistics are crucial and useful in many fields.

(a) fraught
(b) lopsided
(c) lenient
(d) salutary

해석 A: 통계 자료들은 지속적인 변화율을 한눈에 보고 싶은 사람들에게 유익해.

B: 맞아, 통계는 많은 분야에서 굉장히 중요하고 또 쓸모 있지.

해설 통계 자료, 또는 통계에 대해 공통된 의견을 말하고 있다. 중요하고 유익하다고 했으므로 그와 비슷한 뜻을 가진 단어는 salutary(유익한, 효과가 있는)이다.

어휘 fraught 가득찬 lopsided 한쪽으로 치우친
lenient 관대한

---

14 유형 이디엄

A: I am sorry that he was given his walking papers.

B: He's so upset about it! I guess that he is so reserved that he'll never ___________.

(a) have a ball
(b) come down hard on
(c) live it down
(d) be loaded for bear

해석 A: 그가 해고돼서 유감이야.

B: 그는 그것 때문에 몹시 화났어! 내 생각에 그는 내성적이어서 결코 잊어버리기 어려울 거야.

해설 내성적인 성격 탓에 실직의 고통을 극복하기가 어려울 것이라고 하는 것이 자연스럽다. live ~ down은 '고통스럽거나 치욕스러운 일을 서서히 잊다'라는 뜻으로 쓰인다.

어휘 give someone one's walking papers 해고하다
have a ball 즐거운 시간을 보내다
come down hard on 엄하게 꾸짖다
live it down (고통이나 치욕을) 시간이 흘러감에 따라 잊어버리다 be loaded for bear 몹시 화가 나다

---

15 유형 고난도 어휘

A: How did she manage to persuade the fastidious contractors from India?

B: She is famous for being ___________ at handling delicate situations and people.

(a) adroit
(b) cumbersome
(c) gratuitous
(d) embellished

해석 A: 그녀는 인도에서 온 깐깐한 계약자들을 어떻게 설득했던 거야?

B: 그녀는 민감한 상황과 사람을 다루는 데 능숙하기로 유명해.

해설 be adroit at은 '~에 능숙하다'라는 뜻으로, 설득이 가능했던 것은 그녀가 그러한 상황과 사람에 대해 능숙하다고 이야기하는 대화이다.

어휘 adroit 능숙한 cumbersome 성가신, 귀찮은
gratuitous 무료의 embellish 장식하다

16 유형 고난도 어휘

A: I can't believe I made such a stupid mistake. Who would trust me now?

B: Shanna, you don't have to ___________ yourself too much for failing. Everyone makes stupid mistakes from time to time.

(a) fabricate

(b) berate

(c) venerate

(d) hiatus

해석 A: 내가 이렇게 바보 같은 실수를 했다는 것을 믿을 수가 없어. 이제 누가 날 믿어줄까?

B: Shanna, 실패에 대해서 스스로를 너무 그렇게 질책할 필요 없어. 사람은 누구나 때때로 바보 같은 실수를 해.

해설 Shanna가 실패에 대해 자책한다는 것을 알 수 있으므로 그러지 말라는 내용이 와야 알맞다.

어휘 fabricate 날조하다 berate 질책하다
venerate 공경[숭배]하다 hiatus (공간, 시간의) 틈

17 유형 고난도 어휘

A: We all have been educated since we were little to ___________ feminity.

B: You sound like a total feminist.

(a) devour

(b) placate

(c) emulate

(d) disparage

해석 A: 우리 모두는 어렸을 때부터 여자라는 점을 낮춰보도록 교육받아왔지.

B: 너 아주 페미니스트처럼 말한다.

해설 페미니스트처럼 들린다고 하였으므로 그들의 생각과 관련된 어휘가 들어가야 한다. 따라서 가장 적절한 단어는 disparage(폄하하다)라는 단어이다.

어휘 feminist 남녀평등주의자 devour 게걸스럽게 먹다
placate 달래다, 진정시키다 emulate ~와 경쟁하다

18 유형 고난도 어휘

A: As a result of your analyzing, what did you come up with?

B: So far we all know that apes and human beings are genetically very much alike and I am trying to find the ___________ between them and us as well.

(a) compatibility

(b) prodigy

(c) anatomies

(d) discernment

해석 A: 당신이 분석한 결과로 무엇을 알아냈습니까?

B: 지금까지 우리는 모두 유인원과 인간이 유전자적으로 매우 비슷하다는 것을 알고 있는데 전 그들과 우리 사이에 공존 가능성을 알아내려고 노력하고 있습니다.

해설 유인원들과 인간 사이에 유전학적 유사점 외에도 다른 것을 알아내려고 노력하고 있다고 말했으므로 문맥상 가장 알맞은 단어는 '공존 가능성'을 뜻하는 compatibility이다.

어휘 prodigy 비범한 사람, 천재 anatomy 해부학(적 구조)
discernment 안목

19 유형 고난도 어휘

A: My indecisive attitude really seems to degrade me both inside and outside of work.

B: It is quite important to be ___________ as you grow up, so try to reduce other factors that confuse you and replace them with your thoughts.

   (a) evenhanded
   (b) insolvent
   (c) unwavering
   (d) endearing

해석 A: 내 우유부단한 성격이 직장 안에서나 밖에서나 정말 면목을 잃게 하는 것 같아.

B: 성장하면서 확고한 태도는 꽤 중요하지, 그러니까 너를 헷갈리게 하는 다른 요인들을 줄이고 네 생각으로 대체해봐.

해설 우유부단한 성격의 부정적인 면을 이야기하면서 고칠 필요가 있다고 말하고 있으므로, 우유부단한 면과 반대되는 특징이 빈칸에 들어가야 한다.

어휘 degrade 면목을 잃게 하다 evenhanded 공평한 insolvent 지급불능인 unwavering 확고한 endearing 사랑스런

20 유형 고난도 어휘

A: Do you know about anyone historically famous enough to be printed on American currency?

B: I learned that one of the most ___________ faces engraved on American currency is a brave Native American woman named Sacagawea.

   (a) subservient
   (b) noteworthy
   (c) strenuous
   (d) pensive

해석 A: 미국 화폐에 인쇄될 만큼 역사적으로 유명한 인물 중 아는 사람이 있니?

B: 미국 화폐에 그려진 가장 주목할 만한 인물 중 한 명은 용감한 북아메리카 인디인 여성 Sacagawea라고 배웠어.

해설 화폐, 통화에 새겨질 만큼 역사적으로 유명한 사람에 대해 이야기하고 있으므로 빈칸에도 이와 비슷한 의미의 단어가 와야 한다.

어휘 subservient 비굴한, 아첨하는 noteworthy 주목할 만한 strenuous 굽히지 않는, 격렬한 pensive 생각에 잠긴

21 유형 의미상 혼동 어휘

A: Do you think it's better to read one book several times or instead spend that time reading several other books?

B: I personally think repetitively reading a single book will mean merely an accumulation of ___________ knowledge, the burdensome accumulation of information without real value.

   (a) significant
   (b) obvious
   (c) superficial
   (d) profound

해석 A: 넌 한 권의 책을 여러 번 읽는 것이 낫다고 생각하니 아니면 그 시간에 차라리 다른 책 여러 권을 읽는 것이 낫다고 생각하니?

B: 난 개인적으로 한 권을 반복적으로 읽는 것은 단지 피상적인 지식만 축적하는 것, 즉 진정한 가치가 없는 정보를 힘들게 축적하는 것이라고 생각해.

해설 쉼표로 연결되는 동격이므로 진정한 가치가 없는 것에 해당하는 내용을 찾아야 한다.

어휘 significant 중요한 obvious 명백한 superficial 피상적인 profound 심오한

22 유형 의미상 혼동 어휘

A: As an educator, I really struggle with the issue of how to create a classroom of similarly adept students.

B: Same here, I guess it's because at any given grade level, there may be wide ___________ in the academic abilities of the students.

(a) discrepancies
(b) margin
(c) variation
(d) gap

해석 A: 교육자로서, 내가 어떻게 해야 실력이 비슷한 학생들을 한 학급으로 구성할지에 대해 고민이야.
B: 나도 그래, 내 생각엔 어느 학년의 경우라도 학생들의 학습 능력에는 큰 편차가 있기 마련이어서 그런 것 같아.

해설 A는 어떻게 비슷한 실력의 학생들로 한 반을 구성할지가 고민이라고 했다. 그것에 대해 둘 다 동의하고 있는 상황이므로 이와 비슷한 의미가 되도록 문장을 구성해야 한다. 그렇다면 서로간의 차이를 말하는 (a)와 (d) 가운데 답은 복수 discrepancies가 적합하다.

어휘 margin (득표수 등의) 차이 variation 변화, 변종, 변이
gap (두 집단 간의) 차이

23 유형 이디엄

A: Making students take the test and letting those who pass the exam graduate and those who don't stay another year at school is not very wise.

B: It is quite a ___________ approach, but we have no other choice.

(a) back and forth
(b) top and tail
(c) black and white
(d) head and toe

해석 A: 학생들에게 시험을 보게 하고 통과하는 사람은 졸업을 시켜주고 나머지는 일 년을 더 학교에 남게 하는 것은 별로 현명하지가 않습니다.
B: 좀 흑백논리이긴 하지만 우리도 다른 방법이 없습니다.

해설 시험을 통과한 사람은 졸업을 하고 그렇지 못한 사람은 졸업을 못한다고 했으므로 이분법적인 사고의 예를 말하고 있다. 따라서 '흑백논리의, 이분법적인'의 뜻이 있는 black and white가 답이 된다.

어휘 top and tail 전체, 전부
back and forth 앞뒤로 head and toe 머리와 발가락

24 유형 형태상 혼동 어휘

A: I realized that nobody in the West asks or knows about the relationship between blood type and personality.

B: Well that's because in this country, asking an ___________ for his blood type is somewhat bizarre.

(a) ancillary
(b) aberrance
(c) adversary
(d) acquaintance

해석 A: 서양에서는 아무도 혈액형과 성격의 관계에 대해 묻는 사람도 아는 사람도 없다는 걸 깨달았어.
B: 바로 그 때문에 이 나라에서는 지인에게 혈액형을 묻는 건 좀 이상하지.

해설 서양 사람들끼리 혈액형에 대해 논하지 않는 문화를 말하고 있으므로 지인에게 묻는 것은 이상하다는 의미가 되어야 한다.

어휘 ancillary 조수 aberrance 일탈
adversary 상대방, 적수 acquaintance 아는 사람

25 유형 연어

A: Why is it convenient?

B: Because the shoulder ___________ for the bag is adjustable for the user's body size.

   (a) strap

   (b) line

   (c) lane

   (d) stream

해석 A: 어째서 그게 편해?
B: 그 가방의 어깨끈은 사용자의 체형에 맞출 수 있는 것이니까.

해설 여기서의 끈이나 선, 특히 가방끈 등은 strap을 사용한다. 나머지 선택지들도 다 '선'의 의미를 포함하고 있기는 하나 조금씩 의미가 다르다.

어휘 adjustable 조절 가능한 lane (육상 등의) 줄, 선 line (그림 등의) 선 stream 흐름, 줄

Part Ⅱ   Questions 26-50

26 유형 고난도 어휘

Scientists studying cells often encounter the same ___________ problem: it is difficult to examine live specimens under a microscope.

   (a) hampering

   (b) ubiquitous

   (c) emulating

   (d) credulous

해석 세포를 연구하는 과학자들은 아주 흔한 동일한 문제에 종종 직면한다. 현미경으로 살아 있는 표본을 연구하기가 어렵다는 것이다.

해설 뒤에 설명한 것과 같은 문제를 모든 과학자들이 공통적으로, 자주 직면한다는 의미가 필요하다.

어휘 specimen 표본 microscope 현미경
hamper 훼방 놓다, 방해하다
ubiquitous 어디에나 있는 emulate 모방하다
credulous 쉽게 믿는, 잘 속는

27 유형 고난도 어휘

The ___________ of Senator El Lore from the party was a cruel blow to the prime minister.

   (a) defection

   (b) migration

   (c) transformation

   (d) outgoings

해석 El Lore 상원의원의 탈당은 총리에게 치명타였다.

해설 defection은 '탈당, 변절'의 의미이고 동사 defect는 '도망치다, 변절하다'의 의미이다.

어휘 cruel blow 치명타 migration (물리적) 이동
transformation 변형 outgoings 지출, 비용

28 유형 고난도 어휘

Cab drivers ___________ at such a thought, denouncing the system as an infringement of privacy.

   (a) cringe

   (b) vaporize

   (c) disconsolate

   (d) promulgate

해석 택시 운전자들은 그 생각이 사생활을 침해하는 시스템이라며 질색했다.

해설 택시 운전자들이 어떠한 체제에 대해 반대를 하고 있는 내용이다. 따라서 의미상 '반대하다, 싫어하다'라는 뜻이 와야 한다.

어휘 cringe 움츠리다, 질색하다 vaporize 증발하다[시키다]
disconsolate 설낭석인, 불행한 promulgate 공표하다

29 [유형] 형태상 혼동 어휘

Poe's ___________ stories are sometimes too morbid for reading in bed, that's why I do not recommend his works for the night.

    (a) clement
    (b) coalescent
    (c) chimerical
    (d) credulous

[해석] Poe의 기상천외한 이야기들은 가끔씩 잠자리에서 읽기에는 너무 끔찍하기 때문에 나는 그의 작품을 밤에는 추천하지 않는다.

[해설] 자기 전에 읽기에는 부담스러운 이야기를 묘사할 적절한 형용사를 찾으면 된다. '괴기스러운' 이야기라고 해야 뒤에 나오는 morbid(소름이 돋을 정도로 무시무시한)와 어울린다.

[어휘] clement 온화한 coalescent 연합한
chimerical 기괴한, 공상적인 credulous 속기 쉬운

30 [유형] 고난도 어휘

Loss of vision is not ___________, and there is no reason why the human eyes cannot maintain good vision beyond the age of 80.

    (a) unprecedented
    (b) inevitable
    (c) impeccable
    (d) embraceable

[해석] 시력 상실은 불가피한 것이 아니다. 인간의 눈이 여든 살 넘어서까지 좋은 시력을 유지하지 못할 이유는 전혀 없다.

[해설] 시력을 계속 좋게 유지하지 못할 이유는 없다고 얘기하고 있다. 따라서 앞뒤가 상응하도록 의미를 만들어 주기 위해서는 inevitable(불가피한)이 와야 한다.

[어휘] unprecedented 전례가 없는
impeccable 나무랄 데 없는, 흠이 없는
embraceable 사랑스러운, 기꺼이 받아들일 수 있는

31 [유형] 형태상 혼동 어휘

10 minutes later your skin would be _________ and cracked as all the natural oils in it would have been washed away.

    (a) parched
    (b) fetched
    (c) patched
    (d) wretched

[해석] 피부의 천연오일이 모두 씻겨나갔을 것이기 때문에 10분 후에는 당신의 피부가 메마르고 갈라질 것이다.

[해설] 뒤에 cracked라는 표현이 있기에 피부가 갈라지기 전, 즉 메마른(parched) 상태라는 것이 정답이다.

[어휘] parched 바짝 마른 fetch 보내다 patch 때우다
wretch 난파시키다

32 [유형] 고난도 어휘

In a considerable number of households, the level of waste is too high, ___________ a significant danger for those with respiratory conditions.

    (a) posing
    (b) bewailing
    (c) disparaging
    (d) infringing

[해석] 꽤 많은 가정에서 쓰레기의 양이 훨씬 더 많아서 호흡기 질환이 있는 사람들에게 심각한 위험을 불러일으킨다.

[해설] 부정적인 요인이 위험을 야기시킬 수 있다는 내용이 되어야 하므로 문맥상 가장 알맞은 것은 '(문제 · 위험 등을) 불러일으키다'는 의미의 pose의 현재분사 형태이다.

[어휘] considerable 상당한 excrement 배설물
respiratory condition 호흡기 질환
bewail 몹시 슬퍼하다 disparage 헐뜯다, 비난하다
infringe 어기다, 침해하다

33 유형 형태상 혼동 어휘

Individuals ___________ with Alzheimer disease ultimately forget who they are.

- (a) infringed
- (b) infirm
- (c) infused
- **(d) inflicted**

[해석] 알츠하이머병으로 괴로워하는 사람들은 결국 자신이 누군지조차 잊게 된다.

[해설] be inflicted with는 '~로 괴로움을 당하다'라는 뜻이 있다. 따라서 병으로 괴로워한다는 의미가 되어야 하므로 답은 inflicted가 되어야 한다.

[어휘] infringe 위반하다 infirm 병약한, 노쇠한
infuse 주입하다 inflict 괴로움[상처]을 가하다

34 유형 형태상 혼동 어휘

Banning alcohol would only ___________ Mafia groups who would seek methods to smuggle it illegally.

- (a) relapse
- **(b) reinvigorate**
- (c) remonstrate
- (d) remunerate

[해석] 주류를 금지시키는 것은 불법으로 밀수할 방법을 물색할 마피아 세력에게 새로운 힘을 실어주기만 할 것이다.

[해설] 마피아 집단에게 이익이 될 일이므로 다시 활동할 것이라는 이야기를 하고 있다.

[어휘] smuggle 밀수하다 relapse (병이) 재발하다
reinvigorate 새로운 힘[활기]를 불어넣다
remonstrate 항의하다, 불평하다
remunerate 보수를 지불하다

35 유형 고난도 어휘

Although the technology that now ___________ our modern lives can be seen as beneficial, there are some questionable aspects to it as well.

- (a) obstructs
- (b) relents
- **(c) permeates**
- (d) obtrudes

[해석] 지금 우리의 현대적 삶에 스며든 기술이 유익해 보이지만 그에 대한 몇 가지의 의문점 또한 존재한다.

[해설] 우리 삶에 '들어와 있는'이라는 의미가 되어야 하므로 문맥상 permeate가 가장 알맞다.

[어휘] obstruct 막다, 방해하다 relent 가엾게 여기다
permeate 스며들다, 침투하다
obtrude 참견하다, 강요하다

36 유형 형태상 혼동 어휘

Why should only wealthy celebrities have the opportunity to have ___________ weddings?

- **(a) lavish**
- (b) licit
- (c) laxative
- (d) laudatory

[해석] 왜 부유한 명사들에게만 호화로운 결혼식을 할 기회가 주어져야 하는가?

[해설] 부유한 계층의 결혼식을 묘사하는 말이므로 lavish(호화스러운)가 들어갈 것을 알 수 있다.

[어휘] licit 허가 받은, 합법적인 laxative 설사하게 하는
laudatory 칭찬의

37 유형 2어 동사

Chocolate may ___________ up ideas of sweet candy bars and syrupy milkshakes, but the original chocolate was a dramatically different concoction.

    (a) illumine

    (b) grapple

    (c) garrote

    (d) conjure

해석 초콜릿은 달콤한 초코바와 시럽이 든 밀크셰이크를 떠올리게 하겠지만 본래의 초콜릿은 아주 다른 혼합물이었다.

해설 conjure up은 '~을 상기시키다, 떠올리게 하다'의 뜻이 있다. 초콜릿이 뒤에 나오는 대상을 떠오르게 할 수 있다는 의미로 이어진다.

어휘 syrupy 시럽이 든 concoction 혼합물
illumine 비추다, 밝히다
grapple (해결책을 찾아) 고심하다

38 유형 고난도 어휘

Some people try ___________ to keep us from getting back to our land.

    (a) factiously

    (b) vehemently

    (c) bubbly

    (d) redundantly

해석 몇몇 사람들은 우리가 우리 땅으로 다시 돌아가는 것을 막기 위해 엄청난 노력을 한다.

해설 사람들이 노력하는 태도를 묘사하는 말이 들어가야 하는데, 뭔가를 막기 위해 노력하는 것이므로 문맥상 '격렬하게, 열심히'가 답이 되어야 한다.

어휘 factiously 장난스럽게 bubbly 거품이 많은
redundantly 쓸모없게

39 유형 고난도 어휘

Mark Twain grew as a writer to produce dark chronicles of the ___________, hypocrisies and murderous acts of humankind.

    (a) aliases

    (b) agilities

    (c) vanities

    (d) alloys

해석 Mark Twain은 인간의 허영심, 위선, 그리고 흉악한 행동을 담은 어두운 내용의 연작을 내놓은 작가가 되었다.

해설 인간의 부정적인 면들에 대해 이야기하고 있으므로 문맥상 가장 알맞은 단어는 허영심의 뜻을 가진 vanities이다.

어휘 hypocrisy 위선 murderous 살인의, 흉악한
vanity 허영심 alias 가명 agility 민첩성 alloy 합금

40 유형 연어

Students who wish to learn English by ___________ themselves abroad had better realize that there is more to English-speaking countries than just the language.

    (a) immersing

    (b) agonizing

    (c) grieving

    (d) resonating

해석 외국에 나가 영어를 공부하고 싶어하는 학생들은 영어가 모국어인 나라에는 단지 영어뿐만이 아니라 더 많은 것이 있다는 것을 알아야 한다.

해설 immerse는 '담그다, 몰두하다'라는 뜻이 있지만 immerse themselves abroad라고 하면 타지나 외국에 자신의 몸을 담근다는 표현에서 '유학을 가다, 외국으로 가다'라는 의미가 된다.

어휘 immerse 몰두하다, 담그다 agonize 괴로워하다
grieve 마음을 아프게 하다 resonate 공명하다, 울리다

41 유형 고난도 어휘

Russell encountered a very ___________ environment in jail, but he still managed to author a book at the time.

    (a) manageable

    (b) conventional

    (c) sophisticated

    (d) adverse

해석 Russel은 감옥에서 매우 불리한 환경에 처해 있었지만 그래도 그때 책을 쓸 수는 있었다.

해설 안 좋은 상황에 처해 있었지만 그래도 책을 썼다는 내용이므로 불리한 환경이라는 의미가 와야 한다.

어휘 adverse 불리한, 부정적인 manageable 다루기 쉬운 conventional 전통적인 sophisticated 정교한

42 유형 고난도 어휘

Dewey was an early ___________ of the philosophy that people must link new experiences to old experiences.

    (a) assonance

    (b) proponent

    (c) consonant

    (d) transplant

해석 Dewey는 새로운 경험을 옛 경험에 연결시켜야 한다는 철학의 초기 옹호자였다.

해설 철학적인 내용을 한 인물과 연결지어 이야기하므로 답은 proponent(옹호자, 지지자)가 되어야 한다.

어휘 assonance 음의 유사 consonant 자음 transplant 이식

43 유형 고난도 어휘

Adult male lemurs allow females priority and display ___________ when eating, grooming, and going to sleep.

    (a) dominance

    (b) submissiveness

    (c) coherence

    (d) rage

해석 다 큰 수컷 여우원숭이들은 암컷에게 우선권을 주며 먹을 때, 털 손질할 때, 그리고 잘 때 고분고분한 태도를 보인다.

해설 priority(우선권)을 준다는 내용을 앞에 썼으므로 암컷에 대해 이와 비슷한 태도를 나타내는 단어가 와야 한다.

어휘 dominance 우선권, 지배 submissiveness 순종적임, 고분고분함 coherence 일관성 rage 분노

44 유형 고난도 어휘

Those insects are not sexually ___________, meaning that there is no significant difference between the females and the males.

    (a) reconciled

    (b) inherent

    (c) dimorphic

    (d) versatile

해석 그 곤충들은 성적으로 이형태성을 갖추고 있지 않다. 즉 수컷과 암컷 사이에 큰 차이가 없다는 것이다.

해설 뒤에 설명에 알맞은 단어를 선택 하는 문제이다. 수컷과 암컷 사이에 큰 차이가 없는 것은 dimorphic(이형태성의)이라 한다.

어휘 reconcile 조화시키다 inherent 내재하는 versatile 다재다능한, 다용도의

45 유형 연어

A new study has ___________ the popular theory that moderate wine consumption lowers the chance of developing heart disease, thus accepting the last conception.

(a) validated
(b) famished
(c) desponded
(d) rebutted

해석 와인을 적당히 마시면 심장병에 걸릴 확률을 낮춰준다는 유명한 가설을 새로운 연구가 입증함에 따라, 최근의 개념을 인정한 셈이 되었다.

해설 validate the theory는 주로 '가설을 증명하다'는 뜻으로 쓰인다. 따라서 문맥상 가장 알맞은 단어는 validated이다.

어휘 heart disease 심장병 famish 굶주리게 하다
despond 낙담하다 rebut 논박하다, 반박하다

46 유형 연어

Kim doesn't deserve to ___________ the position because he was connected with the corruption.

(a) secure
(b) lock
(c) reach
(d) place

해석 Kim은 그 부패사건과 관련이 있다는 얘기가 있어서 그 직위를 얻을 자격이 없다.

해설 지위나 자격을 얻을 때는 secure를 쓴다. (c)나 (d)의 연어는 쓰이지 않는다.

어휘 secure 확보하다 corruption 부패 lock 채우다

47 유형 고난도 어휘

Hoping to give its young citizens a(n) ___________ in the global economy, many governments have begun subsidizing early education programs.

(a) cipher
(b) edge
(c) handicap
(d) damnification

해석 국제 경제에서 자국의 어린 시민들에게 우위를 제공하기 위한 바람으로 많은 국가들이 조기 교육 프로그램을 보조하기 시작했다.

해설 조기 교육을 보조하기 시작했다고 하였으므로 아이들의 발전을 위한 것임을 알 수 있다. 가장 알맞은 단어는 edge(우위)이다.

어휘 subsidize 보조하다 cipher 암호, 하찮은 것
handicap 장애 damnification 손상

48 유형 고난도 어휘

When learning becomes a(n) ___________, many students lose the motivation to study.

(a) excitement
(b) abstraction
(c) extravaganza
(d) bacchanal

해석 학습이 재미없게 되면 많은 학생들이 공부할 동기를 잃는다.

해설 abstraction은 '추상적 개념'이란 뜻이 있는데 의미상 '지루한 것'이라는 뜻이 될 수 있다. 학습이 이런 것이 되면 동기를 잃을 것이라고 했으므로 이에 어울리는 의미의 단어를 찾아야 한다.

어휘 motivation 동기 excitement 흥분
extravaganza 호화로운 오락물
bacchanal 떠들썩한 술잔치

49 유형 고난도 어휘

I believe that the realization of our ambition is merely one of many factors in our ___________ for fulfillment.

    (a) adequacy

    (b) research

    (c) quest

    (d) abundance

해석 야망의 실현은 우리가 만족을 찾기 위한 많은 요인 중 하나일 뿐이라고 믿는다.

해설 '만족'이라는 단어를 바탕으로 많은 요인들 중 하나라고 했으므로 만족을 '찾기 위한'이란 뜻이 되어야 알맞다.

어휘 realization 실현 fulfillment 성취, 만족
adequacy 적절, 타당성 research 연구, 조사
quest 탐색, 추구 abundance 풍부

50 유형 이디엄

Heart disease is a serious health problem across the globe, and without aggressive prevention measures, problems will only become more serious later ___________.

    (a) down the road

    (b) for now

    (c) in the meantime

    (d) without care

해석 심장병은 세계적으로 심각한 건강상 문제이며 강력한 예방 조치를 취하지 않으면 미래에는 문제가 더 심각해지기만 할 것이다.

해설 예방 조치를 취하지 않으면 문제가 더 심각해 질 것이다, 라고 미래형으로 표현했으므로 가장 적절한 표현은 down the road(미래에)이다.

어휘 for now 우선은, 현재로는
in the meantime 그동안, 그 사이에
without care 태평하게

고난도 Actual Training 10

1. (a)	2. (a)	3. (b)	4. (a)	5. (b)	6. (a)	7. (c)	8. (d)	9. (d)	10. (b)
11. (a)	12. (c)	13. (c)	14. (c)	15. (c)	16. (b)	17. (a)	18. (a)	19. (d)	20. (b)
21. (d)	22. (a)	23. (b)	24. (d)	25. (a)	26. (a)	27. (b)	28. (c)	29. (d)	30. (b)
31. (b)	32. (a)	33. (c)	34. (c)	35. (a)	36. (a)	37. (a)	38. (d)	39. (c)	40. (a)
41. (b)	42. (b)	43. (b)	44. (d)	45. (a)	46. (a)	47. (d)	48. (a)	49. (b)	50. (b)

Part I Questions 1-25

1 유형 고난도 어휘

A: What kind of assignments would I have if I get this opportunity?

B: ___________ mostly. Nothing too demanding, but it isn't the most interesting work either.

(a) Clerical
(b) Intricate
(c) Arduous
(d) Judicial

해석 A: 제가 이 기회를 얻으면 어떠한 업무를 하게 되나요?
B: 주로 사무직이에요. 너무 부담되지는 않겠지만 아주 재미있지도 않을 겁니다.

해설 이 기회를 얻으면 어떤 일을 하게 되는지 물어보는데 B는 그 일이 재미있지도 않고 너무 부담되지 않을 것이라는 말을 덧붙인다. 따라서 간단한 사무직에 대한 설명이라고 보는 것이 적절하다.

어휘 clerical 사무직의 intricate 복잡한
arduous 고된, 힘든 judicial 사법의

2 유형 2어 동사

A: I guess I need to choose one country and compare several factors for the one country.

B: Or if you want to compare several countries, you probably need to ___________ one factor.

(a) zero in on
(b) rub it in
(c) lay it off
(d) act it out

해석 A: 한 나라를 정해서 몇 개의 요소를 비교해야겠네요.
B: 아니면 여러 나라를 비교하고 싶으면 한 가지 요소에 집중해야 할 거야.

해설 A에서 여러 개의 요소를 비교하자고 했지만 B의 처음에 Or(아니면)가 왔기에 그 반대가 되는 하나에 초점을 맞춘다(zero in on)라는 내용이 와야 한다.

어휘 zero in on 초점을 맞추다 rub it in 반복해서 말하다
lay it off 해고하다 act it out 행동으로 표출하다

3 연어

A: How was the interview?

B: It certainly was spontaneous in the sense that it happened very quickly and the answers that I gave were ___________ responses.

  (a) off limits

  (b) split second

  (c) waste

  (d) storm-prone

해석 A: 인터뷰 어땠어요?

B: 아주 빠르게 진행되고 짧은 순간에 대답을 해야 했다는 점에서 굉장히 자발적이었어요.

해설 인터뷰에 대해서 물어보았는데 아주 빠르게 진행되었다는 점에서 대답도 split second(짧은 순간)에 했다는 표현이 빈칸에 적절하다.

어휘 **off limits** 제논의 금지된 **waste** 여분의, 쓰레기의 **storm-prone** 폭우가 발생하기 쉬운

---

4 연어

A: You can just stop by during my office hours and maybe I can give you some references, or at least I can be a ___________.

B: Thank you so much for being a great help!

  (a) sounding board

  (b) curriculum vitae

  (c) pilot test

  (d) draft-dodger

해석 A: 업무시간에 잠깐 들르면 참고자료를 주거나 최소한 무슨 얘기인지는 들어볼게.

B: 큰 도움이 되어서 너무 고마워요!

해설 B의 대답은 도움이 되어 고맙다는 얘기이므로 무엇인가 도움이 될 만한 내용이 들어가야 한다. 따라서 sounding board가 적절한 답이다.

어휘 **sounding board** 어려울 때 의견을 얻을 수 있는 사람 **curriculum vitae** 이력서 **pilot test** 사전시험 **draft-dodger** 징집 기피자

---

5 연어

A: If you are really serious about that lab assistant position, I can give you some information about that when I see you.

B: I can't thank you ___________.

  (a) so much

  (b) enough

  (c) little

  (d) a lot

해석 A: 그 실험실 보조업무에 정말 관심이 있다면, 다음에 만날 때 정보를 줄 수가 있어.

B: 정말 고마워요!

해설 충분하게 고마워할 수가 없다고 말하고 있다. 특히 긍정적으로 표현을 하자면, (a)가 오는 것이 자연스럽겠지만, 앞이 can't 의 모습이 되었기에 enough가 오는 것이 자연스럽다.

어휘 **lab** 실험실 **assistant** 조수, 보조

---

6 연어

A: Is anything wrong?

B: I have no idea why your volunteer work was not recorded. It might have been a computer ___________.

  (a) glitch

  (b) velocity

  (c) crouch

  (d) docility

해석 A: 무슨 문제가 있어요?

B: 왜 당신의 봉사활동 경력이 기록되어 있지 않은지 모르겠어요. 컴퓨터 오류인 거 같아요.

해설 무슨 문제가 있냐고 물어보니 왜 봉사활동 기록이 없는지 모르겠다고 하므로 컴퓨터 오류가 난 것으로 알 수 있다.

어휘 **glitch** 오류 **velocity** 속도 **crouch** 웅크림 **docility** 온순함

7 유형 고난도 어휘

A: How did your slides in PowerPoint help in your presentation?

B: Some of the titles ___________ my memory.

  (a) extracted

  (b) parched

  (c) jogged

  (d) suffused

해석   A: 파워포인트에 있는 슬라이드가 발표하는 데 어떻게 도움이 되었나요?
B: 제목들이 제 기억들을 되살렸어요.

해설   파워포인트가 어떤 도움이 되었냐는 물음에 기억을 되살렸다고 해야 적절한 문맥이 된다. 그러므로 jogged가 적절하다.

어휘   extract 뽑아내다 parch 바짝 마르게 하다
jog (기억을) 되살리다 suffuse 뒤덮다, 가득 채우다

---

8 유형 이디엄

A: Can I tell you something? I'm embarrassed to ask you questions.

B: Why in the ___________ would that be?

  (a) globe

  (b) road

  (c) string

  (d) world

해석   A: 뭐 하나 말해줄까요? 질문하기 부끄러워요.
B: 도대체 왜 그래요?

해설   '도대체 왜~?'라고 말할 때는 why in the world라는 표현을 쓴다. 특히 이 문제는 빈칸 뒤에 would가 나와서, 왠지 world가 되지 않을 것 같다는 시각적 고려까지 감안해서 출제한 문제이다.

어휘   embarrassed 쑥스러운, 당황스러운 globe 지구

---

9 유형 고난도 어휘

A: I'm having a hard time following what we've been discussing the past week.

B: If you've taken the ___________ for my class, then you shouldn't be having any problem.

  (a) complacencies

  (b) repulsions

  (c) notorieties

  (d) prerequisites

해석   A: 교수님, 지난주에 우리가 토론한 내용을 따라가기가 힘들어요.
B: 만약에 예비과목을 들었다면 전혀 문제가 없을 텐데.

해설   수업을 따라가기 힘들다고 하고, 또한 taken이라는 단어가 있으므로 과목의 의미가 있는 단어가 빈칸에 와야 한다. 그러므로 필수과목이 적절하다.

어휘   complacency 자기만족 repulsion 반감, 증오
notoriety 악명, 악평 prerequisites 필수과목

---

10 유형 이디엄

A: Whose fault do you think it was?

B: Beats me. I merely saw the accident from the ___________ of my eye.

  (a) verge

  (b) corner

  (c) edge

  (d) mercy

해석   A: 그게 누구 잘못이라고 생각해?
B: 모르겠어. 난 단지 우연히 그 사건을 목격했을 뿐이야.

해설   from the corner of one's eye 우연히 곁눈질로

어휘   Beats me. 모르겠다(= Search me.)
happening 이상한 일[사건]

11 `유형` 이디엄

A: I suppose it'll be hard to get a reservation.

B: The peak season for tennis is over. It should be ____________ to get a reservation.

(a) a cinch

(b) off base

(c) out of bounds

(d) in hot water

`해석` A: 예약하기 힘들겠지요.
B: 테니스 치는 성수기가 끝나서 예약하기 쉬울 거예요.

`해설` 테니스장을 사용하는 성수기가 끝나서 이제는 예약이 쉽다는 내용이 빈칸에 들어가야 한다.

`어휘` cinch 누워서 떡먹기 off base 크게 잘못하여
out of bounds 지정구역 밖에서, 금지된
in hot water 어려움에 빠진, 곤경에 처한

---

12 `유형` 의미상 혼동 어휘

A: How would you define noise?

B: It can even have psychological and social ____________ because it affects people's quality of life.

(a) accommodations

(b) applications

(c) implications

(d) declaration

`해석` A: 소음을 어떻게 정의할래요?
B: 사람들의 삶의 질에 영향을 주기 때문에 심리적 · 사회적 영향까지도 미칠 수 있죠.

`해설` 소음이 삶의 질에 영향을 준다고 하므로 사람에게 영향을 준다는 의미가 빈칸에 적절하다. 따라서 implications가 적절하다.

`어휘` accommodations 숙박 시설 application 적용
implication 영향, 결과 declaration (세관) 신고서

---

13 `유형` 연어

A: Hey, Susan. I heard that Tim had a crush on you at first sight.

B: I don't believe you. You're ____________. I saw him dating with Jessica yesterday.

(a) pushing me out

(b) pushing it

(c) pulling my leg

(d) pulling me up

`해석` A: 이봐, Susan. Tim이 너에게 첫눈에 반했다고 들었어.
B: 난 너를 믿지 않아. 농담하지 마. 어제 Tim이 Jessica랑 데이트하는 것을 봤는걸.

`해설` A의 말을 B가 믿지 않는다는 말에 이어질 적절한 표현은 '농담하지 마'라는 뜻의 You're pulling my leg. 또는 Don't try to pull my leg. 정도가 될 것이다.

`어휘` push somebody out (장소 또는 조직에서) ~을 밀어내다
push it 생각대로 되어 우쭐하다
pull somebody up (잘못한 것에 대해) ~을 비난하다

---

14 `유형` 형태상 혼동 어휘

A: Is there an extra cup I can use?

B: I'm afraid not. There is a ____________ one that you can use.

(a) derivable

(b) discarded

(c) disposable

(d) decayed

`해석` A: 우리가 사용할 여벌 컵이 없나요?
B: 없는 것 같아요. 근데 일회용 컵은 있어요.

`해설` 일반 컵은 없고 일회용 컵은 있다는 내용이다. 일회용품은 disposable goods라고 한다.

`어휘` derivable 추론할 수 있는 discarded 버려진
disposable 처분할 수 있는, 일회용의
decayed 부패한, 썩은

15 유형 의미상 혼동 어휘

A: You do not look so good.

B: Yesterday, I drank until I got drunk and now I have a severe ___________.

(a) malady

(b) disorder

(c) hangover

(d) intoxication

해석 A: 좋아 보이지 않네요.
B: 어제 취할 때까지 마셔서 지금 숙취가 심해요.

해설 '숙취'라는 표현은 hangover이다. 술을 많이 먹어서 나타나는 현상을 말한다.

어휘 malady 질병 disorder 질병 intoxication 취한 상태 severe 심한

16 유형 연어

A: There are not enough souvenirs to ___________ to all participants.

B: There are more in the other box.

(a) brush up

(b) go around

(c) play sick

(d) head over heels

해석 A: 기념품이 모든 참가자들에게 다 돌아가지 못할 것 같아요.
B: 다른 박스에도 있어요.

해설 기념품이 사람들에게 돌아간다는 것을 나타내는 상황을 파악하는 것이 이 문제의 요점이다. 그래서 정답은 go around 가 된다.

어휘 brush up 몸단장하다, 학문을 다시 시작하다
go around 골고루 돌아가다 play sick 꾀병부리다
head over heels 거꾸로

17 유형 연어

A: Are you going to work with John for this team project?

B: Never! He ___________ for the whole session and does not participate.

(a) fiddles about

(b) breaks a leg

(c) flares up

(d) gets an inkling

해석 A: 이번 팀 프로젝트 John이랑 할 건가요?
B: 절대로 안 해요. 그는 회의 내내 농땡이 치고 참여하지도 않아요.

해설 팀 프로젝트에 참여도 안하고 빈둥거린다는 의미가 빈칸에 적절하다.

어휘 fiddle about 농땡이 치다 break a leg 힘내다
flare up 버럭 화를 내다
get an inkling 어렴풋이 눈치채다

18 유형 고난도 어휘

A: What do I have to do in order to get a good grade in the writing class?

B: The professor will like very ___________ and persuasive writing.

(a) cohesive

(b) creepy

(c) dispatched

(d) classified

해석 A: 작문시간에 좋은 성적을 받으려면 어떻게 해야 해?
B: 교수님은 아주 응집력 있고 설득력 있는 글을 좋아할 거야.

해설 작문 시간에 좋은 성적을 받을 수 있는 글의 조건으로 언급된 '설득력 있는'과 비슷한 의미의 형용사가 있어야 한다. 따라서 cohesive가 적절하다.

어휘 cohesive 응집력 있는 creepy 혐오스러운
dispatched 파견된 classified 분류된

19 유형 2어 동사

A: Do you want to do extra work for a better grade?

B: Since I have an 18-unit course load I don't think I can ___________ a paper like that.

  (a) sound off

  (b) go off

  (c) touch on

  (d) squeeze in

해석 A: 더 좋은 점수를 위해 과제를 하나 더 내줄까?

B: 18학점을 들어야 하기 때문에 그 과제를 할 짬이 안 날 것 같아요.

해설 더 좋은 점수를 위해 과제를 하나 더 내주겠다고 하지만 너무 할일이 많아서 그럴 시간이 없을 것 같다는 의미가 들어가야 한다.

어휘 sound off (신호나 나팔을) 불다
go off (자명종, 경보기가) 울리다
touch on ~에 대해 간단히 언급하다
squeeze in 짬을 내서 하다

20 유형 2어 동사

A: He is not patient enough to ___________ for an hour.

B: I guess so. He doesn't like being bored.

  (a) lay through

  (b) sit through

  (c) skim through

  (d) cut through

해석 A: 그는 한 시간 동안 오래 앉아 있을 만큼 참을성이 있지 않아요.

B: 그런 것 같아요. 지루한 것도 싫어해요.

해설 차분하지가 않고 지루한 것을 싫어한다고 하므로 빈칸에 '오래 앉아 있다'라는 표현이 적절하다.

어휘 patient 참을성 있는 lay through 통과하다
sit through 오래 앉아 있다 skim through 대충 읽다
cut through 관통하다

21 유형 연어

A: What we have to do today is to clean up our room and do the laundry and ventilate our room.

B: Sorry. I didn't ___________ the last part. What was it again?

  (a) get

  (b) see

  (c) retrieve

  (d) catch

해석 A: 오늘 우리가 해야 할 일은 청소와 빨래 그리고 우리 방을 환기시키는 거야.

B: 죄송해요, 마지막 부분을 못 들었어요. 뭐였죠?

해설 didn't catch the last part라고 하면 마지막 부분을 못 들었다는 뜻이다.

어휘 do the laundry 빨래하다 ventilate 환기시키다
retrieve 회수하다

22 유형 이디엄

A: I don't like Tom's rash behavior.

B: Neither do I. He ___________ about our surprise party for Samantha in front of all the others.

  (a) mouthed off

  (b) cut the mouth

  (c) put a cork in it

  (d) spread out

해석 A: 나는 Tom의 경솔한 행동이 싫어.

B: 나도 그래. 그는 우리가 Samantha를 위해 준비한 깜짝 파티를 다른 사람들이 다 있는 데서 떠벌렸어.

해설 Tom의 경솔한 행동을 보여주는 표현으로 적절한 것은 '말하다, 떠벌리다'라는 뜻의 mouth off가 적절하다.

어휘 rash 경솔한 cut the mouth 입을 다물다
put a cork in it 잠자코 있다
spread out 몸을 뻗나, 넓은 공산을 차지하다

23 유형 이디엄

A: I'm going on a holiday to the beach.

B: You need to get into ___________ if I am to go with you.

(a) health

(b) shape

(c) condition

(d) mind

해석 A: 이번 휴가는 바닷가로 가기로 했어.
B: 내가 같이 가면 넌 몸 만들어야겠네.

해설 get into shape는 '몸을 만들다'라는 뜻이다.

어휘 get into shape 몸을 만들다 condition 상태

24 유형 연어

A: Sam, how do you like your new roommate, Chris?

B: Well, he's quite dirty and freaky. I cannot really ___________ him.

(a) keep away from

(b) swear off

(c) take with

(d) hit it off with

해석 A: Sam, 네 새 룸메이트 Chris는 어떠니?
B: 글쎄, 걔 꽤 지저분하고 괴상해. 그 애와는 정말이지 사이좋게 지낼 수가 없어.

해설 새로운 룸메이트에 대해 지저분하고 괴팍스럽기 때문에 '친해지기 어렵다'라는 표현이 가장 적절하다. hit it off with는 '~와 죽이 맞다, 사이좋게 지내다'라는 뜻이다.

어휘 freaky 기이한, 괴팍한 keep away from ~를 멀리하다
swear off (담배, 술 등을) 끊다
take with ~에 인기가 있다, 평판이 좋다

25 유형 이디엄

A: Park Ji Sung was dominant among the players in the Korean National Soccer Team.

B: He ___________ in the World Cup.

(a) was a Triton among minnows

(b) passed with flying colors

(c) stood us up

(d) walked on air

해석 A: 박지성은 한국 축구국가대표 선수들 사이에서 돋보였어.
B: 그는 월드컵에서 선전했지.

해설 Triton among minnows는 '군계일학'이라는 뜻이다. A가 박지성이 축구 국가대표 선수들 중 뛰어나다고 했으니 B의 말에도 박지성이 특히 잘했다는 의미가 와야 한다.

어휘 pass with flying colors 훌륭하게 해내다
stand sb up 바람맞히다 walk on air 매우 기뻐하다

Part II Questions 26-50

26 유형 고난도 어휘

Most people have two trillion of platelets in them and they work to help the blood to ___________, which means to stop bleeding.

(a) clot

(b) flourish

(c) thrive

(d) perish

해석 대부분의 사람들에게는 2조 개의 혈소판이 있어서 혈액이 응고되도록 도와주는데, 그것은 출혈이 멈춘다는 뜻이다.

해설 여기서 혈소판의 역할이 피를 멈추게 한다고 했으니 빈칸에 perish는 올 수 없다. 또한 혈소판은 혈액을 응고시키는 역할을 하므로 clot이 적절하다.

어휘 clot 응고되다 flourish 번성하다
thrive 번창하다, 잘 자라다 perish 사라지다

27 유형 고난도 어휘

The diagram on the next page in your text shows a
___________ match with no clumping.

    (a) permeating

    (b) compatible

    (c) ephemeral

    (d) flaunting

해석 교재 다음 페이지에 있는 이 도표는 응집되지 않고 양립하는 조화를 보여준다.

해설 no clumping이 힌트이다. 응집되지 않으므로 양립할 수 있다는 것을 파악해야 한다.

어휘 clumping 응집, 군집 permeate 스며들다
compatible 양립할 수 있는, 모순되지 않는
ephemeral 덧없는 flaunting 과시하는

28 유형 고난도 어휘

Many minor reactions can occur like fever or chills,
but some reactions are so severe that they lead to a(n)
___________ destruction of the red blood cells from
the donor and that can result in shock or even death.

    (a) eternal

    (b) tampering

    (c) spontaneous

    (d) overrated

해석 여러 경미한 반응은 오한과 열처럼 나타날 수 있지만, 어떤 반응은 너무 심각해서 기증자에게 받은 적혈구가 자연적으로 파괴되면서 쇼크나 심지어 사망까지 초래할 수 있다.

해설 여기서 but이 힌트이다. minor한 반응이 일어날 수 있지만 뒤에서는 조금 더 심각한 destruction이 일어날 수 있다고 말한다. 선택지 중에서는 자연발생적인 이라는 뜻의 (c)가 적절하다.

어휘 eternal 영원한 tampering 쓸데없이 참견하는
overrated 과대평가된

29 유형 고난도 어휘

You can do this because so much of a written text
is ___________ which means that there's a lot of
repetition, so quite a few words can be skipped
without losing the meaning.

    (a) lifelike

    (b) unabated

    (c) reluctant

    (d) redundant

해석 글이 반복이 많이 되어 불필요한 부분이 넘치기 때문에 상당수의 단어를 건너뛰더라도 의미를 잃지 않게 할 수 있다.

해설 뒷부분이 빈칸에 들어갈 단어의 의미를 설명해준다. 반복도 많고 그래서 몇몇의 단어는 그냥 지나쳐도 의미가 상실되지 않는다고 하므로 '불필요한'이라는 의미가 적절하다.

어휘 lifelike 실물과 똑같은
unabated 줄지 않은, 약해지지 않은
reluctant 내키지 않는 redundant 불필요한

30 유형 형태상 혼동 어휘

Although California currently leads the US in
___________ wind power, there are several other
areas that also hold considerable potential for
increased production.

    (a) abdicating

    (b) harnessing

    (c) abstaining

    (d) abominating

해석 캘리포니아가 현재 미국의 풍력발전 활용을 주도하고 있음에도 불구하고, 생산을 증대시킬 엄청난 잠재력을 보유하고 있는 지역도 여럿 있다.

해설 풍력을 이용하는 것이기 때문에 harness(동력으로 활용하다)가 가장 적절하다.

어휘 abdicate 퇴위하다, 포기하다
harness 동력화하다, 이용하다 abstain 삼가다
abominate 혐오하다

31 유형 고난도 어휘

When musicians were not creating pieces for religious occasions and performing at church functions, they were playing in the chambers of ___________ homes of nobility.

   (a) secure

   (b) stately

   (c) heartfelt

   (d) convinced

해석 음악가들이 종교적 의식이나 교회행사에서 악보를 쓰지 않을 때면 귀족의 웅장한 집들의 실내에서 연주했다.

해설 뒤에 귀족계급의 집이 언급되므로 웅장한 집이라는 것이 적절한 표현이다.

어휘 secure 안전한 stately 위풍당당한, 웅장한 heartfelt 진심어린 convinced 확고한 nobility 귀족층

32 유형 고난도 어휘

As agricultural land is sold for development, hydroponics has become a ___________ alternative for almost every country in the world.

   (a) viable

   (b) gnawing

   (c) tortuous

   (d) devouring

해석 농경지가 개발을 위해 매매되면서, 수경재배는 거의 대부분의 나라에서 실행 가능한 대안이 되었다.

해설 대부분의 나라에서 채택한 대안이므로 빈칸에는 '실행 가능한'이라는 형용사가 와야 한다.

어휘 hydroponics 수경재배 gnawing 신경을 갉아먹는 tortuous 비틀린, 복잡한 devouring 열렬한 agricultural land 농경지

33 유형 고난도 어휘

In the past, it was considered adequate for a building not to collapse during an earthquake, now insurance companies and even clients are demanding buildings that will be able to maintain their structural ___________ through an earthquake and remain sound after the earthquake.

   (a) inspection

   (b) utility

   (c) integrity

   (d) inhibition

해석 과거에는 빌딩이 지진이 일어났을 때 무너지지만 않으면 충분했지만, 지금은 보험사뿐만 아니라 고객들도 지진이 일어난 후에 빌딩이 구조적으로 온전한 모습을 유지할 것을 요구하고 있다.

해설 과거에는 지진이 일어나면 무너지지만 않으면 되었지만 지금은 온전해야 한다는 의미를 말한다. 그러므로 integrity가 적절하다.

어휘 inspection 검사 utility 공과금 integrity 진실성, 온전함 inhibition 금지

34 유형 고난도 어휘

The wind in Texas is so ___________ that wind power alone would be unreliable as a primary source of continuous energy.

   (a) aboriginal

   (b) ambiguous

   (c) variable

   (d) puissant

해석 텍사스의 바람은 너무 변덕스러워서 풍력만으로는 중요한 지속적 에너지 공급원으로 의지할 수 없다.

해설 풍력 하나로는 에너지 공급원이 될 수 없다고 하는 이유를 설명하는 말이 필요하다. 풍력은 바람이 있어야 발전이 가능한데, 변덕스러운 바람이 안정적인 공급을 막는다고 보는 것이 자연스럽다.

어휘 aboriginal 토착의 ambiguous 불확실한 variable 변덕스러운 puissant 힘센

35 고난도 어휘

It's true that some species of bacteria do cause diseases, but for most part, bacteria are ___________.

   (a) benign
   (b) virulent
   (c) avid
   (d) lethal

[해석] 박테리아의 어떤 종들은 질병을 유발하는 게 사실이지만, 대부분 박테리아는 양성이다.

[해설] but을 기준으로 앞에서는 박테리아가 질병의 원인이라고 한다. 뒷부분에는 반대되는 이야기가 나와야 한다. benign bacteria라고 하면 '몸에 좋은 박테리아'를 말한다.

[어휘] benign 양성의, 무해한 virulent 악성의 avid 열심인 lethal 치명적인

36 유형 고난도 어휘

After extensive debate, representatives of the thirteen political bodies eventually ___________ the Constitution of the United States of America, a document that represented a compromise between the rights of the states and the need for a strong centralized system of governance.

   (a) ratified
   (b) acknowledged
   (c) reversed
   (d) contended

[해석] 긴 시간에 걸친 회의 후에 13개 정치단체의 대표들은 주의 권리와 강한 중앙집권 통치체제의 필요성 사이의 절충안을 나타내는 문서인 미국 헌법을 마침내 비준했다.

[해설] 빈칸 뒷부분에 절충안을 의미하는 문서가 언급되었으니 거절하거나 싸운다는 의미는 빈칸에 어울리지 않는다. 헌법을 비준하다고 하는 것이 더 정확하므로 (a)가 답이 된다.

[어휘] ompromise 타협안, 절충안 ratify 비준하다 acknowledge 인정하다 reverse 반대하다 contend 다투다

37 유형 고난도 어휘

Frontier home design in the US was greatly influenced by the ___________ of the Homestead Act of 1862.

   (a) provisions
   (b) footnote
   (c) manifestation
   (d) denomination

[해석] 미국의 국경지역 건축 디자인은 1862년 주택법 조항에 의해 영향을 많이 받았다.

[해설] 건축법 앞에 of가 있으므로 Act(법령)와 비슷한 의미의 단어여야 한다. 따라서 '조항, 규정'을 의미하는 provisions가 적절하다.

[어휘] benign 인자한, 양호한, 온화한 footnote 각주 manifestation 표현 denomination 단위, 액면가 frontier 국경

38 유형 의미상 혼동 어휘

Remote areas, especially islands, and other regions at a distance from electrical ___________ are vigorously exploring wind options.

   (a) transfusions
   (b) irritation
   (c) rhetoric
   (d) grids

[해석] 특히 섬과 같은 외딴 지역이나 전기시설에서 멀리 떨어진 다른 지역에서 풍력을 활발히 연구하고 있다.

[해설] 전기나 가스의 시설망을 말할 때는 grids나 facility, infrastructure를 쓴다.

[어휘] vigorously 활발히, 열심히 transfusions 수혈 irritation 짜증, 경악 rhetoric 화려한 문체

39 유형 고난도 어휘

Although there are three major classifications, within these basic groups there are virtually hundreds of variations that make them somewhat more difficult to identify and classify than the rather __________ specimens.

(a) laidback
(b) tempted
(c) **straightforward**
(d) crossed

해석 주로 세 가지로 분류하는 방법이 있지만, 이 기본 그룹 내에는 사실상 수백 가지의 변종이 있어서 분류하고 확인하는 것이 보다 간단한 표본들보다는 다소 어렵다.

해설 빈칸 앞에 rather라는 단어가 있으므로 more difficult의 반대말이 오는 것이 적절하다. 따라서, '수월한, 간단한'이라는 뜻인 sraightforward가 답이다.

어휘 classification 분류 virtually 사실상 variation 변종 laidback 느긋한, 한가로운 tempted 유혹하는 crossed 방해 받는

40 유형 고난도 어휘

The frontier settlers had __________ the hardships of their first five years, and they'd received their claims.

(a) **tolerated**
(b) inflamed
(c) dissolved
(d) defamed

해석 국경의 이주자들은 처음 5년간의 고통을 견디고 그들의 권리를 받았다.

해설 뒷부분에 권리를 받았다고 하므로 문맥상 앞부분에는 고난이 있었지만 '참았다'라는 의미가 필요하기 때문에 (a)가 적절하다.

어휘 tolerate 견디다 inflame 불붙이다 dissolve 사라지다, 흩어지다 defame 명예를 훼손하다

41 유형 고난도 어휘

The expansion and shrinking of icebergs is caused by freezing and __________.

(a) sprinkling
(b) **thawing**
(c) adversing
(d) improvising

해석 빙하의 확장과 수축은 빙하가 얼고 녹는 것 때문에 생긴다.

해설 앞부분에 나온 확장과 수축은 상반되는 현상으로 인한 빙하의 크기 변화를 나타낸다. 그러므로 freezing과 반대되는 의미가 빈칸에 들어와야 한다.

어휘 sprinkle 뿌리다 thaw 녹다 adverse 거스르는, 반대의 improvise 즉흥적으로 하다

42 유형 형태상 혼동 어휘

Some types of depression appear to be genetically inherited, but often there's no family history of depression, or, __________ a person with a family history may never develop a depressive disorder.

(a) comparably
(b) **conversely**
(c) impassionately
(d) congenially

해석 어떤 우울증은 유전적으로 물려받은 것처럼 보이지만, 종종 가족 중에 우울증 이력이 없거나 반대로 있다고 하더라도 우울증이 결코 나타나지 않을 수 있다.

해설 or 앞부분은 '가족이 우울증을 가진 적 없어도'라고 했고 or 뒷부분은 '가족이 이력이 있더라도'라고 하므로 거꾸로 말한 것이다. 따라서 (b)가 적절하다.

어휘 comparably 동등하게 conversely 반대로 말하면 impassionately 열정적이게 congenially 알맞게

43 `유형` 고난도 어휘

All of these conditions have converged to
___________ an enormous number of species at the
same time, which is mass extinction.

    (a) hamper

    (b) extirpate

    (c) foster

    (d) defy

`해석` 이 모든 조건들이 한데 모여 엄청난 수의 종을 동시에 전멸시킨 것이 대량멸종이다.

`해설` 맨 뒤에 mass extinction이 힌트이다. 모든 종의 멸종이니 빈칸에는 많은 종들을 '전멸시키다'라는 의미의 단어가 적절하다.

`어휘` hamper 훼방 놓다, 방해하다 extirpate 멸종시키다
foster 촉진하다 defy 무시하다, 거부하다

---

44 `유형` 연어

Studies indicate that gang behavior is probably
caused by normal ___________.

    (a) nonaggression pact

    (b) motion sickness

    (c) illiteracy rate

    (d) adolescent insecurities

`해석` 연구결과는 비행 집단 행동이 일반적인 사춘기의 불안정에 의해 유발된다는 것을 알려준다.

`해설` 폭력 집단 행동에 대한 설명을 하는 문장인데 (a) 불가침조약, (b) 멀미, (c) 문맹률은 관계가 없으며 (d) 사춘기의 불안정은 관련이 있다.

`어휘` nonaggression pact 불가침 조약
motion sickness 멀미 illiteracy rate 문맹률
adolescent insecurities 사춘기의 불안정

---

45 `유형` 고난도 어휘

The signal causes the gland to suppress the
___________ of a hormone called melatonin.

    (a) secretion

    (b) direction

    (c) correlation

    (d) commotion

`해석` 그 신호는 분비기기관으로 하여금 멜라토닌이라는 호르몬 분비를 억제하게 만든다.

`해설` gland의 의미는 '분비기관'이므로 이것의 기능은 즉 분비(secretion)인 것이다. 따라서 빈칸에는 (a) secretion이 적절하다.

`어휘` direction 방향 correlation 상관관계
commotion 동요, 폭동

---

46 `유형` 고난도 어휘

It appears that there are long periods in which
not very much change occurs; then ___________
periods in which there are mass extinctions of
species followed by diversification of the groups that
survived.

    (a) sporadic

    (b) humiliated

    (c) diversified

    (d) incidental

`해석` 많은 변화가 일어나지 않는 긴 기간이 있는 것 같다. 그리고 단발성 기간에는 종의 대량 멸종이 일어나고 그 이후에 생존한 집단들의 다양화가 이어진다.

`해설` 앞부분에서는 long periods(긴 기간)이고 뒤에서는 반대의 의미가 문맥상 적절하다. 그러므로 '때때로 일어나는'이라는 뜻의 sporadic이 가장 잘 어울린다.

`어휘` humiliated 굴욕감을 느끼는
diversified 다양한, 변화의
incidental 우연히 일어나는

47 유형 고난도 어휘

The theory is that a decrease in light during the long winter months may be responsible for triggering a chemical imbalance that in turn may cause depression among those people with a ____________ to depression.

- (a) mediator
- (b) hideout
- (c) gimmick
- **(d) predisposition**

[해석] 그 이론은 아주 긴 겨울 동안에는 빛의 감소가 화학적 불안정을 유발하는 원인일 수 있고 그에 따라 우울증에 걸리기 쉬운 소인이 있는 사람들에게는 우울증을 일으킬 수 있다는 것이다.

[해설] 겨울에 빛이 없으면 사람이 우울해진다는 내용이다. 그러므로 병에 대한 '소인, 소질'이라는 단어가 빈칸에 적절하다.

[어휘] trigger 유발하다 imbalance 불균형
mediator 중재자 hideout 은신처
gimmick 속임수, 궁리 predisposition 소인, 소질

48 유형 고난도 어휘

About 75 percent of those developing seasonal affective disorder are women, with a typical age of ____________ about thirty years old.

- **(a) onset**
- (b) smattering
- (c) agitation
- (d) deference

[해석] 계절적 정서 장애를 갖고 있는 사람 중 75퍼센트가 여성이고, 전형적 발병 연령은 약 30살이다.

[해설] seasonal affective disorder(계절성 우울증) 환자의 75%가 여성이고 전형적 연령이 30살 가량이라고 하고 있다. 따라서 빈칸에는 '발병'이라는 뜻의 onset이 적절하다.

[어휘] smattering 얕은 지식
agitation 동요, 흥분 deference 복종

49 유형 고난도 어휘

Defenders of the climate change theory say the droughts sparked a chain of events that eventually led to the ____________ of the Maya.

- (a) barren
- **(b) demise**
- (c) frugality
- (d) hindrance

[해석] 날씨 변화 이론의 옹호자들은 가뭄이 결국에는 마야 문명의 멸망으로 이어진 일련의 사건들을 촉발했다고 말한다.

[해설] 가뭄으로 인해 여러 가지 일들이 일어났으므로 마야 문명이 멸망했다는 단어가 빈칸에 적절하다.

[어휘] spark 자극하다, 고무시키다
barren 불모지(보통 복수를 씀)
demise 멸망 agitation 동요, 흥분
frugality 절약, 감소 hindrance 방해

50 유형 고난도 어휘

This group is larger, called the "social group" and it's made up of co-workers, ____________ and so on.

- (a) condolences
- **(b) acquaintances**
- (c) venerations
- (d) acquisitions

[해석] 이 집단은 더 크고 사회적 집단이라고 불리며, 직장 동료, 아는 사람 등으로 구성된다.

[해설] co-worker와 비슷한 단어를 찾아야 한다. 따라서 acquaintance(아는 사람)가 적절한 단어이다.

[어휘] condolence 조문, 애도 acquaintance 아는 사람
veneration 숭배, 존경 acquisition 획득